Sex and Religion in the Bible

CALUM CARMICHAEL

*Sex and Religion
in the Bible*

Yale UNIVERSITY PRESS
New Haven &
London

BS
680
.S5
C36
2010

Published with assistance from the foundation established in memory of Philip Hamilton McMillan of the Class of 1894, Yale College.

Copyright © 2010 by Yale University.

All rights reserved.

This book may not be reproduced, in whole or in part, including illustrations, in any form (beyond that copying permitted by Sections 107 and 108 of the U.S. Copyright Law and except by reviewers for the public press), without written permission from the publishers.

Set in Sabon type by Westchester Book Group.

Printed in the United States of America.

Library of Congress Cataloging-in-Publication Data

Carmichael, Calum M.
  Sex and religion in the Bible / Calum Carmichael.
     p. cm.
  Includes bibliographical references and indexes.
  ISBN 978-0-300-15377-4 (hardcover : alk. paper)   1. Sex—Biblical teaching. I. Title.
  BS680.S5C36 2010
  220.8'3067—dc22

                                                                         2009024288

A catalogue record for this book is available from the British Library.

This paper meets the requirements of ANSI/NISO Z39.48-1992 (Permanence of Paper).

10 9 8 7 6 5 4 3 2 1

Contents

Preface vii

Introduction ix

1. Procreation 1
2. The Marriage at Cana 12
3. A Sexual Encounter 28
4. Seduction 44
5. Contamination 64
6. Adultery 85
7. The Suspected Adulteress 108
8. Incest 135
9. Desexing 158

Abbreviations   177

Notes   181

Index of References   201

Subject Index   208

Preface

Close reading of biblical texts pays rich dividends for the obvious reason that the texts are compellingly interesting in their complexity and appeal. This literature is rightly thought to be classic—it is never fully understood, and those who study it in depth always want to have more from it. I have published on some of these texts before, but usually as part of a wider inquiry into the origin of biblical law. In this volume I concentrate on a limited range of material in order to highlight sexual matters that arise within it.

Biblical quotations are from the King James Authorized Version of 1611 because it adheres to as literal a translation as possible of the original Hebrew and Greek texts and its archaic character reminds us that we are dealing with a time long past. Sometimes I alter the translation for reasons that I shall cite.

Introduction

If we go to the Bible to find out how people in that time lived their sexual lives, we make a profound error. While the rules and narratives surely do give some idea about prevalent customs, the biblical text was never meant to give a factual account of life back then. Most scholars assume that the varied materials that constitute the Bible give an accurate portrayal of sexuality and religious belief in an ancient society. That kind of historical reconstruction is, indeed, the aim of much scholarly work.[1] My purpose here is to focus on certain well-known narratives in both the Hebrew Bible (for example, Jacob being tricked into intercourse and marriage with Leah, and Abraham encouraging his wife to become another man's wife) and the New Testament (the marriage at Cana of Galilee and Jesus' encounter with a woman at a well), and to bring out notions about sex and marriage underlying these stories. An analysis of the narratives need not exclude some sense of historical reality. But with regard to the Hebrew Bible in particular, I shall stress how it is not pressing social problems that inspire sexual rules, but extraordinary developments arising in the narrative tradition.

Our methods of reconstructing the past using ancient sources did not develop until the emergence of sixteenth-century French legal humanists who tried to work out what life in ancient Rome was like by probing Roman legal and other texts. Those sixteenth-century thinkers, however, ran into problems when they found that the classical sources did not lend themselves satisfactorily to constructing a factual account of the past.[2] The same problem emerges when we try to work out what life was like in ancient Israel by using biblical texts. A common mode of communication in the Bible takes the form of historical and biographical information, but we should not read the text as history and biography as we have come to think of these disciplines. The primeval history recounted in Genesis 1–11 has a chronological scheme and portraits of individuals, but these are mythical events and persons being described. In my view, myth in the form of an explanation and often justification of some event, real or imagined, characterizes most biblical material where a different vision for understanding the world from ours prevails. Whereas our style today emphasizes investigative inquiry to establish facts, the biblical authors are storytellers whose intent is to formulate a mythical account of the origin of their people. A spirit of inventiveness characterizes their work, and we consequently should avoid overmuch effort in constructing actual history and social life from the texts they created.

My purpose, then, is to enter into the spirit of the material and engage the imagination and intelligence of the original minds behind the texts. This type of inquiry is likely to interest modern readers, because storytelling at all times has a compelling appeal. The brilliance of those who forged into a single coherent narrative the law codes and stories in Genesis through 2 Kings is in their "eye for resemblances," as Aristotle says of the genius demonstrated in the making of metaphors (*Poetics* 1459.6–8). By their comparisons and contrasts, the unknown compilers of Genesis through 2 Kings take rules familiar to them and reformulate them in response to unusual issues that arise in the narrative material available to them. This profound link between law and narrative has a felicitous consequence. Because an issue arises in a particular narrative, the legal historian is uniquely able to pinpoint in the most precise way why an ancient rule takes up the problem it does. The rules relate not to an unknowable historical past but to a body of stories with which we are well familiar. The bedrock of biblical and Jewish law turns out not to be family and national life of a historical entity called ancient Israel, but dramatic moments in the legendary and mythical history that is recounted in the continuous narrative Genesis through 2 Kings.

There is a further dimension to be taken into account in emphasizing the importance of biblical storytelling. In one of the last conversations we had before he died, my own teacher, David Daube, spoke rather sadly because he could not follow up on a breakthrough he had made in observing a striking difference between the (loosely labeled) Indo-European languages and the Semitic languages. The former languages permit prefixing, suffixing, and compounding. Marcus Aurelius can say in Greek that no virtue is *katexanastatikos*, "down-out-re-sist-ant," to justice and that a part cut off from a plant is more often than not *dysapokatastatos*, "scarce-re-in-stat-able." We can say in English that a book is un-put-down-able and that something is un-forget-able. The linguistic options available to users of languages such as Greek, Latin, German, and English prove productive in furthering analytical thinking. The meaning at the core of a verb can be expanded extensively with the outcome that all sorts of nuances are achievable. This remarkable capacity to make distinctions enhances philosophical reflection.

Different are the Semitic languages, Daube observed, for they do not permit such ease of distinction making. They go in, rather, for modifying the verb by changing the vowels of the trilateral root that constitutes the word. The verb *'abhadh*, "to perish," can take on the meaning "to destroy," *'ibbhedh* or *he'ebhidh*, a causative form: "to cause to perish, to destroy." The core sense of the verb remains and contributes to the potential of drawing us further into the communication being conveyed. The result is that we are more likely to find in Hebrew a compactness of communication that, in the hands of a sophisticated teller of stories, has profound impact on the recipient. The hearer of a biblical story has to work through the significance of its contents because "it is half the art of storytelling to keep a story free from explanation as one reproduces it."[3] Whereas Greek rationalism and its later Western offshoots appear to favor explanation, balance, clarity, and systematization, the ancient Near Eastern approach has probably more affinity for the intuitive and the inventive. The New Testament was written in Greek, but it retains all of the imaginative inventiveness of its Near Eastern cultural background. Two of the most famous stories in the Gospels, the marriage at Cana of Galilee and

Jesus' encounter with the woman of Samaria at a well (in the Fourth Gospel), will make this fictional freedom abundantly clear.

I shall discuss problems biblical texts bring up in all their particularity, why religious ideas are sometimes central to a story but at other times play no role at all. Mainly, I wish to convey just how extraordinarily sophisticated the ancient writers are.[4] Two points, among many, might be cited to underline that sophistication. First, the stories at some historical moment must have undergone a passage from oral tradition to written form. Such a transition would have been accomplished with utmost care and entail considerations similar to what John Locke comments on about the writing of letters. To commit to writing, Locke states, is to lay the writer "open to severer examination of his breeding, sense and abilities than oral discourse, whose transient faults, dying for the most part with the sound that gives them life, and so not subject to strict review, more easily escape observation and censure."[5] Second, Goethe (or at least the view is attributed to him), when a half-yearly newssheet became a monthly one, remarked that he foresaw with horror the time when it would appear once a week. His capacity to think and reflect would be diminished by so much information coming to him. How could he relate it to what had gone before and anticipate what would happen in the future? The biblical writers had no such concerns. Lacking the means to cultivate a historical sense as we know it, they had ample time to reflect to the finest degree on what was available to them. Little wonder that their compositions are "miniatures of major content."[6]

I have recently completed the compilation of the *Collected Works of David Daube* and am indebted to many of the insights he produced in so many areas of knowledge.[7] A rabbinic notion holds that to take up the views of a departed scholar is to make his spirit live again, even to have him participate in the discourse (*Pesikta Rabbati* 2.4; *b. Yeb.* 97a).[8] I like to think that this fine idea shows up in some of the following discussion.

I

Procreation

And God blessed them, and God said unto them, Be fruitful and multiply.

—*Genesis 1:28*

I begin with a discussion that raises the question of developments in social history: the duty to procreate. The observations bring out, however, the difficulty in writing much that is actually historical about the topic.[1] Emerging instead are ideas that prove compelling at all times and reveal just how sophisticated biblical narratives are in conveying them.

The first text in the Bible to raise the topic of sex and religion is in Genesis 1:28. There is increasing recognition that Genesis through 2 Kings is a fully coherent composition and that we should view its chronicle of events through the eyes of its composer, who probably produced the work at the end of Israel's existence as a nation, either just before or shortly after the Babylonian exile.[2] Attempts to use Genesis through 2 Kings for dating events to satisfy our historical curiosity are consequently fraught with difficulties. It is best to go along with the narrator's chronological account so that we can enter into his world of thought.

We immediately encounter a surprise. Both Judaism and Christianity traditionally view the text in Genesis 1:28 as laying down a duty to procreate, and even modern scholars take its words to be a commandment. But, as David Daube observed, the words do not in fact command. Rather, the full text of the passage constitutes a blessing: "And God blessed them, and God said unto them, Be fruitful and multiply." When we wish a person good fortune, we understandably use the language of command, rather than some authoritative remark that may meet with resistance, because the addressee will be receptive of a wish to participate in the blessing. The phrase "Have a nice day" does not leave one duty bound to do so. The same is true for the statement "Be fruitful and multiply." Ordinarily, one will feel inclined, even bound, to participate in the pleasure of producing offspring (or having a pleasant day), but such an inclination is quite different from being under a requirement to do so. We have, then, in Genesis 1:28 a blessing, not a duty.[3]

Are there texts in the Bible that lay down a duty to produce children? Daube duly took up the question and found none. To be sure, if an Israelite's firstborn son is married and dies without having produced a male child, a law in Deuteronomy 25:5–10 requires a living brother to have intercourse with the widow so as to produce one by her. The child so born continues the name and estate of the dead husband, an outcome that doubtless also contributes to a better life for the widow. A legal fiction comes into play: a matter is interpreted as a fact, a dead man has a son, but remove the construal put on it and it is no fact at all; he is the living brother's son.

If a man is under an obligation to produce a child for a dead brother, does it not follow that he is also duty bound to perpetuate his own name and inheritance? Would the levirate rule not point to a general duty to procreate in the Bible? The answer is that it does not, and in making the distinction between the specific and the general we confront a universal phenomenon. Duties are laid on persons to help others, but as far as one's own person is concerned, one is free to receive or reject a blessing. There is a biblical requirement to aid a person with a broken-down beast (Deut 22:1–4), but if an Israelite's own animal breaks down it would be quite in order for him to leave it to die. Israelites are to assist others if they lack food, but they are free to starve themselves (Deut 24:19–22), the Bible recognizing no prohibition against suicide. It was only later that the rabbis read one into Genesis 9:5, "And surely your blood for your lives I will require," and Augustine into Exodus 20:13 (=Deut 5:17), "Thou shalt not murder."[4] In a parable in Luke's Gospel, a host who is out of bread to serve to a guest arriving at midnight asks his neighbor for some. The host is under an obligation to be hospitable, though if he himself were in need, he would never make a request of his neighbor at that time of night (Luke 11:5–7). The duty to help others will, in fact, have its origin in the primordial instinct to procreate. The powerful compulsion to look after the resulting helpless infant spills over into many other areas of life.

Although no duty to produce children is found in biblical sources, it is worth asking what historical factors might eventually have made for such a requirement. Why, in particular, does procreation eventually become a duty in Judaism and Christianity? The answer points to down-to-earth political realities, although a religious dimension is not lacking. Where those who govern perceive a state interest to increase the birthrate, they lay down a duty to procreate, which, we might note in passing, raises the issue of centralized control over marriage. In our own time we might not come upon a particular state that imposes an actual duty to procreate, but we are familiar enough with the problem a government faces because of the lack of future workers to fund pensions for an increasingly aging population. Governments typically respond to the problem by offering inducements to encourage an increase in the birth-rate.

In ancient Greece, the shortage of fighting men to do battle in the Persian wars (ca 500 BCE) is such that a duty to procreate is imposed. Further, the duty comes wrapped in the sentiment that those who produce offspring will partake in immortality as well as ensuring a continuous stream of worshipers of God.[5] It has to be pointed out, however, that the support of religion in the form of philosophical and theological beliefs enters in as a second best by way of justifying state policy. The military-political necessity comes first, and religious sentiment serves to buttress it. To be sure, high-minded reflection may be around long before the need for political action. What occurs is that a necessary change in policy brings in its wake a need to assert that the topic has always been of great significance. Cynically, one could say that often religion confers respectability on an unpleasant requirement—for example, to produce more fighting men. A religious belief in immortality through one's descendants is exploited because the belief, related as it is to death (including death in battle), gives comfort by its primary focus on a future renewal of life (including the production of more male children to ensure a strong military). Less cynically, the necessity to increase the birthrate brings out what may have been taken for granted all along and now needs to be articulated, namely, that the production of children constitutes a great blessing.

Sometimes the duty to procreate comes with sanctions. Sparta, for instance, imposes both a fine and a measure of civic disgrace on single men, and Plato's *Laws* do the same.[6] Single women at Sparta are not penalized, but in Plato's *Republic* women as well as men come under a duty to procreate.[7] Various schools of thought, especially the Stoics, spread Plato's views on the topic throughout the Mediterranean world, and later generations would have articulated them to adherents of Judaism and Christianity.

Closer to the inception of Christianity, the legislation in 18 BCE of Augustus, the first Roman emperor, imposes a legal (as against a moral) duty to procreate. In previous centuries in Rome, the concern with a low birthrate shows up, but no general legal sanction befalls those refraining from producing children. Augustus brings about change. He penalizes men between twenty-five and sixty and women between twenty and fifty if they are unmarried or married but childless, but he rewards parents producing three or four children.[8] The influence of Greek philosophy and statecraft is readily detectable in the presentation of the legislation. What differs at Rome is that the primary motivation is the need to do something about the declining birthrate among the ruling classes.

At some point, from the second century on, the obligation to procreate begins to appear in Jewish and Christian sources, but not in the New Testament.[9] The fateful destruction of the Temple in 70 CE and the Bar Kochba revolt in 132–135 CE, with their accompanying loss of Jewish life, are probably decisive in the duty being taken over into Judaism from the surrounding culture. The task is confined to males. The peculiarity of the emerging Christian position, which we primarily associate with Paul in 1 Corinthians 7, is the view that if you cannot do without sex, marriage for the sake of procreation is the proper course to pursue. Abstention is superior because of a view that goes back to Jesus: marital union falls short of the ideal type of union, which is to remain celibate for the sake of the kingdom of heaven (Matt 19:10–13). Essentially the view is that, in mystical embrace, the Christian should unite with Jesus only. A deviation from the Jewish position is that the post-Pauline Church Fathers require both males and females to fulfill the duty.

As an exercise in social history, the inquiry into when the duty of procreation comes into Christianity and Judaism is less than satisfying, because the sources limit us in pursuing it.[10] More stimulating is Daube's insight in noting that, down through the centuries, there are countless examples of blessings becoming transformed into duties: acquiring wealth; receiving an education; saving for old age; undergoing medical checkups; and prolonging life. The topic brings to our attention the ebb and flow of attitudes and values at different periods and in different milieus and sharpens our awareness of modern life. Duties wane as circumstances change, for example, that of procreation in the face of concern about overpopulation or in deference to women achieving parity with men in the workplace. Or duties may proliferate: in Australia, the duty to vote, and in the United States, the duty to wear a seat belt. In any event, a topic of vast scope begins from a single observation on an ancient text that is almost universally interpreted wrongly. Daube's correction of the error opens up the possibility of thinking about an idea, the relationship between blessings and duties, which has never previously come under scrutiny, and how it plays out in many areas of life, ancient and modern.[11]

Jesus on Marriage and Procreation

In a discussion between Jesus and some Pharisees, Jesus rejects the institution of divorce. He argues on the grounds that Moses permitted divorce only as a concession to human sinfulness, but because the end-time exists in their current situation, the accommodating attitude no longer applies. His position is contrary to the plain meaning of a law in Deuteronomy 24:1–4, where Mosaic permission to divorce a wife is taken for granted ("writes her a bill of divorcement, and giveth it in her hand, and sendeth her out of his house"). After the interchange, the disciples of Jesus, puzzlingly in some ways, react by saying that in light of his dismissal of divorce it is consequently not expedient for a man to marry in the first place. Jesus responds: "All men cannot receive this saying, save they to whom it is given. For there are some eunuchs, which were so born from their mother's womb: and there are some eunuchs, which were made eunuchs of men: and there be eunuchs, which have made themselves eunuchs for the kingdom of heaven's sake. He that is able to receive it, let him receive it" (Matt 19:12).

When Jesus enunciates to his disciples the second-best nature of marriage in Matthew 19:10–13 and asserts the ideal of sexless existence in the kingdom (as in Mark 12:25: "For when they rise from the dead, they neither marry nor are given in marriage"), we should bear in mind that he does so in his role as a master with a circle of disciples. A major aim of the master is less to lay down an actual duty to avoid marriage, which if he had the power he would require in real life, than to oblige his disciples to seek spiritual enlightenment. It is instruction, nonetheless, of a kind that seeks to transform their way of being in the world. The master takes up ordinary matters, marriage and the production of children in this instance, and pursues analogous spiritual ideas. These disciples, some at least, will have wives and children, but in their pursuit of learning they are to contemplate another kind of union, namely, a disciple with his master. The sense communicated is not all that different from the claim of Alexander the Great. He revered his tutor Aristotle no less than his father because "to the one he owed life, to the other the good life."[12] By becoming like your master in thought and practice, you become not just like him but in a way one with him.

What I am pointing to here is the intellectual liveliness inherent in the position of Jesus. In suggesting such an element it is important to stress the original setting in the life of Jesus, namely, a master with his disciples and how instruction is conveyed in the culture of the time. The influence of the death of Jesus on the writing up of the Gospels will have so colored the presentation of his life that Matthew, in this instance, may have no interest in highlighting any original liveliness of mind. The quality is detectable when, after Jesus makes known his elevated view of marital union, we learn that the disciples rebuke those who bring children to appear before him in order that he might lean his hands on them (Matt 19:13). We go from a learned dispute about the legal topic of divorce and the fallout from Jesus' view on it to the physical appearance of children. Their presence at this point seems somewhat out of place after certain Pharisees have asked him about divorce and his disciples, in turn, about marriage. While the children's appearance may ring false, the actual subject of children is in line with the preceding topic of marriage. The point is that the narrative account exists more to convey ideas than to record what might have actually occurred. The emphasis is on Jesus' opposition to his disciples' restraint of the children and on his speaking positively about their appearing before him "for of such [the nature of children] is the kingdom of heaven" (Matt 19:14).

The disciples express their negative stance about marriage because they draw the inference from the master's teaching. To become a eunuch is to downgrade marriage and diminish the standing of children. The master then sees an opportunity to lay down another teaching, which derives from his raising the status of children. The implicit rebuke he delivers to the disciples is to the end that they think further. As disciples who have repented of their past sins and live in expectation of the Kingdom of God, they are becoming transformed into new beings in the sense familiar to them from the world of conversion to their Jewish religion. Converts to that religion undergo a passage from death to life and become newborn little children: "begotten again," "a newborn babe," "a new man," "a new creation" (*b. Yeb.* 22a, 48b; 1 Peter 1:3, 2:2; Col 3:10; 2 Cor 5:17). John the Baptist (or Baptizer) is given this nickname precisely because he applies proselyte baptism to people who are already Jewish. Repentance, for which he calls, is like conversion, a movement from the death of one's old life to a new life.[13] It is an idea powerful enough to spill over into the situation where a teacher instructs his pupils in new ways of thinking. The initiate to a new spiritual world, Judaism, early Christianity, or special knowledge of one kind or another, is but a child in his first exposure to it. He receives milk before being fed meat (1 Cor 3:2; Heb 5:12; 1 Peter 2:2).

The Creation of Male and Female

The text in Genesis 1:28 about being fruitful and multiplying might be the first biblical reference to the topic of procreation but a more profound probing of the subject is also present in Genesis 1. I refer to the view underlying the notion that "God created man in his image, in the image of God created he him; male and female created he them" (Gen 1:27). No text exceeds this one in influencing later thinking, for example (as I shall shortly note), the detailed argument underlying Jesus' view of marriage and divorce, but also much later notions about human dignity and equality. We even see the idea brought into economics. "The image of God," says Michael Novak, "underlying socialist thought is *Nous*: the all-seeing, commanding intelligence. The image of God underlying both the free market and the triune system of democratic capitalism is *Phronimos*, the practical provident intelligence embodied in singular agents in singular concrete situations."[14]

What has not been appreciated is the narrow focus of Genesis 1:27. Its aim, I submit, is to explore the question of why males and females are essentially the same, yet the differences that exist between them are so important that they serve to bring them together. Rabbinic interpreters are accurate when, puzzling over why the text switches from the use of the singular to the use of the plural—from "so God created man in his own image, in the image of God created he *him*" to "male and female created he *them*"—they see a reference to an original, androgynous being (*Gen. Rab.* on Gen 1:26; *Mek.* on Exod 12:40). The first human is both male and female in one body according to Genesis 1:27.

The next section of Genesis, the Adam and Eve story, continues to explore the topic of sameness and difference, first, between man and animals and then between male and female. After Adam unsuccessfully seeks a companion from among the animals, God creates Eve from Adam's anatomy. Why, we might ask, does the Genesis myth depict Adam as seeking a mate among the animals? The answer is that the ancient author perceives humans as showing features of animals. He contemplates, in turn, the differences between humans and animals, males and females, humankind and divinity, not by means of philosophical inquiry but by imagining that the developments of the kind in question took place in primeval history. Robert Graves and Raphael Patai take Adam's congress with the beasts for granted but explain it differently: "the tradition that man's first sexual intercourse was with animals, not with women, may be due to the widely spread practice of bestiality among herdsmen of the Middle East." They infer from the *Gilgamesh Epic* that Enkidu, too, first mates with the animals until civilized by Aruru's priestess.[15]

What has not been fully understood is that the reference to God's image refers not to a human being as we now recognize him or her but to the first mythical, pre-Eve created being that possesses the image of God. A pre-sexual state is in focus. One reason why the ancient writer suggests that this unique first being has God's image is that he is puzzling over the gender of God. Typically in biblical sources, God is portrayed as a male, a father, a judge, and a warrior, for example. He is but rarely likened to a mother (Isa 49:15, 66:13). In certain contexts, then, it suits the purposes of the authors to portray the deity by means of male and female metaphors. The text in Genesis 1:27 is different and is the result of conscious reflection not just on the essential sameness of males and females but also on the issue of God's gender. In that the first created being lacks sexual differentiation, so too does God because he creates that being in his own image. By postulating that the first being ever is both male and female the Genesis author avoids the attribution of a specific gender to God.[16]

When Jesus in Matthew 19:4 quotes the verse in Genesis 1:27 (the creation of man in God's image, male and female) as "proof" that God did not originally intend that married couples should divorce, he is doing so because of his view that marriage is a return to the original androgynous state that God created at the beginning of time. In marriage, the man reunites with his lost female part and so becomes like the first created being that was made male and female in one. Marriage in Jesus' eschatological view restores the original androgynous being at creation. As we will see in Chapter 9 on the topic of desexing, an anti-sexual attitude underlies his view. How much of the attitude should be attributed to his own personal psychology and how much to the religious views current in his time cannot be decided. There is perhaps a combination of both these factors, although the only one we can recognize, and it is a most powerful one, is the religious idea. As Paul spells out in 1 Corinthians 7, sexual attraction is contrary to spiritual union with the Christ figure. Eschatology, the doctrine of last things, which is perceived as a coming back to the beginning of things, involves this radical thinking. A return to an androgynous state is but the penultimate step on the way to some final, wholly mysterious union in God. The pre-sexual, first being that possesses the image of God is of a higher order than the males and the females who come after Eve issues from Adam's body. The eventual, end-time reversal of the separate conditions of maleness and femaleness represents the return to the ideal of a sexually free state, the attainment of an original, undifferentiated gender ready for incorporation into God.[17] It is why, according to Jesus, after the Resurrection the institution of marriage will not exist (Mark 12:25). Jerome's remark captures the contrast well: "If marriage replenishes the earth, virginity replenishes paradise."[18]

Another text that contains a reference to God's image is Genesis 9:6: "Whoever sheddeth man's blood, by man shall his blood be shed: for in the image of God made he man." Contrary to the common view, the focus is, I submit, not on the murder victim but on the man who will carry out the lawful punishment—it is he who is the antecedent of "for in the image of God made he [the executioner] him." The reason for introducing the idea of the image of God in this context is that the judicial executioner must possess a status higher than the man to be killed in order to act as the representative of God. The image of God is a necessary component of the authority to execute. Cain's slaughter of Abel is wrongful precisely because in killing him he does not possess a status that raises him above his brother. He is not his brother's keeper in the sense in which Abel, as a keeper of animals, could kill one because as human to animal Abel possesses the necessary difference in status to do so. In Numbers 16, God is the executioner of Korah and others who rebel against the authority of Moses and Aaron because as Korah and company challenge their leadership, the judgment has to come from God who stands above both parties.

The issue of equal status is important in so many matters, especially in the area of what we term human rights (the "honor of creatures" in rabbinic sources, *b. Ber.* 19b; *b. Men.* 37b; *Mek.* on Exod 21:37). Talmudic texts tell of Raba's famous rhetorical question addressing the issue as to when some special circumstance may warrant the suspension of the commandment against murder (*b. Pes.* 25b; *b. Sanh.* 74a). When consulted by someone whom a governor had ordered to kill a certain man, lest he be killed himself, Raba responded: "Let him kill you but you shall not kill; what have you seen [to hold] that your blood is redder?" Raba enunciates what appears to him the gist of the rule in Leviticus 19:16 about "not standing against the blood of thy neighbor": the utter impropriety of putting oneself above a fellow being in this situation.

The use of a text in Genesis 5:1–2, with its reference to the image of God, by Simeon ben Azzai, a third-generation Tannaitic rabbi, is also worth noting because it is the basis of a command to love universally, enemies included. The text reads: "This is the book of the generations of Adam. In the day that God created man, in the likeness of God made he him; male and female created he them; and blessed them, and called their name Adam, in the day when they were created." Whereas Rabbi Akiba sees the essence of the law in the commandment "Thou shalt love thy neighbor as thyself," Azzai sees it in the Genesis verse, that is, he finds it in the teaching that all humankind comes from Adam, who was created by God in his likeness (*Siphra* 89b; *Gen. Rab.* on Gen 5:1–2). Impressively, a universal law of love, nonsexual in scope, is traced back to the time when God created the first being.[19]

2

The Marriage at Cana

And the third day there was a marriage in Cana of Galilee; and the mother of Jesus was there.

—*John* 2:1

The use of marriage as a metaphor for the intimate relationship between a master and his disciples is brilliantly exploited in one of the strangest and most compelling narratives in the New Testament, the account in John 2:1–11 of a marriage at Cana in Galilee. The narrative reveals just how powerful the metaphor is. That the account is owing to the inventive genius of a Gospel writer reflecting on matters long after the death of Jesus is a sure indication that it would be unwise to speculate about the attitude to sexuality on the part of the historical Jesus. The pursuit of spiritual ideas, whether by the Jesus of history or, in this instance, by the writer of the Fourth Gospel, is the primary motivation for the use of the marriage metaphor. As with Jesus' teaching on marriage, what drives the application of the metaphor is the appeal to the nature of the created order in Genesis 1.

The term *metaphor* comes from the Greek *metaphorein* and means "to carry something from one place to another."[1] Metaphors can confuse rather than clarify, and their extended use in the Fourth Gospel certainly contributes to the difficulty of comprehending its contents. Aristotle says that "everything said metaphorically is unclear" (*Topics* 139.34). Lord Mansfield, the eighteenth-century Scottish lawyer, states: "Nothing in law is so apt to mislead as a metaphor."[2] When it comes to the expression of religious ideas, however, there can be no alternative but to deal in metaphors. John's switching back and forth between the literal and the metaphorical, between ordinary language and spiritual ideas, is uncommonly impressive. His aim is to initiate an elite group into spiritual mysteries.

The elitist aspect of an ancient work has a long pedigree. There is the fable, attributed to Aesop, about how the eyes envied the mouth the honey it was fed. When the eyes were given some, however, they smarted and found it repellent. Dio Chrysostom (in the first century) applies the fable to philosophy. That discipline is for the few, not for the many, because the latter would not really like to hear what is being said (33.16). John comes close to Chrysostom's play upon the literal and the metaphorical in the fable and its application: "For judgment I [Jesus] am come . . . that they which see not [the uninformed] might see [understand]; and that they which see [the informed] might be made blind [metaphorically]. And the Pharisees . . . said, Are we [the informed] blind also? Jesus said . . . If ye were blind [uninformed] ye should have no sin: but now ye say, We [who possess all information and understanding] see; therefore your sin remaineth" (John 9:39–41). Immediately preceding this contretemps is an episode about Jesus literally causing a blind man to see.

The richness of ideas that reflection on Genesis 1 inspired comes out in a strikingly imaginative way in the Fourth Gospel. The Jewish, Hellenistic author of this work comes from a background steeped in the cosmological speculation of his time. John, to whom the work is ascribed, records much of the life of Jesus in light of the notion that Jesus is the Logos (Word), the original voice that gave existence to the created order in Genesis 1. As stated in the Prologue to the Fourth Gospel: "In the beginning was the Word, and the Word was with God, and the Word was God. The same was in the beginning with God. All things were made by him; and without him was not any thing made that was made. In him was life; and the life was the light of men. And the light shineth in darkness; and the darkness comprehended it not" (John 1:1–5). Far from being an isolated identification that portrays the Jesus of history as the preexistent agency creating everything in the known universe, John has this equation play out throughout his account of the life of Jesus. John's notion is that the creator Jesus is again active in the sense that events in his lifetime re-create the world according to the pattern of the seven days of creation in Genesis 1. We have the following, merest indication of a scheme that stretches from John 1:6 to John 5:47.[3]

The opening five chapters of John recount the beginnings of Jesus' life and record at the outset how the person of the Baptist is a lone, confused voice in the wilderness who seeks light in the dark. Eventually encountering that light at the moment when the Spirit descends dovelike on Jesus at his baptism by water, the Baptist has two of his disciples spend the day with Jesus, a day that begins at four in the afternoon (John 1:1–42). The history is so relayed that each step matches the detailed developments of the first day of creation in Genesis 1:1–5: the formlessness of the universe, the light coming out of the darkness at the moment when the Spirit moves over the water like a bird, and the time span of the first day of the creation, evening and morning. To jump to the final, seventh day of the scheme: in John 5 a healing on the Sabbath occurs because Jesus is depicted as having work to do on that day. The issue at stake, whether God really rests from his work on the Sabbath, is one that was much debated at the time.

The engine driving the inventiveness of John's seven-day scheme is the allegorical mode of interpreting the Hebrew (more probably the Greek) Bible as exemplified in the work of Philo of Alexandria (ca. 20 BCE 20–50 CE). John, like Philo, does not discount the plain meaning of the sacred text; rather, he sees it as having a supernatural origin that requires a deeper layer of meaning to be extracted from it. Only on the basis of the view that the text has such a supernatural origin can interpreters derive allegorical meaning from it. Without that view the meaning is but a figment of the imagination. Light, according to Genesis 1:3, does literally emerge from darkness in the created world, but it also allegorically points to Jesus in his role as the Word or Logos, the light in the darkness that is quite different from the light of the luminaries of day four of Genesis 1:14, 15.[4]

In John 2:1 the reference to a third day, "And the third day there was a marriage in Cana of Galilee; and the mother of Jesus was there," begins an account of a village wedding. On closer inspection, the narration of the event parallels in every particular the third day of creation in Genesis 1:9–13. Here are the two texts:

> And God said, Let the waters under the heavens be gathered together unto one place, and let the dry land appear: and it was so. And God called the dry land Earth; and the gathering together of the waters called he Seas: and God saw that it was good. And God said, Let the earth bring forth grass, the herb yielding seed, and the fruit-tree yielding fruit after his kind, whose seed is in itself, upon the earth: and it was so. And the earth brought forth grass, and herb yielding seed after his kind, and the tree yielding fruit, whose seed was in itself, after his kind: and God saw that it was good. And the evening and the morning were the third day. (Gen 1:9–13)

> And the third day there was a marriage in Cana of Galilee; and the mother of Jesus was there: And both Jesus was called, and his disciples, to the marriage. And when they wanted wine, the mother of Jesus saith unto him, They have no wine. Jesus saith unto her, Woman, what have I to do with thee? mine hour is not yet come. His mother saith unto the servants, Whatsoever he saith unto you, do it. And there were set there six waterpots of stone, after the manner of the purifying of the Jews, containing two or three firkins apiece. Jesus saith unto them, Fill the waterpots with water. And they filled them up to the brim. And he saith unto them, Draw out now, and bear unto the governor of the feast. And they bare it. When the ruler of the feast had tasted the water that was made wine, and knew not whence it was, but the servants which drew the water knew, the governor of the feast called the bridegroom, And saith unto him, Every man at the beginning doth set forth good wine; and when men have well drunk, then that which is worse: but thou hast kept the good wine until now. This beginning of miracles did Jesus in Cana of Galilee, and manifested forth his glory; and his disciples believed on him. After this he went down to Capernaum, he, and his mother, and his brethren, and his disciples; and they continued there not many days. (John 2:1–12)

The miracle story of the water turned into wine has proved to be one of the most elusive to interpret. C. H. Dodd points out that on the face of it, the story appears to be a naive tale about a marvel at a village wedding.[5]

He notes its realism. There is an eye for character and for seemingly trivial detail—the water pots hold from seventeen to twenty-five gallons apiece—and there is the homely humor in the remark of the governor or steward of the banquet: "Everyone puts the best wine on the table first, and brings on the poor stuff when the company is drunk; but you have kept your good wine to the last" (Dodd's translation). We then find the typical Johannine comment that brings out his theological interpretation of a tale: "This beginning of the signs did Jesus in Cana of Galilee, and manifested forth his glory." The verse commonly cited in assessing the meaning of this statement is the one in the Prologue about how "the Word was made flesh, and dwelt among us, and we beheld his glory, the glory of the only begotten of the Father, full of grace and truth" (John 1:14). The Word is the agency that spoke at creation (Gen 1), the uttered speech resulting in activity in the material world. The miracle story in John is not to be taken at face value; its true meaning lies deeper, but where has been difficult to fathom.

The usual approach of commentators is to contrast the new Christian order with the entire system of Jewish ceremonial observance.[6] It is hardly a proper comparison. The tendency to think of Judaism solely in terms of its ritual law is a strange prejudice. Ignored are the equally important areas of private law, the law of procedure, family law, and the moral law. What causes confusion is that when New Testament sources declare their opposition to Jewish law, their focus is solely on ceremonial, ritual law, and, up to a point, moral law. The chief reason for the very restricted focus is that, in appealing to Gentiles, Christian missionaries could not expect them to observe all the ceremonial rules of Judaism, for example, circumcision as a sign of a special bond between the convert and God. It is unlikely that even Jewish ceremonial law is being targeted at this point in John, because the practice of washing hands is too minor a matter.

The water pots are there in accordance with the Jewish manner of purifying, and because this water is turned into wine, we have, according to these commentators, the supposed contrast between a religion that is lower than the new religion of truth.[7] In other words, to them the water represents the Judaism of Jesus' time, which was characterized by ceremonial observance, and the wine represents a "higher" form of religion, which concentrates on spiritual matters. Yet we note that Jesus directs the servants to fill the pots with water. He does not break or discard them, and thus the imagery used in the tale does not fit well with such a broad and sweeping contrast between two religions. Nor is the contrast that the steward of the banquet draws between the old and the new wine all that strong. In fact it is quite benign. The steward even emphasizes that the drinkers of the second round of wine will hardly notice the difference. Usually, when interpreters resort to large perspectives, they are admitting, as Dodd does, the difficulties of breaking into the substance of the story.

An approach through the creation story proves illuminating.[8] In the Genesis account, up to and including the third day, water plays an important role: there are the waters of day one over which the Spirit moves like a bird (Hebrew *rḥp*, "to hover," as in Deut 32:11), and there is on day two the separation of the waters below the firmament from those above it so that the upper waters are held back. Water plays an equally important role in John up to this miracle story: there is, corresponding to day one, the water of the Baptist's ceremony when the Spirit like a bird, a dove, rests on Jesus (John 1:32). Corresponding to day two, there is the location by the Sea of Galilee at Bethsaida of one Nathanael, who is sitting under a fig tree. Rabbinic literature constantly compares the Torah to water. Since in rabbinic sources a favorite place for someone to search scripture is sitting under a tree, the idea is probably that he is drinking the waters of the Torah.[9] A preoccupation with scripture seems all the more likely because Philip (the third disciple of Jesus to be named in John and who is also from Bethsaida) comes upon Nathanael under the tree and immediately refers to what scripture has revealed about Jesus. Philip states: "We have found him, of whom Moses in the law, and the prophets, did write, Jesus of Nazareth, the son of Joseph" (John 1:45). This lower, earthly Jesus then comes upon Nathanael and tells him about the upper realm of day two of creation: Nathanael will see the heaven mysteriously open and will receive visions, that is, the knowledge that is identified with the waters of the upper firmament (John 1:51).

In John's time the belief is widespread that special knowledge, *gnosis*, resides in the heavenly realm above the firmament, which came into existence on the second day of creation. For example, 1 Enoch 17:4, "And they [the angels] took me to the living waters" is a reference to the symbolical water above the firmament. Philo refers to the words of God that have been "poured like rain out of that lofty and pure region of life to which the prophet [Moses] has given the title of 'heaven'" (*Leg. All.* 3.163). In that ordinary humans cannot relate to the notion that there are waters above the firmament of the created universe, it is understandable how the description of the second day of creation in Genesis 1:6–8 invited symbolic meaning to be attributed to these waters. The light of day one, which differed from the sunlight of day three, similarly invited allegorization, as we noted.

Dodd points out that the contrast between Torah and Jesus as the incarnate Word is one of the governing ideas of the Fourth Gospel.[10] Nathanael is to anticipate progress from enjoying first the waters of the Torah under the fig tree to savoring next the special waters that are above the firmament of the heavens. These upper waters are offered only to those reborn of the Spirit. For Philo, because the firmament provides access to heavenly knowledge of the kind that Jesus promises Nathanael, the firmament of day two is the best part of the created world (*De Opic.* 27, 82; *Ques. Gen.* 4.215).

If we assume that the events at Cana mirror the activity of day three of Genesis 1:9–13, much that is suggestive emerges for a great many details of the Johannine story. The first time the topic of a union resulting in fertility emerges in the Genesis creation story occurs on day three: earth and water unite to bring forth the fruits of the earth. John's description of how Jesus miraculously causes the water in the *stone* pots to produce the juice of the vine is, I suggest, the equivalent of the union of water and earth on day three of creation. We might emphasize how the focus of the story is not much, if at all, on the actual bride and the bridegroom but on the water that, through some mysterious union, is turned into wine. In the cosmological speculation that the creation story stimulated in the rabbinic circles of John's time, the water of day three of Genesis represents the masculine, generative source of life and the receiving earth is female (e.g., *Gen. Rab.* 13:13, 14; *y. Taan.* 64b).[11]

Philo's understanding of the miraculous nature of what took place on the third day of creation—he too compares the dry land to a fertile woman (*De Opic.* 38, 39; *De Plant.* 15)—is directly pertinent to the miracle at Cana. Philo states, "And after a fashion quite contrary to the present order of Nature all the fruit trees were laden with fruit as soon as ever they came into existence" (*De Opic.* 40). The author of 2 Esdras 6:43, 44, expresses a similar view when he describes how on day three of creation God's word went forth: "And at once the work was done. For immediately fruit came forth in endless abundance and of varied appeal to the taste." David Winston persuasively argues that in Wisdom 19:7 the "leafy plain" that emerged when the Israelites crossed the Red Sea at the time of the exodus from Egypt is a continuation in this section of Wisdom 19 of the motif of a refashioning of the days of creation in Genesis 1, in this instance the third day (Gen 1:11–13).[12]

In the close parallel of John's account, water has turned into a great abundance of wine, so much so that its quantity is hugely out of proportion to the needs of those attending a village wedding. The abundance is, astonishingly, in addition to the wine that has already been drunk. The marvel corresponds, I suggest, to the superabundance that Jesus as God's Word accomplished on the third day of creation: the water miraculously turns into wine without the intermediate processes involving the planting, watering, growth, and harvesting of vines. In commenting on the miracle of day three of creation, Philo contrasts the ordinary way of things: "For now the processes take place in turn, one at one time, one at another, not all of them simultaneously at one season" (*De Opic.* 40; *Ques. Gen.* 2.47). Nothing in John's narrative suggests how the miracle is brought about: no act of Jesus other than his word is required, as is true again at Cana when he heals the nobleman's son (John 4:49–53)—and as was true at the creation of the world when, according to John, Jesus as the Word made all things (John 1:3). What Jesus as the Logos does at Cana is bring forth from the earth the same extraordinary, fertile abundance of day three of creation.[13]

Water and wine are indeed associated with the third day of creation, when the waters under the firmament were gathered together into one place and the dry land—and the fruit trees—appeared. The link between wine and the events of the third day of creation is explicit in the hymn to God the Creator in Psalm 104. The Psalmist describes how "the waters stood above the mountains" before God sent them to the "place founded for them" (Ps 104:6–8). This is the creation of the sea, as opposed to the dry land. The Psalmist goes on to describe "grass to grow for the cattle, and herb for the service of man that he may bring forth food out of the earth, and wine that maketh glad the heart of man" (Ps 104:14, 15). The link between the creation of the sea (water) and vegetation or the vine (wine) is thus affirmed as belonging to the third day of creation.[14] In his discussion of Noah as the first tiller of the soil, when he planted the first vineyard, Philo states that agriculture began with Noah—and on day three of creation (*Ques. Gen.* 2.66).

In the description of the third day of creation in 2 Esdras 6:42—a work that is generally dated around the time of the composition of the Fourth Gospel—the focus is on God's command to assign one-seventh of the space to water and the remaining six parts to dry land. As Joan E. Cook points out, vegetation such as the vines comes forth but is not the result of a direct command.[15] Moreover, unlike the account in Genesis 1:12, 2 Esdras 6:44 specifies that the plants had taste, color, and scent. In the incident at Cana of Galilee, Jesus' only command is that the stone pots be filled with water. What follows is that, something having occurred indirectly to this water, it now has the taste of wine.

What is also worth pointing out in the Fourth Gospel is how Jesus has the water fetched and poured into water pots whose capacities are cited in line with the measurements of the time (John 2:6). According to *Genesis Rabba* 5:1, God used a standard of measurement for the waters that were gathered together into one place at creation, a view inspired by texts such as Job 38:5–8; Isaiah 40:12; and 2 Esdras 16:57, 58. Equally interesting is the rabbis' understanding of the miracle whereby God pours the water that covers the world into one place. To draw out exactly what the marvel is, the rabbis use the following illustration with water pots. Whereas a human empties a full water pot into an empty one, God at creation empties a full water pot into a full one without spillage. That is the nature of the miracle when the waters are gathered together. The rabbis' thinking, presumably, is that after the second day of creation water is everywhere under the firmament. The next day God miraculously moves all of this water into a lesser area without creating a deeper place to accommodate it all. The result is the dry land in one place and the water in another. It is as if a man takes a full pot of water and pours it into another full pot that is miraculously able to accommodate it. In the rabbis' implicit metaphor, the resulting empty pot is the dry land of day three of creation. If they had expressed the belief in pseudohistorical, Johannine guise, Jesus, the Logos active at creation, would have been the cause of the miracle.

I am suggesting that in citing water pots in his story John uses a metaphor similar to the one used by the rabbis to allude to day three of creation. John's text, which explicitly draws attention to the fullness of the pots—"Fill the waterpots with water. And they [the servants] filled them up to the brim" (John 2:7)—is comparable to the rabbis' explanation of the miracle of fullness on day three of creation. Full pots of water astoundingly become full pots of wine.

The fact that there are six water pots specified in John's account reveals an interesting link to a view found in 2 Esdras 6:42: the waters that are gathered together into one place at creation come from six out of the seven parts of the entire area of water that is under the heaven.[16] In other words, in 2 Esdras, six parts of water are poured into one already filled part, and in the place of the six appears land that is instantaneously fruitful. I emphasize that the development occurs immediately ("For thy word went forth, and at once the work was done" v. 43): water instantly becomes fruitful abundance ("For immediately fruit came forth in endless abundance," v. 44). We should probably understand that the pots used by Jesus already have water in them, as a literal reading of the Greek suggests (John 2:6, 7), and that more water is then added. If that is so, the parallel illustrates well the supposed activity on day three of Genesis when, for the rabbis, God adds water to water. Commentators, for example, R. E. Brown, are puzzled by the use of the verb *antlēsate* in reference to drawing water from the pots. The verb is normally used to refer to drawing water from a well (John 4:7, 15), that is, the water lodged in the earth. B. F. Westcott goes so far as to suggest that the water came from a well and not from the pots. The point is, I think, that the verb is employed because the water and the pots symbolize the water and earth of the created order.[17]

So skillful is John's art that it is always difficult to know when to cease imputing significance to details in his narrative. Thus the location of the miracle at Cana of Galilee can be viewed as a place on dry land between two seas, the Sea of Galilee and the Mediterranean. The name Cana, which Birger Olsson thinks is significant and which may derive from *qanah*, "to create," might tie into this observation about Cana's location. Cana, this "created place," recalls how at creation dry land appeared in the midst of the waters. The symbolical significance attributed to places in John's topographical references by second-century exegetes of John's Gospel suggests that these interpreters, for example, Heracleon, were extending a process already at work in the Gospel. John 9:7 provides an example: "Go wash in the pool of Siloam" [from *šlḥ*, "to send"], which is translated "one who has been sent." As Thomas Brodie well states, "While the theological dimension of John's cities is strong, their hold on history is often fragile."[18]

Another line of interpretation also leads us to the theme of union and fertility that is the topic of the third day of creation. John comments that what happened at Cana is the first of the signs Jesus made by way of manifesting his glory, and "his disciples believed in him." The words of the steward of the wedding feast to the bridegroom convey the sign: how he, the bridegroom, gave first the good wine, but now he provides the best and not, as is the customary way of bridegrooms, the less good. The significance of the comment is that Jesus himself is to be thought of as a bridegroom. He, after all, provided the outstanding wine. We should note that the words of the Baptist in John 3:29 well convey the notion of Jesus as having a bride: "He that hath the bride is the bridegroom: but the friend [the Baptist] of the bridegroom, which standeth and heareth him, rejoiceth greatly because of the bridegroom's voice: this my joy therefore is fulfilled." When John writes as the climax to the episode that the disciples believed in him, he is suggesting that Jesus is a bridegroom and his disciples a bride and that they metaphorically become one as in a marital union.[19]

Symbolism involving the vine permeates the account of the water turned into wine at Cana in a way that has not been observed. In the Old Testament (and many other bodies of literature) the vine is a well-established symbol of a woman as a wife and mother, for example, a man's wife is a fruitful vine (Ps 128:3).[20] When Jesus says to his mother, "Woman, what have I to do with thee [literally, What to me and to you, Woman]? mine hour is not yet come" (John 2:4), we are dealing with what John thinks of as the lower order of creation. She is his mother, a vine that gave him birth, an act of lower, earthly creation. The use of the designation "Woman," so problematic to interpreters, brings out the fundamental feature that she, a woman, gave birth to a son. This relationship of mother and son is even more explicit in John 19:26: "Woman [says Jesus], behold thy son." R. Alan Culpepper states, "Whatever the precise connotation of his words to his mother during the wedding at Cana (2:2), there is a certain coldness about them."[21] This attempt, however, to speak about the emotions of Jesus misses the point of the cosmological character of the work. The ideas John works with are primary, their presentation being but a skillful guise.

In rabbinic thought the hour of a man can be spoken of as the hour of his birth.[22] The idea turns up in John 16:21: "A woman when she is in travail hath sorrow, because her hour is come: but as soon as she is delivered of the child, she remembereth no more the anguish, for joy that a man is born into the world." Although the mother's situation is under scrutiny, there is the accompanying spotlight on the hour of the birth of the child, especially so because the real focus is Jesus' forthcoming resurrection, the hour of his rebirth. Jesus is assuring his disciples that their sorrow over his death will be superseded by their joy when they see him again in his risen state. That joyful time will be his hour that was yet to be when he spoke to his mother at the wedding at Cana. Jesus' mother, unnamed, appears in but two scenes (2:1–5, 12; 19:25–27, there being no birth narrative in the Fourth Gospel). Culpepper points out how the paucity of description about her has encouraged a variety of symbolic interpretations. He thinks that the overtones of both the scenes in which she appears do indeed point to something significant. In the second scene she is given over by the dying Jesus to the ideal (the "beloved") disciple. Culpepper cites R. E. Brown's reference to these two figures of the mother and the disciple as "the two great symbolic figures of the Fourth Gospel." Culpepper continues, "The impact of this scene has been tremendous. Here are the man and 'woman,' the ideal disciple and the mother he is called to receive, standing under the cross of the giver of life. There is the beginning of a new family for the children of God."[23] I would point out that John's underlying theme of procreation is what determines his write-up in both scenes.

Paul's comment in Galatians 1:15 is comparable to Jesus' remark to his mother about how his hour has yet to come (John 2:4). In discussing the history of his conversion, his becoming newborn, Paul refers to how God "separated him from his mother's womb." His conversion was a second birth, one that was of a different order than the birth he experienced when issuing from his mother's womb.[24]

A sequel to the state of unity between Jesus and his disciples is that when his hour (of resurrection) has come he will be glorified "with the glory which I had with thee [his father] before the world was" (John

17:1–4). Moreover, he will have glorified his father at that point because he will have completed the work—of re-creation, we might add—that his father had given him to do. John interprets the transformation of the water into wine as: "This beginning of miracles did Jesus in Cana of Galilee, and manifested forth his glory" (John 2:11). Later in his Gospel, John gives symbolic expression to the idea of the unity that exists between Jesus and his disciples when he has Jesus speak of himself as the true vine and his disciples as its branches (John 15:1–8). Jesus is the male-female element in one.

In John 2:4, then, when Jesus converses with his mother about his new "hour," he is implicitly contrasting it with the hour he experienced with her when she delivered him as her offspring. He is hinting that the old order of earthly creation is passing away. His hour, which was actually the hour of his birth, is, oddly, yet to come: he awaits his new or second birth, the resurrection.

The symbolism of Jesus' mother as the vine that produced him can be observed from another angle. We might first note that for her to be concerned about the shortage of wine at the wedding is odd.[25] This aspect of the story alerts the reader that John is pursuing some surprising meaning. When she points out to her son that the wedding company has no wine, his response, "Woman, what have you to do with me, my hour has not yet come," seems impossibly disconnected. Why should a remark by a mother to her son about lack of wine prompt the son to talk about the topic of birth? If the meaning of his odd remark about his "hour" has to do with reproduction, as seems certain, we can infer that her reference to wine triggers the underlying symbolism about the vine as a metaphor for human reproduction.

The mother of Jesus is the vine that produced him. She in turn anticipates that he will do something when she says to the servants: "Whatsoever he saith unto you, do it" (John 2:5). He does—he miraculously produces wine from water. As a consequence of the miracle or sign, "his disciples believed in him" (John 2:11). Just as the mother of Jesus anticipated the production of wine, so the miracle anticipates something significant about to happen—Jesus himself is a vine that produces branches, his disciples. "I [Jesus] am the vine, ye [his disciples] are the branches," (John 15:5). Jesus himself as a vine thus metaphorically produces offspring. It follows that the disciples are both bride and offspring. Three comments might be made.

First, John does go in for such conflated metaphors, for instance, Jesus is both shepherd and gate to the sheepfold (John 10:7, 9, 11).[26] Second, a vine as a metaphor for marital union and birth encourages this interchange between a producer and those who are produced (although one can see the point of Lord Mansfield's complaint about nothing being so apt to mislead as a metaphor). The branches can be thought of as part of the vine in the sense that they are united with it, as a wife to a husband, but they can also be thought of as the fruit-bearing part of the vine, hence as offspring of the vine. Third, and very much to the point, Jesus as the Word is the creator of the vine. From this perspective, just as the fruit trees of day three of creation in Genesis appear simultaneously both as fruitfulness and as fruit producing, so Jesus' disciples at the same time are both united with him and his offspring. The sign manifests his glory and, as Dodd claimed, the statement in the prologue, one that also evokes mysterious beginnings, is recalled where Christ's glory is that of the only begotten of the Father. The sign at Cana points to the glory he will achieve because those who believe in him, as his disciples do, are begotten of him. We have a remarkable continuity of theme, namely, union and procreation, in all of these manifestly related texts in John (1:14, 2:11, 15:5).

The incident at Cana closes with a transitional statement about how Jesus goes to Capernaum with his mother and brothers and his disciples. The statement becomes much more significant in light of the interchange between the mother, who produces sons at the lower earthly level of biological creation, and Jesus, who produces disciples at the higher level of spiritual creation. The imagery of the vine as powerfully reproductive underlies the statement. The apparently simple description about Jesus, his mother, brothers, and disciples constitutes a choice illustration of John's use of a literal statement to bear great import. A "historical" detail means so much more than meets the eye. The distinction between the initial wine that is given to the wedding guests and the wine that Jesus produces is comparable. The former belongs to the old creation and the latter to the new.

John's clever interplay between literal statements and allegorical meanings is, as I indicated, along the lines of his predecessor Philo's view of a biblical text. Philo does not discount the ordinary meaning of the biblical text but seeks its deeper significance: "Some merely follow the outward and obvious. . . . I would not censure such persons, for perhaps the truth is with them also. Still, I would exhort them not to halt there, but to press on to allegorical interpretations and to recognize that the letter is to the oracle but as the shadow to the substance, and that the higher values therein revealed are what really and truly exist" (*De Confus.* 190; cf. *De Abr.* 18). For John, there is a powerful sense in which, like the Hebrew Bible, the historical details of the life of Jesus constitute a supernatural story that has two layers of meaning, a plain and an allegorical. This is so because Jesus at any one time during his life is the Word made flesh, and the Word does indeed include the words of scripture. That is why John draws a connection between Jesus as the Word and the words of the Mosaic writings: "For had ye [his fellow Jews] believed Moses, ye would have believed me [Jesus]: for he wrote of me. But if ye believe not his writings, how shall ye believe my words?" (John 5:46, 47). In various parts of the Gospel John presents Jesus as the living embodiment of these words. The view underlying the portrayal is that not only did Jesus as the Word speak at the creation of the world, but as that same personified Word he continues to be active in the world that scripture depicts. That is why John can relate Jesus to so many texts in the Old Testament.[27] Equally important, John has Jesus function not just in the prior world of Old Testament events and developments but also as the Word in his own historical life.

To evaluate the description of the event at Cana of Galilee as if it were an actual occurrence is to miss the highly sophisticated purpose that John has in recounting the incident. By recognizing his aim we can account for a miracle in a way that avoids the naivety of raising questions of modern science such as: do the laws of nature exclude miracles? The whole point of the miracle at Cana of Galilee is to suggest that the disciples' master—in reality John with his circle of initiates who probe the significance of the life of Jesus—repeats a miracle equivalent to what he accomplished at creation. First and foremost, we must appreciate that ancient Near Eastern thinkers use storytelling, not philosophical writing, as their way of communicating profound ideas. What appears to be historical and biographical narration serves this end. Events are recounted as if they occurred—with emphasis on the "as if."

Unlike the Synoptic Gospels, for example, in which Jesus dies on Passover day, John in his pursuit of meaningful connections chooses to have him die on the day before, because that is the day when the Passover lamb is sacrificed (John 19:14).[28] The theological claim trumps a commitment to chronological accuracy. Our interest in historical investigation, however compelling, is more often than not besides the point in assessing biblical sources. The ideas conveyed through narrative art are really everything. The beliefs behind the ideas often create events—Jesus as the Passover lamb in John's Gospel—in a way that is similar to what Albert Schweitzer attributed to the historical Jesus. By his dogmatic beliefs, Schweitzer argued, Jesus consciously aimed to bring about dramatic events, appointing, for example, twelve disciples as the new Israel and thinking that he could usher in the Kingdom of God by his actions.[29] It is a cast of mind that continued to inspire because it was imbedded in the cultural climate of the time. John provides a prime instance of such inspiration.

3

A Sexual Encounter

> *And upon this came his disciples, and marvelled that he talked with the woman: yet no man said, What seekest thou? or, Why talkest thou with her?*
>
> —*John 4:27*

The appeal to the nature of the created order in Genesis 1 continues to exercise its hold in another famous narrative that, of all the events related in the four Gospels, unquestionably brings out a sexual relationship between Jesus and an unnamed woman of Samaria. The very boldness of the depiction of the liaison plus the mode of interpretation employed by the author of the Fourth Gospel are sure indicators that he uses the sexual encounter in a special way. The narrative is, nonetheless, one of the most remarkable in biblical literature. I should point out that the use of sexuality to communicate serious notions is not without precedent. In order to make the play acceptable to a male audience, Aristophanes' *Lysistrata* presents in bawdy fashion women's ideas about true human values.

The best way to approach John's extraordinary narrative and to explain the prominence of the sexual dimension is to observe that its contents mirror the events of the sixth day of creation, when the male and the female first appeared. I shall cite the two texts at appropriate points to show how the constituent parts of Genesis 1:26–31 (the sixth day of creation) receive detailed treatment in Jesus' encounter with the Samaritan woman (John 4:1–54).

I turn to Jesus' central role at this point in John's narrative. The Baptist has produced new beings, allegorically speaking, by water baptism at a level that corresponds to the activity of day five of creation when he made disciples "at Aenon near to Salim where there was much water" (John 3:23).[1] Jesus, in turn, produces at the highest level. As the Word of God, he re-creates the Samaritan woman by making her "a well of living water," that is, he restores her to the ideal male-female creation of the sixth day of Genesis 1:27, the day when God's Word made man in his image, male and female "creating he them." The male-female dimension of the sixth day of creation inspires John to allegorize Jesus' meeting with the woman of Samaria at the well and explains the remarkable concern about Jesus' interest in her marital history and how his disciples are taken aback that he is in the company of a woman with no one else present (John 4:27).[2]

A Sexual Encounter

A correspondence between John's narrative and day six of Genesis 1:24–31 can be seen in the contents of the conversation between Jesus and the woman. Here are the two texts in Genesis and John:

> And God said, Let us make man in our image, after our likeness: and let them have dominion over the fish of the sea, and over the fowl of the air, and over the cattle, and over all the earth, and over every creeping thing that creepeth upon the earth. So God created man in his own image, in the image of God created he him: male and female created he them. (Gen 1:27)

> There cometh a woman of Samaria to draw water: Jesus saith unto her, Give me to drink. For his disciples had gone away unto the city to buy meat. Then saith the woman of Samaria unto him, How is it that thou, being a Jew, askest drink of me, which am a woman of Samaria? for the Jews have no dealings with the Samaritans. Jesus answered and said

unto her, If thou knewest the gift of God, and who it is that saith to thee, Give me to drink; thou wouldest have asked of him, and he would have given thee living water. The woman saith unto him, Sir, thou hast nothing to draw with, and the well is deep: from whence then hast thou that living water? Art thou greater than our father Jacob, which gave us the well, and drank thereof himself, and his children, and his cattle? Jesus answered and said unto her, Whosoever drinketh of this water shall thirst again: But whosoever drinketh the water that I shall give him shall never thirst; but the water that I shall give him shall be in him a well of water springing up into everlasting life. The woman saith unto him, Sir, give me this water, that I thirst not, neither come hither to draw. Jesus saith unto her, Go, call thy husband, and come thither. The woman answered and said, I have no husband. Jesus said unto her, Thou hast well said, I have no husband: For thou hast had five husbands; and he whom thou now hast is not thy husband: in that saidst thou truly. (John 4:7–18)

We recall that the marriage at Cana of Galilee pays little or no attention to the actual bride and bridegroom. The reason is that John's focus is on the third day of creation in Genesis, when the first union of water and earth occurred. A wedding is but a screen to present an incident from the life of Jesus that occasions a miracle to correspond to the one that occurred at creation. By contrast, the focus on an actual sexual encounter when Jesus meets the Samaritan woman is attributable to the explicit interest in the origin of the attraction between the sexes on the sixth day of creation in Genesis 1:26–28.

The way John presents Jesus' sexual encounter is remarkably subtle. The woman is not named but time and again is referred to as "Woman," even when Jesus addresses her in John 4:21: "Woman, believe me the hour cometh." As in Jesus' references to his mother as "woman" at Cana and to his coming hour, here he is encountering a woman in the universal sense of womanhood, a product of the original, lower order of creation. He meets her at Jacob's well at high noon. It is precisely the odd time—as commentators point out, it is the hottest part of the day and consequently to be avoided—when the patriarch Jacob met his future wife, Rachel (Gen 29:7).[3] Jesus is alone with her and one indication that we are meant to focus on the sexual nature of the encounter is the later reflection of the disciples that they "marvelled that he talked with the woman" (John 4:27).

The conversation about the water at the well between Jesus and the woman turns on the sexual symbolism attaching to water. Water has proverbial associations with female sexuality. Counsel given to a married man is of the kind: "Drink waters out of thine own cistern, and running waters out of thine own well" (Prov 5:15), and "Let thy fountain be blessed: and rejoice with the wife of thy youth" (Prov 5:18). He is to resist the temptation that "Stolen waters are sweet" (Prov 9:17). The advice is to the end that a husband should steer clear of "strange [*zar, nokri*] women" (Prov 2:16, 5:3, 20, 7:5, 22:14, 23:33).[4] When Jesus asks the female stranger at the well to "Give me to drink," he is using the language of sexual love. When he invites her to partake of "living water," so that she will become "a well of living water," at one level he is speaking of her sexuality along the lines of the bride in the Song of Songs, who is similarly described (Cant 4:12). Hugo Odeberg draws attention to the richness of "water" as a procreative symbol in the rabbinic and Hellenistic literature that is pertinent to the mystical concepts that show up in the Fourth Gospel. For example, the upper waters in 1 Enoch 54:8 and *Genesis Rabba* 13:13, 14 are masculine, whereas the waters beneath the earth, well water, for instance, are feminine.[5]

Decisive confirmation that sexual symbolism associated with water is playing a major role in the narrative about the Samaritan woman comes from pondering how the subject of the woman's marital history—bewilderingly, it would appear—comes into the conversation. After she requests to become a well of living water, Jesus asks her to call her husband. When she responds that she has no husband, he informs her that she has had five. We can grasp the sense of the apparently disjointed nature of the narrative only by following through on the sexual symbolism of the conversation about water. Five men, previous to Jesus, had asked, "Give me to drink," and she had duly distributed her "water" to each in turn.

In characteristic fashion the evangelist then switches from the down-to-earth meaning of Jesus' encounter with the woman to a dizzyingly elevated one. When, oddly, Jesus says to her, "And now he whom thou hast is not thine husband" (John 4:18), he is probably referring to his own person. He is removing himself from an ordinary sexual association with her so that she can comprehend who he really is. Her response to his talk about husbands is, "Sir, I perceive that thou art a prophet" (John 4:19). He is more than that as she comes to appreciate. Not only is he greater than the patriarch Jacob, who met his bride at the place Jesus and she stand (John 4:12). As emerges in a later contretemps with the Jews when they allege that he is a Samaritan (John 8:48–58), he counters by claiming that he is greater even than Abraham: "Before Abraham was, I am" (John 8:58). He is in fact above the level of ordinary male-female sexuality, because as the Word at creation he is the one who originally created the first human, that is, the androgynous being: "male and female created he them" (Gen 1:27). As I noted in Chapter 2 regarding the relationship between Jesus and his disciples in the context of the wedding at Cana, Jesus is again both bridegroom and the one who gives birth to the bride. His role as a historical person and as the preexistent Word accounts for this rather bewildering manner of thinking.

The withdrawal of Jesus from an actual marriage to the Samaritan woman finds an interesting echo in a view (probably contemporary with or a little earlier than John's Gospel) expressed in *m. Sheb.* 8:10: "Moreover they declared before him that R. Eliezer used to say: He that eats the bread of the Samaritans is like to one that eats the flesh of swine. He replied: Hold your peace; I will not say to you what R. Eliezer has taught concerning this." A later rabbi understood Rabbi Eliezer's reference to eating bread as a euphemistic circumlocution for marriage. Joachim Jeremias thinks that this is indeed the correct interpretation, that is, antagonism to any marriage of a Jew and a Samaritan.[6]

The switch from Jesus' sexual relationship with the woman to his role as re-creating her as a well of living water has a parallel in a rabbinic interpretation of Proverbs 5:15, the original meaning of which is about sexual relations between a man and his wife. The text, as Hugo Odeberg points out, came to be interpreted as, "Drink waters out of thine own cistern [*boreka*], that is, drink of the waters of thy Creator [*bore'eka*]."[7] The thinking appears to be that drinking water can refer to union with one's wife, and this act is linked to the original creation of the world because sexual intercourse, leading to procreation, is our only connection with the world's origin.

When Philo comments about Moses' second birth, he provides a parallel to the thought underlying the woman's transformation from a deformed order of living in her current state to a higher spiritual one. Moses' original birth came from a "body and had corruptible parents," whereas his second birth was a divine one, which had no mother but only a father,

God (*Ques. Exod.* 2.46). The reborn Moses represents pure mind (*ho katharōtatos nous*). *Au fond,* what the Samaritan woman believes in her head is what makes her a new being. We might compare how in rabbinic sources, even though the rabbis know from the biblical record about Moses' birth from Amram and Jochebed, they have Moses nonetheless experience a virgin birth (Josephus *Ant.* 2:205–23; *b. B. B.* 120a; *Exod. Rabba* 1:19). His miraculous origin inspires the story in Matthew about the virgin birth of Jesus, as Dale Allison convincingly shows (see Chap. 9).[8] Luke and especially Matthew are perfectly aware that Mary had an illegitimate encounter and that a comparable higher meaning has been achieved, just as the biblical lawgiver has Moses know that (in Lev 18:12, 13) he condemns as incestuous the very union his parents had contracted, a man with his father's sister (Exod 6:20; Num 26:59).

Jesus as the Prophet Jeremiah and the Restoration of the Created Order

In a noticeably abrupt change of direction, John turns from a description of the earthly male-female aspect of Jesus' relationship with the Samaritan woman to the topic of true worship and how the Samaritan nation has fallen short of the requirement. That is, he treats her as standing for the nation. What accounts for this seemingly disjointed switch is John's treatment of the biblical prophetic tradition about the northern kingdom of Israel, that is, according to the Hebrew Bible, the historical Samaria when it was independent of the southern kingdom of Judah. Jacob-Israel is the eponymous ancestor of the northern kingdom, and the woman and her fellow Samaritans are his descendants. When the woman perceives that Jesus is a prophet, John probably has him take on the mantle of the prophet Jeremiah.[9] Like that prophet, Jesus addresses himself to the Samaritans' departure in the person of the woman from the true religion of the Jews of Judah.

The relevant section in John's account reads:

> The woman saith unto him, Sir, I perceive that thou art a prophet. Our fathers worshipped in this mountain; and ye say, that in Jerusalem is the place where men ought to worship. Jesus saith unto her, Woman, believe me, the hour cometh, when ye shall neither in this mountain, nor yet at

> Jerusalem worship the Father. Ye worship ye know not what: we know what we worship; for salvation is of the Jews. But the hour cometh, and now is, when the true worshippers shall worship the Father in spirit and in truth: for the Father seeketh such to worship him. God is a Spirit: and they that worship him must worship him in spirit and in truth. The woman saith unto him, I know that Messias cometh, which is called Christ: when he is come, he will tell us all things. Jesus saith unto her, I that speak unto thee am he. (John 4:19–26)

Jeremiah speaks of the early history of God's relationship with Israel (Samaria) in terms of a bridegroom with a bride (Jer 2:2). Israel, however, became a harlot, unable to restrain her thirst for lovers, and forsook her fountain of living waters, namely, God (Jer 2:13, 20–25). Speaking the Word of God and hence, for John, speaking about Jesus, Jeremiah seeks to restore Israel to her original pristine state (Jer 3). Strikingly, just as Jeremiah depicts God as both bridegroom and creator, so John depicts Jesus, in his transforming encounter with the Samaritan woman, in an identical way. Thus Jesus as a bridegroom approaches a sexual relationship with her but, because of her past love life, he requires that she first return to a divine fountain of living water. John, that is, has searched the scriptures, which testify of Jesus as the Logos or Word that extends back in time (John 5:37) and, identifying Jesus with the prophet Jeremiah, proceeded to shape the narrative about the Samaritan woman.

The explicit comparison in John 4:12 between Jesus and Jacob—"Art thou [Jesus] greater than our father Jacob?" asks the Samaritan woman of Jesus—takes on more meaning in light of John's focus on the history of the Samaritans (cf. also John 8:48–58). Jacob was the father, the creator of the old Samaria; Jesus, the creator of the new Samaria. The beginnings of the first Samaritans occurred when Jacob met a woman (Rachel) at the well, just as the beginnings of the new Samaritans took place when Jesus meets a woman at this same well. Jeremiah had indicated that an act of re-creation was required for the transformation of the old Samaria (Israel). Jesus proves to be the agent of just such a transformation in producing the new Samaria.

When we note John's use of Old Testament material at this point in his Gospel, we must emphasize that John draws a connection between Jesus, who is the Word, and the words of the Mosaic writings. It is a feature that critics well recognize. C. K. Barrett, for example, refers to the multivalent character of John's references: a scriptural citation is intended to link up with a number of Old Testament passages; or, if no citation is actually given, a thematic relationship exists between the Johannine subject matter and episodes in the Old Testament.[10]

Reproduction

A clear correspondence between John's narrative and the sixth day of creation centers on the winning over of the woman's fellow Samaritans to belief in Jesus as the Messiah. The development suggests that she is reproducing because of her spiritual union with Jesus. Here are the pertinent texts:

> And God blessed them, and God said unto them, Be fruitful, and multiply, and replenish the earth, and subdue it: and have dominion over the fish of the sea, and over the fowl of the air, and over every living thing that moveth upon the earth. (Gen 1:28)

> And upon this [Jesus telling the woman that he is the Messiah she is talking about] came his [Jesus'] disciples, and marvelled that he talked with the woman: yet no man said, What seekest thou? or, Why talkest thou with her? The woman then left her waterpot, and went her way into the city, and saith to the men, Come, see a man, which told me all things that ever I did: is not this the Christ? Then they went out of the city, and came unto him. (John 4:27–30)

In Genesis, the blessing upon the instantaneously sexualized male and female of the sixth day of creation is to result in their being fruitful and multiplying. In John, after the personal encounter between Jesus and the newly transformed Samaritan woman, there is no more mention of any sexual partner in her life. Yet she produces offspring—in the sense of new believers in Jesus as the Messiah.[11] The male and the female are being fruitful and multiplying. In her new state, one that is imbued with the spirit of the Logos or Word, she has gone to her own people and won them over. Hugo Odeberg's statement about those who have been born "from above" is relevant: "He who has been born from above and entered the spiritual world and eternal life, he will himself be a source of eternal, spiritual life. The all-inclusiveness of the spiritual world implies that all spiritual beings partake in the eternal generation of life, *hudōr hallomenon eis zō'n aiōnion,* that proceeds from God."[12]

Jesus' involvement with a woman might have been expected because of the Baptist's earlier, anticipatory comment about how he, the Baptist, is but the friend of the bridegroom (John 3:29). He means Jesus as bridegroom. When the Baptist goes on to state that Jesus must increase while he must decrease—that is, in terms of the numbers of disciples each will have—the underlying idea is the anticipated number of offspring that comes from a marital union. The multiplication of believers that results from Jesus' involvement with the Samaritan woman is exactly what the Baptist anticipated, and, as just indicated, harks back to the blessing of the sixth day of creation that the male and the female should be fruitful and multiply.

Sickness in the Lower Order of Creation

The fruitfulness and multiplication among the Samaritans who come to believe in Jesus is of a figurative, higher order than what occurs for ordinary sexual beings. Indeed, what the Samaritans achieve at this higher level stands in sharp contrast to the fate that the lower order of creation experiences. The Samaritans arrive at their elevated position because they are convinced that their previous path to salvation, their state before re-creation, was imperfect. In the lower creation, if human beings reproduce and the resulting child suffers an illness that threatens death, there is manifest imperfection and it too requires a remedy. In typical fashion, because John never fails in dealing with some specific matter to go back and forth between the literal and the metaphorical, he turns to just such an aspect of the lower creation.

Just after Jesus' interaction with the Samaritans—and we would want to know why there is a switch to such an apparently different topic—he heals a nobleman's son. The text reads:

> Now after two days he departed thence, and went into Galilee. For Jesus himself testified, that a prophet hath no honour in his own country. Then when he was come into Galilee, the Galileans received him, having seen all the things that he did at Jerusalem at the feast: for they also went

unto the feast. So Jesus came again into Cana of Galilee, where he made the water wine. And there was a certain nobleman, whose son was sick at Capernaum. When he heard that Jesus had come out of Judea into Galilee, he went unto him, and besought him that he would come down, and heal his son: for he was at the point of death. Then said Jesus unto him, Except ye see signs and wonders, ye will not believe. The nobleman saith unto him, Sir, come down ere my child die. Jesus saith unto him, Go thy way, thy son liveth. And the man believed the word that Jesus had spoken unto him, and he went his way. And as he was now going down, his servants met him, and told him, saying, Thy son liveth. Then inquired he of them the hour when he began to amend. And they said unto him, Yesterday at the seventh hour the fever left him. So the father knew that it was at the same hour, in the which Jesus said unto him, Thy son liveth: and himself believed, and his whole house. This is again the second miracle that Jesus did, when he was come out of Judea into Galilee. (John 4:46–54)

By healing the nobleman's son, Jesus restores at the ordinary level of family life the blessing of fruitfulness to the distressed parents. John draws attention to the fact that geographically Jesus has returned to Cana of Galilee "where he made the water wine" (John 4:46). That incident is about the marriage of a couple, which is the preliminary stage to the birth of children. In other words, while John focuses on the healing of the child in John 4:46–54, he also manages to allude to the larger picture of marriage and reproduction, in particular, to the creation of the male and the female on day six of creation and the blessing on them to bring forth offspring in the ordinary sense of human reproduction.

John states that the healing of the nobleman's son is the second miracle that Jesus does (John 4:54). The first is the changing of water into wine at Cana. Central to each miracle is the notion of procreation. The disciples believe in Jesus because of the miracle with the wine, which is about his "hour," namely, the hour of his death followed by his rebirth. Their belief betokens that they are his offspring, the branches of the vine. The nobleman's son, in turn, experiences a passage from death to life and the nobleman and his household come to believe in Jesus (John 4:50). In becoming believers they too are offspring of Jesus in a sense similar to how the disciples (and the Samaritans) become offspring.

Harvesting

Another clear correspondence between John's Gospel and the sixth day of creation is the shared interest in food. In Genesis, food for the human creations of day six is to consist in the harvest of the earth. In John, when the disciples return to Jesus with actual food, after he brings about the re-creation of the Samaritan woman, he chooses to launch into a discourse not just about food of a different kind but about harvesting it. The relevant texts are:

> And God said, Behold, I have given you every herb bearing seed, which is upon the face of all the earth, and every tree, in the which is the fruit of a tree yielding seed: to you it shall be for meat. And to every beast of the earth, and to every fowl of the air, and to every thing that creepeth upon the earth, wherein there is life, I have given every green herb for meat: and it was so. (Gen 1:29, 30)

> In the mean while his disciples prayed him, saying, Master, eat. But he said unto them, I have meat to eat that ye know not of. Therefore said the disciples one to another, Hath any man brought him aught to eat? Jesus saith unto them, My meat is to do the will of him that sent me, and to finish his work. Say not ye, there are yet four months, and then cometh harvest? behold, I say unto you, Lift up your eyes, and look on the fields; for they are white already to harvest. And he that reapeth receiveth wages, and gathereth fruit unto life eternal: that both he that soweth and he that reapeth may rejoice together. And herein is that saying true, One soweth, and another reapeth. I sent ye to reap that whereon ye bestowed no labour: other men laboured, and ye are entered into their labours. And many of the Samaritans of that city believed in him for the saying of the woman, which testified, He told me all that ever I did. So when the Samaritans were come unto him, they besought him that he would tarry with them: and he abode there two days. And many more believed because of his own word; And said unto the woman, now we believe, not because of thy saying: for we have heard him ourselves, and know that this is indeed the Christ, the Saviour of the world. (John 4:31–42)

We have in the matter of food for created beings the typical back and forth between the lower and higher realms of creation. The many Samaritans who accept him as Messiah because of the woman's testimony are equated with a harvest. We have, that is, an allegorical discourse that is inspired by the miraculous harvest of day six of creation. Immediately noteworthy is that in Jesus' reference to food in John 4:32 the term used is *brōsis* and not *brōma;* as Birger Olsson points out, however, although the two may often be synonymous, the latter would give the more natural meaning.[13] The term used in John 4:32 happens to be the one used in Genesis 1:29 about God's provision of food to serve the needs of all creatures. Also noteworthy is that the language Jesus employs about food has close association with reproduction, the very topic that John has just focused on. In giving expression to the implied transformation of the Samaritans into new beings because of their newly acquired knowledge, Jesus employs the language of sowing and harvesting. (In Chap. 4 I discuss the universal association between harvesting and human reproduction.) Philo compares food, in the form of plants and trees, to the mind and what has been sown and planted in it (*De Agric.* 8–10).

The ordinary fact that the disciples return with food obviously inspires the figurative language about how the believing Samaritans constitute a harvest. We would still wish to know, however, why the agricultural metaphor is given such extensive treatment. The focus on the administration of food on the sixth day of creation provides the answer. When John has Jesus state that his food is to do the will of God and to accomplish his work (John 4:34), the work is that of creation. Indeed the verb used is *teleioō* ("to complete") and the notion is that Jesus brings to completion the work of creation in keeping with the cosmological perspective that so far dominates John's presentation of all the work of Jesus. It is the same work that he is about to do even on the Sabbath day, along with his father, God, who also works on that day.[14] Thus we have in John 5:16–18: "And therefore did the Jews persecute Jesus, and sought to slay him, because he had done these things on the sabbath day. But Jesus answered them, My father worketh hitherto, and I work. Therefore the Jews sought the more to kill him, because he not only had broken the sabbath, but said also that God was his father, making himself equal with God."

When Jesus describes his task among the Samaritans in terms of sowing and harvesting, it is possible to pinpoint precisely how the work is thought of as a process comparable to the way in which food at the time of the creation of the world came into existence. That food was characterized by Philo in the following terms: "And, after a fashion quite contrary to the present order of Nature, all were laden with fruit as soon as ever they came into existence. For now the processes take place in turn, one at one time, one at another, not all of them simultaneously at one season" (*De Opic.* 40, 41). Jesus suggests a comparable miracle is occurring among the Samaritans: "Say not ye, There are yet four months, and then cometh harvest? behold, I say unto you, Lift up your eyes, and look on the fields; for they are white already to harvest" (John 4:35). Jesus contrasts the normally experienced time difference between sowing and harvest with what happens to the Samaritans, namely, the entire process takes place at one time.[15] The felicitous consequence is that sower and reaper are able to rejoice together. This joy is both an expression of the completed order of creation, to wit, the spontaneous abundance of the sixth day of creation and a celebration of the births that the Baptist anticipated in his role as the bridegroom's friend.

Rabbi Simlai, a Palestinian Amora of the third century, interprets Genesis 1:26 (the sixth day of creation), "Let us make man in our image, after our likeness," for his disciples to mean that the man, the woman, and the divine Spirit jointly produce offspring (*Gen. Rab.* 8:9). Jesus, the woman, and the divine Spirit accomplish this task precisely in accordance with the injunction of Genesis 1:26. G. F. Moore thinks that Rabbi Simlai's interpretation was directed against Christians as heretics.[16] I think it more likely that both John and Rabbi Simlai are interpreting the enigmatic reference to "us" in Genesis 1:26 as alluding to maleness and femaleness in the godhead (see Rabbi Samuel's view, which I shall cite shortly). Simlai's apparent reference to an ordinary man and an ordinary woman makes no sense in that they have not yet come into being. The focus is on those (heavenly) beings who produced the first man, or rather the first male-female. The sexuality of the Samaritan woman may stand for femaleness that has to be, and is, transformed by heavenly water into divine female sexuality.

Following through on his focus upon the joy that is appropriate at the harvesting of the Samaritans, Jesus quotes a proverb: "And herein is that saying true, One soweth, and another reapeth" (John 4:37). Commentators note that the saying in its usual application refers to a distressing situation, but Jesus, who is aware of this usual application, is able to achieve the opposite effect.[17] There is thus an intended surprise in the words "And herein is that saying true": a situation of joy, not trouble, has been established because there is a newly transformed state of nature that is similar to what occurred at creation.

Elsewhere in John there is a parallel to his thinking about trouble and joy in the saying about one sowing and another reaping. In John 16:21 there is the explicit contrast between trouble and joy in regard to the topic of human fruitfulness: "A woman when she is in travail hath sorrow, because her hour is come: but as soon as she is delivered of the child, she remembereth no more the anguish, for joy that a man is born into the world." Jesus is the one speaking about this aspect of human birth and, comparable to when he addresses his disciples about the Samaritans, his intention is to direct his disciples to the new order of creation.

There is also a rabbinic parallel. In *Genesis Rabba* 42:3, Rabbi Samuel ben Nahman engages in a semantic exercise regarding the story of creation. He draws a distinction between the expressions "And it came to pass" and "And it shall come to pass." The former, referring to the past, denotes trouble, the latter future joy. The former expression is used in descriptions of the days of creation in Genesis, for example, "And evening came to pass and morning came to pass, a sixth day." Rabbi Samuel argues that, contrary to his opponents' view, these days were not occasions for joy because they lacked completion. As proof of the future, completed order of creation, he cites Zechariah 14:8: "And it shall come to pass in that day, that living waters shall go out from Jerusalem." His views constitute a remarkable echo of those that John has Jesus express. In Jesus' discussion with the Samaritan woman there is reference to living waters and the role of Jerusalem in the lives of Jews and Samaritans. Even should there be no connection between the two sources, as is likely, we can still see how the image of water in the creation story was treated at a time later than John's Gospel.

Rabbi Samuel, a Palestinian Amora of the earlier part of the third century, also expresses views that tantalizingly reveal much in common with what we find in John's account of Jesus with the Samaritan woman. Similar to Jesus' contrast between worship at Jerusalem and worship of God in spirit and truth, Samuel directs attention away from supplicating at the ruined site of the Temple in Jerusalem and seeking the *Shechinah* (female Divine Presence) in heaven. His view is contrary to that of those who believe that the Divine Presence still abides at the ruined site. He is interested in the notion of androgyny, the union of the male and the female in the first man, and thinks of God as possessing both male and female characteristics. His Messianic interests are also unconventional. He speculates about an Ephraimite Messiah from the tribe of Joseph.[18] The Samaritan woman in John 4:25 refers to the Messiah, and from a Samaritan perspective it seems reasonable to assume that their Messiah would be linked to Ephraim. After all, they traced their own descent from Ephraim. He, we recall, is the son of Joseph who is cited in John 4:5 in a reference to the parcel of ground that is near the city of Samaria, where Jesus meets the Samaritan woman.

The next development in John's account of Jesus' life is his healing of a crippled man on the Sabbath day (John 5). This action arouses hostility, and Jesus justifies his deed by arguing that both he and his father, God, must work on the Sabbath (John 5:17). The account is, I claim, John's description of the equivalent of the seventh day of the original creation in Jesus' re-creation of the world.[19] John has Jesus tell his opponents that they should search the scriptures, for they "testify of him" (John 5:39). John 5:46, in turn, claims that a study of the writings of Moses is really an account of what Jesus does in his life. The implication is not just that the dispute about working on the seventh day revolves around the issue as to how to interpret the institution of the Sabbath at the creation of the world. It is a statement to the effect that to examine the days of creation in Genesis 1 is to read about Jesus. That is, John's description of the life of Jesus is indeed an account about the completion of the original order of creation, because his deeds duplicate and perfect the scheme laid out in Genesis 1. Moses, for John, is the one who wrote the story of creation in Genesis 1.

John uses, then, the creation story to convey the cosmological significance of the deeds of Jesus. Philo before him reveals a similar mode of thought. His view is that, whereas contemplative pagans got so far in comprehending the nature of the creator from the created universe, a full disclosure was given to the Jewish nation through the writings of Moses (*Leg. All.* 3.97–103; *De Praem.* 46). For John, in turn, this role is played by Jesus, because Moses wrote about him. The notion that Moses in the form of his writings accuses Jesus' opponents is reminiscent of the rabbinic use of the device of hypostatization. In the examples we have, a document from which parts have been unfairly omitted takes up its own defense, speaks out, and attacks the culprit. The use of the device in regard to biblical texts by Simeon ben Jochai, for example, in the second century CE, can be traced to Hellenistic rhetorical instruction.[20] John's Gospel embodies a similar rhetorical conceit and also contributes to his persistent personification of the natural world.

The Synoptic Gospels contain a parallel of sorts to how John switches from some extraordinary characterization of Jesus to the primary subject matter. It may not be about sexuality, but it comes close enough. All three Gospels record complaints about the unworthy company Jesus keeps at meals and how, unlike the disciples of John the Baptist and of certain Pharisees who fast, Jesus' disciples do not (Matt 9:10–17; Mark 2:15–22; Luke 5:29–39, 7:36–50, 15:1–10). In Matthew and Luke, Jesus takes up the complaint and chides the people because they put down the Baptist as one who possesses a malign spirit, and they condemn him as one who is seriously out of control. Jesus, they claim, is "a glutton and a winebibber, a friend of publicans and sinners" (Matt 11:19; Luke 7:34).

Why, we might ask, is the possibility even raised that Jesus is given to heavy drinking and gluttony? That he did so party in real life is unlikely in the extreme. The point is that the emphasis is on the final part of the denunciation, on his keeping company with undesirable, dissolute types who diminish his supposed saintliness. The indictment, which Jesus attributes to his opponents, is viewed as an attempt to characterize him as the rebellious son of the rule in Deuteronomy 21:20: one who disobeys parents and who engages in excessive drinking and eating. By rabbinic times, the law was only enforced if a rebellious son also associated with unsatisfactory, untrustworthy types. In Jesus' case, these would be the publicans and the sinners. To bring Jesus under the rule, it was necessary to characterize him as a glutton and a winebibber.[21]

4

Seduction

> *I am Ruth thine handmaid, spread therefore thy skirt over thy handmaid.*
>
> —*Ruth 3:9*

The sexual seduction of the Samaritan woman by Jesus leads—and it was so intended—to a religious conviction on her part that he is the Messiah. The link between sexual seduction and religious conviction is, in fact, such a common one that John's mode of presenting how she came by her belief need not be so surprising. Yet it is surprising for at least three reasons.

First, where wrongful religious attachment is thought of in terms of sexual seduction, the aim is to depict a negative development: the person seduced becomes an idolater. That is, when a writer speaks of idolatry as sexual seduction he is borrowing the vocabulary of the latter. John's extraordinary boldness is to have Jesus appear to seduce the woman sexually—except that he stops short of any physical contact with her. The drama of his account doubtless enables John to highlight what Jesus is about, namely, to win over the woman and her fellow Samaritans to believe in him as the Messiah (John 4:25, 26, 39–42). We must constantly be alert to a rhetorical technique that comes from John's first- or second-century Jewish-Hellenistic milieu, and we should not forget that already in the Book of Proverbs wisdom is presented as an attractive, seductive woman. (There is no figure of wisdom as a beguiling male who wins over women by his charms.)

Second, there is another difference between John and any biblical precedent. Foreign women are often the agents by which Israelite men are seduced into idolatry (Exod 34:16; cf. Deut 7:4; Num 25; 1 Kgs 16:31; 2 Kgs 8:17; 2 Chron 21:6). The Samaritan woman, half-foreign in a way, plays no such role. Jesus is the seducer, but it is not to idolatry.

Third, it is true that John's depicting Jesus' approach to the woman as sexual is not without a biblical precedent. The prophet Hosea depicts the bond between God and Israel as a marriage between a husband and wife. The relationship becomes interesting when she is unfaithful to him and he wants her back. When that happens we read that God "infatuates, entices" *(pitta)* his wayward wife, that is, he uses seductive ways to win her back: "I will entice her and bring her into the wilderness, and speak tenderly to her" (Hos 2:14). There is, however, an obvious major difference between Hosea and the Fourth Gospel. Hosea's account of God's enticement of his unfaithful wife is inevitably metaphorical, whereas John relates that Jesus does in fact entice the Samaritan woman.

Jesus' successful seduction at the religious level means that his intercourse with the woman in the nonsexual sense results in offspring—through her belief that he is the Messiah she brings her fellow townspeople to believe in him too. The winning over is described as a harvesting: "Look on the fields; for they are white already to harvest" (John 4:35). Metaphors drawn from agriculture to speak of human sexuality are universal. In biblical material, such metaphors dominate the story of Ruth, but the extent of that author's use of them when recounting her sexual seduction of Boaz has not been appreciated.

The Book of Ruth

The threshing-floor scene when Ruth approaches the sleeping, inebriated Boaz at midnight and lies down beside him is one of the best known in world literature. Goethe's comment that the story was the sweetest idyll composed in antiquity is much quoted: "das lieblichste kleine Ganze, das uns episch und idyllisch überliefert worden ist" (the loveliest of examples in epic and idyllic poetry which has been handed down to us).[1] As early as the Gospel of Luke the scene inspires a section of the narrative of the annunciation: "And the angel said . . . The Power of the Highest shall overshadow you . . . and Mary said, Behold the handmaid of the Lord" (Luke 1:35). The allusion is to Ruth 3:9: "I am Ruth thine handmaid, spread therefore thy skirt over [overshadow] thy handmaid." Ruth prefigures Mary. The conduct of each woman invites suspicion: Ruth's nocturnal visit to Boaz to whom she is not married, and the unmarried Mary's pregnant state by someone not even her betrothed. For the narrator of the Gospel, however, such suspicion is beside the point. In the Jewish cultural setting from which Luke draws, Boaz is viewed as a redeemer figure who is associated with bringing about ultimate redemption and Ruth's action on the threshing floor at midnight expresses, despite appearances, the most exalted chastity. By Luke's time, she has become a suitable model to depict Mary's seemingly precarious moral position.[2]

The original biblical story of Ruth is quite different. The art and sophistication that have gone into its composition are striking, and the details deserve fullest attention. Running through the entire story is a deft interplay between harvests and human birth, an association that is a staple among agricultural societies ancient and modern. Famine strikes the land of Judah, and Elimelech's family (his wife, Naomi, and two sons, Mahlon and Chilion) leave their home in Bethlehem to sojourn in the neighboring land of Moab. There Elimelech dies, and the sons take wives, Orpah and Ruth, of the women of Moab. The two sons-husbands also die there.

Through his use of language the narrator is intent on evoking certain associations. The loss of a man's seed and his death are the bleak counterparts to the failure of agricultural seed in his hometown of Bethlehem, which means "house of [grain] bread." Elimelech is an Ephrathite of Bethlehem-Judah, who, having left because of the failed harvest, has come into the country, literally fields, of Moab (Ruth 1:2). The name Ephrathite reinforces the association with fruitfulness, the meaning having been derived from the Hebrew *parah,* "to be fruitful." Moab, in turn, is the place proverbially associated not only with a patriarch's lack of offspring to perpetuate his name but with a deviant remedy for the problem. One of the two daughters of Lot gets her father drunk in order "to preserve seed of the father" (Gen 19:30–38)—hence the name Moab, "from father" (at least that is how its meaning would have been understood).

So is set out the grim situation facing the future of Elimelech's family line: "Call me not Naomi [pleasant one], call me Mara [bitter one]: for the Almighty hath dealt very bitterly with me" (Ruth 1:20). From this point on in the story each aspect of the problem of continuing a family line will be taken up in a similarly adroit and allusive fashion. Hearing that there are again harvests in Bethlehem (*beth leḥem*)—Yahweh has "visited his people in giving them bread (*leḥem*)"—Naomi decides to return from the country (field, singular this time) of Moab (Ruth 1:6). Although she and her two daughters-in-law actually start out to return to the land of Judah, Naomi appeals to them "to return each to her mother's house" (Ruth 1:8). She wants them to marry husbands from among their own people, the Moabites. Oddly, Naomi does not direct them to go each to her father's house. There is lacking the expected reference to the patriarchal home (Gen 38:11; Lev 22:13; Num 30:16; Deut 22:21). To suggest, as critics do, that *both* fathers must be dead seems especially weak.[3] More likely, we are to pick up an allusion to Lot's daughters. Faced with a similar male-deprived situation these daughters sought a remedy by getting their father drunk and becoming pregnant by him. Naomi is eventually going to have Ruth, who is consistently referred to as a Moabitess, remedy their forlorn state by approaching a drunken Boaz in a setting heavy with sexual overtones. Naomi's instruction to Ruth and her sister not to go to their fathers' houses may well carry an innuendo associated with what Lot's daughters did to their father.

Naomi then informs Ruth and Orpah about a development so beyond any likely chance of realization that they should not even consider it. Naomi asks this question: even should she acquire a husband that very night and produce sons by him who would grow up and become their husbands, would they wait for such an improbable development to come about? Orpah returns—no doubt to her mother's house—but Ruth opts to accompany Naomi back to her own country. They arrive in Bethlehem at, significantly, the beginning of the barley harvest (Ruth 1:22).

If places and names evoke past events and give added import to current actions, the actions themselves begin to elicit remarkable coincidences. Each coincidence, moreover, is associated with aspects of harvesting. Ruth, the Moabitess (Ruth 2:1), has just come from the country (fields) of Moab

(Ruth 1:22), and she requests to glean grain in someone's field. The field she picks happens to belong to Boaz, a wealthy relative of Elimelech. Boaz, who belongs to the generation before Ruth's, learns of and praises her kindness to Naomi, warns young men not to molest her, and gives her grain above and beyond what poor widows are normally given. Ruth beats out what she has gleaned and finds that she has a full measure of grain to take to her mother-in-law, Naomi. This miniature harvest is a harbinger of the most climactic and significant of developments, each of which continues to be intimately tied to agricultural activity.

Boaz has been attending to his harvest, and we find him in his threshing floor winnowing his barley and casting it into a heap. Having finished the annual task, he eats and drinks and "his heart is merry" (Ruth 3:7); he then lies down and falls asleep beside his freshly threshed heap of grain. Responding to Boaz's generous treatment of Ruth, Naomi primes Ruth about paying a nocturnal visit to the inebriated Boaz at his threshing floor. Having dressed appealingly, Ruth approaches Boaz, finds him asleep, uncovers his feet, and lies down there. Awakening, he is startled to find the woman at his feet. When he asks who she is, she replies, "I am Ruth thine handmaid, spread therefore thy skirt over thy handmaid; for thou art a near kinsman" (Ruth 3:9). He responds by invoking a blessing on her, telling her that there is a closer kinsman than he, and, promising to take the matter up in the morning, has her spend the night with him.

To interpret these actions we have to note how agricultural practices can be figurative for human ones. Throughout the story of Ruth what happens to the fertility of the land of Judah parallels what happens to one of its families, to Elimelech and his lineage. As in other languages, the verb "to thresh, to tread," *dûš* in Hebrew, can have the meaning of intercourse. It is said about Onan in *Genesis Rabba* on Genesis 38:9 that "he trod [dûš] within but ejaculated without." The *Oxford English Dictionary* lists the obsolete "to tread" transitively with "out," as "to engender, beget." It cites the idiom "to tread one's shoe awry" as "to fall from chastity," as when a woman's vulva, her "shoe," is worn by the "feet" of, presumably, many lovers. (On a shoe as a common symbol of the female genitals, see Chap. 9.)

Figuratively, then, threshing or treading can refer to the seed to be released and implanted in the woman. Not surprisingly, it is in the erotic poetry of the Song of Songs that we have an allusion to such threshing.

Anticipating union with his bride, the bridegroom describes her features while at the same time imagining how he will engage with them: "How beautiful are thy feet with shoes, O prince's daughter! The joints of thy thighs are like jewels, the work of the hands of a cunning workman. Thy navel is like a rounded goblet, which wanteth not liquor: thy belly is like an heap of wheat set about with lilies. Thy two breasts are like two young roes that are twins" (Cant 7:1–3). In referring to the shoes on her feet, the bridegroom is really alluding to a higher part of her body, to her thighs, and describing what will occur when her "shoes" will adorn his "feet." Note that he does not refer to anatomical parts between feet and thighs, to her ankles or knees, for example, but focuses on her genital region. The lilies allude to her pubic hair, as noted by Wilhelm Rudolph, and the reason why her belly does not lack grain is because he will continually release seed there. [4]

This erotic scene is pertinent to the seduction scene in Ruth 3. Ruth's lying down at Boaz's feet has sexual overtones because in Hebrew, again as in most languages, "feet" can refer to the male genitalia (female, too, depending on the prevailing perspective). It is worth recalling the wider context for Ruth's dramatic and apparently strange action of lying at Boaz's feet. Her beating out seed from what she gleans from Boaz's field suggests to Naomi that Ruth should attempt to have Boaz engage in a comparable act of beating out seed. Only Ruth should be the field this time. That is why Naomi sends Ruth to Boaz after he has finished his own agricultural threshing. Beguiling dress and mood-enhancing drink are involved in the seduction. Since Ruth is commonly described as a Moabitess, as already indicated, an allusion to the origin of her people may be found in this scene—to the time when her first ancestress exploited drunkenness to become pregnant by her father, Lot, with a view to preserving seed for the family line (Gen 19:30–38). Equally noteworthy, Boaz and Lot are one generation removed from the adventuresome women.

Ruth's actions are designed to suggest to Boaz that having finished treading and produced his agricultural seed, he should tread her and produce human seed. Ruth, we recall, uncovers his feet and lies down beside him, that is, she takes off his shoes so as to suggest that he should put her on as his new pair and proceed to tread her to produce seed. Her actions are carried out beside the new seed from his recent threshing, and Boaz's role is to release seed in her to continue the line of Elimelech. That is why when Ruth leaves Boaz's threshing floor in the morning he places in her lap measures of grain such that she looks pregnant with human seed inside her.[5] When a child is eventually born to Ruth from Boaz's seed, Naomi herself takes the child and places it in her lap (Ruth 3:15). The same verb, *šît*, is used in each instance for the placement of the agricultural and human seed.

When Boaz awakes to find the attractively dressed woman at his feet, he is greeted with the request that he spread his covering over her. That is, he should take off his present garment and put her on as his new one. The suggested procedure is exactly analogous to the one hinted at for the shoes. As in most languages, a garment can be figurative for a woman (see Chap. 9). A rule in Deuteronomy 22:30 prohibits a man's intercourse with his father's skirt, his wife, the son's stepmother. When God spreads his garment over the woman Jerusalem to cover her nakedness, the prophet Ezekiel makes it clear that the deity wishes to enter into a marriage with the woman. The notion that Jerusalem becomes God's new garment comes out in the fact that he clothes and adorns her and makes her an international celebrity (Ezek 16:8–14). She is his beautiful garment.

Little wonder that with all this sexual metaphor being applied in the story, Boaz expresses concern that any suggestion of an actual seduction taking place be avoided. In telling Ruth to lie at his feet until the morning he has her depart his threshing place "before one could know another" for "he said, Let it not be known that a woman came to the threshing floor" (Ruth 3:14). Jesus, we saw, does not go to such lengths to avoid suspicion being raised about his involvement with the Samaritan woman. It is left to his disciples to express their concern about it.

In the climax to the story the sexual allusions continue. Boaz appears the next morning at the local city gate to summon the man who is nearer in line to the dead Elimelech to address the issue of the latter's estate. Boaz avoids using the man's name. All the reader learns about Boaz's call to him is something like in English, "Here, so and so, turn aside, sit down here" (Ruth 4:1). The odd expression used in Hebrew, *pelônî 'almônî*, may convey a double reference to virility (*'ôn*) so that the meaning contains an element of mockery: "my virile, virile one" (*'ônî, 'ônî*). The name Onan is itself a doubling of *'ôn*, "the virile, virile one," for a similarly mocking purpose. The author of Ruth is much given to wordplay.[6]

The name Boaz ("in him is strength," as in the LXX) probably also hints at his sexual potency.⁷

The unnamed man does not, in fact, give of his virility to Ruth. In a comparable situation, the proverbial example of a man who refuses to give of his seed, and provides an example of passivity that is culpable, is indeed Onan with Tamar in Genesis 38. To avoid giving her conception, Onan interrupts intercourse with Tamar and ejaculates outside of her. Ruth 4:12, 18 explicitly refer to the outcome of the latter episode when Tamar goes on to trick Onan's father, Judah, to give of his seed. The author, I suggest, so writes up the nearer kinsman's role in the Ruth story that his character is made to echo the part of Onan in the Tamar story, just as the author hints that one of Ruth's roles in the saga is to imitate the first Moabitess, the daughter of Lot, in taking advantage of an inebriated relative. The kinsman is initially happy to possess the land that is Elimelech's, but when he hears that he will have to take Ruth too and raise a child to the dead Elimelech, he demurs on the extraordinary grounds that he does not wish to destroy his own inheritance.

To make sense of his claim, critics invariably water it down and take the term *šḥt* here to mean "to mar, to impair" his inheritance and not "to destroy" as in other biblical contexts (Deut 20:19, 20; Judg 6:4; Jer 11:19; Mal 3:11). But even this weakened meaning of the word makes little sense. If the man did take Ruth and produce a child, he would be in possession of Elimelech's land for many years until such time as the child was old enough to take it over.⁸ The existence of the institution of polygamy can be assumed, so that if he has children by another woman it is difficult to see how producing a child by Ruth would "mar" his inheritance, never mind "destroy" it.

Critics fail to appreciate the subtlety of the ancient author. His intent is to compare the man to the proverbial Onan. Onan acted as he did with Tamar because by not giving a child to his dead brother he stood to gain the latter's share of the father's estate. Onan's sudden death for his disloyalty is to be understood as mirroring punishment. By denying his dead brother a continued share in the family inheritance, his own share is cut off. Each kinsman, then, wishes to acquire material benefit from the dead relative, but Onan's attempt leads to his own destruction at the hands of God. The kinsman in Ruth is made to stop short of what Onan did and therefore not experience the destruction of his life and inheritance. This avoidance of doing what Onan did is why the kinsman uses the strong language about destroying his inheritance. Onan destroys (šḥt, the same verb the nearer kinsman uses) his seed, not spills it, as is the standard translation. In doing so, not only is Onan preventing the restoration of his dead brother's inheritance but he is also unwittingly destroying his own, for God strikes him down on the occasion.

So much of the story of Ruth involves the role of imitation, even if only to oppose. Aside from Ruth playing a role like Rachel's, Leah's, and Tamar's (Ruth 4:11, 12), we have the suppressed comparisons of Ruth playing the role of a daughter of Lot, and Boaz playing Judah's role because each man, having been seduced unexpectedly by a woman from a younger generation, impregnates the woman. The author of Ruth does not, to be sure, have Ruth conscious of behaving like her ancestress in using wine to lie with a relative. The author's intent is to draw the link, and the same consideration applies to the nearer kinsman with his refusal to give conception to Ruth.

The climax to the story of Ruth is all about the success of her seduction of Boaz. There is an emphasis on the positive consequences of procreative strength, in sharp contrast to the nearer kinsman's failure to exercise it on behalf of Elimelech. When Boaz acquires Elimelech's land along with Ruth, the people at the gate witness the transaction, wish Ruth to be fertile like Rachel and Leah on behalf of Jacob-Israel, and express the view that procreative strength (ḥyl, a synonym of ʿoz) not be lacking in Bethlehem. Boaz's house is to be like "the house of Perez whom Tamar bare unto Judah, of the seed which Yahweh shall give thee of this young woman" (Ruth 4:12). Seed, that is, from a man whose accumulation of agricultural seed on his threshing floor was the cue for Naomi, Ruth's mother-in-law, to have the process imitated with Ruth. The women of Bethlehem praise Naomi on her success in acquiring human seed and express the wish that the child be "a restorer of life and a nourisher of thine old age" (Ruth 4:15). Naomi at this point takes the child and lays it in her bosom. As we noted, the use of the same verb šît, as when Boaz places seed in Ruth's lap, recalls the consistent paralleling of human with agricultural reproduction. When the women speak of the child as one who will nourish Naomi, the Hebrew word is *kûl*. The verb is regularly used about providing someone with food (Gen 45:11; 2 Sam 19:32, 33;

1 Kgs 4:7, 5:27, 18:4, 13). At the end of the story, then, the link between human seed and agricultural produce is positively highlighted—in sharp contrast to the loss of harvests in Bethlehem and the decimation of the family of Elimelech at the beginning of the story.

Another Case of Seduction by a Woman with a View to Marriage: Leah Becoming Jacob's Bride

When the people of Bethlehem-Judah wish Ruth to be fertile, they invoke the examples of Rachel and Leah who produced children—Judah, for example—on behalf of Jacob-Israel (Ruth 4:11). The invocation contains no hint of just how dramatic that development was in the life of Jacob, the founding father of the nation (Gen 29). A seduction of a complicated kind by Leah, the mother of Judah, is at the heart of it and will prove very relevant to a strange rule in Deuteronomy 22:13–21 about a bride slandered on her wedding night.

In the story, Jacob wishes to marry Laban's younger daughter, Rachel, and agrees to work seven years for her to become his wife. After the seven years are up, Laban, doubtless taking advantage of Jacob's inebriated state at the wedding festivities, slips the presumably veiled Leah into the bridal tent in place of Rachel. When Jacob comes to his senses after the substitution and discovers his unwanted new wife, he confronts Laban. The latter responds by offering Rachel to Jacob for a further seven years of service, if he remains married to Leah. In the circumstances Jacob has no alternative but to accept the offer, and Rachel becomes his second wife.

Laban must have primed Leah to take her sister's place in the wedding tent. Either she knows her father's intentions, or it really is the case in his country, Aram, that, as Laban explains to Jacob, though only after the fact, a father is bound by custom to marry off the elder daughter first (Gen 29:26). In any event, even though Jacob has already discounted Leah as a wife because of her looks, there is a real sense in which, by taking up her presumed right to marriage as the elder sister, she makes herself sexually available to Jacob and seduces him into a marital union. Delicacy about relating female sexual activity doubtless prevents the ancient author from paying attention to the details of what goes on in the wedding tent. All we learn is, "And it came to pass, that in the morning, behold, it was Leah" who lay beside Jacob (Gen 29:25).

There is manifest cheating on the part of Laban. From an ethical and legal standpoint, the obvious issue arises as to whether Jacob should be obliged to take Leah in that the error comes about through deception. Modern legal systems would decide that he would be justified in returning the woman to her father or guardian. But such an outcome, especially if the custom of marrying off the older daughter before the younger applies, is unfair to her and any child that may have been conceived on the wedding night. Jacob, however, does not even attempt to void the marriage. If Laban chooses to, he could prevent Jacob from having Rachel as a wife, whom he very much wants. Jacob's dilemma does lead to the formulation of a Deuteronomic law that, like the story, centers on the issue of returning an unwanted wife to the father. Both story and law highlight the remarkable phenomenon of brides unwanted after the wedding night. The law reads:

> If any man take a wife, and go into her, and hate her, And give occasions of speech against her, and bring up an evil name upon her, and say, I took this woman, and when I came to her, I found her not a maid: Then shall the father of the damsel, and her mother, take and bring forth the tokens of the damsel's virginity unto the elders of the city in the gate: And the damsel's father shall say unto the elders, I gave my daughter unto this man to wife, and he hateth her; And, lo, he hath given occasions of speech against her, saying, I found not thy daughter a maid; and yet these are the tokens of my daughter's virginity. And they shall spread the cloth before the elders of the city. And the elders of that city shall take that man and chastise him; And they shall amerce him in an hundred shekels of silver, and give them unto the father of the damsel, because he hath brought up an evil name upon a virgin of Israel: and she shall be his wife; he may not put her away all his days. But if this thing be true, and the tokens of virginity be not found for the damsel: Then they shall bring out the damsel to the door of her father's house, and the men of her city shall stone her with stones that she die: because she hath wrought folly in Israel, to play the whore in her father's house: so shalt thou put evil away from among you. (Deut 22:13–21)

In the law, a man refuses to accept his new bride because he alleges that she is not a virgin. The dispute hinges on the wedding-night sheet. If it is bloodstained and therefore evidence of her prior virginity, the husband has to pay her father double the bride-price for the slander he brings on her and her father's house, and he must remain married to her. Jacob, we might note, pays a double bride-price, fourteen years of service, for Rachel and has to remain married to Leah.[9] According to the law, if there is no blood on the sheet, the judgment is severe: the woman is to be put to death because the unstained sheet is evidence that she has engaged in harlotry. Prostitution may be a recognized profession, but for a daughter of Israel to engage in anything like it is such a serious falling away from the standards the Deuteronomic lawgiver sets for her and fellow members of the house of Israel that capital punishment is viewed as the appropriate penalty.

The climactic part of the rule, the bride's lack of virginity, provides the reason, I submit, why the rule is set down at all. It displays the same narrow focus as in the story. In both, a man rejects his bride because of a misconception about her that, in each instance, results from what happens on the wedding night. Jacob is mistaken about his bride's identity, and the man in the rule is mistaken about his bride's virginity. But the story and the rule then diverge. Because of his circumstances, Jacob cannot reject Leah. In the rule, however, the man can reject his bride if no blood has been found on the sheet. The lawgiver, I suggest, crafted the rule as a reaction to Jacob's inability to reject Leah. The situation depicted in the rule is the only one that would permit the man in Jacob's situation to void the marriage. The rule furnishes a valid basis for rejecting a bride—her lack of virginity—that was not available to Jacob. Or, put another way, the lawgiver looking back on the story might have reckoned Leah's lack of virginity the only condition that could have settled the dispute between Jacob and Laban. The law's intent is that if sometime in the future a son of Jacob-Israel seeks to dismiss his newly acquired bride, the one ground entitling him to do so is the production of proof that she is not a virgin.[10]

We can assume that later Israelites were familiar with the story about the founding father's marital problem. Jacob's predicament raises the question about what a man might do if he somehow acquires a wife he does not wish to have. Either the prospective father-in-law cheats in the way Laban does, or there is a genuine misunderstanding as a result of the suitor's prior negotiations over the arrangements to enter the marriage. The rule in turn has come up with a comparable problem that might plausibly occur in ordinary, not legendary, times and lays out the legal outcomes.[11]

Laws on Seduction and Jacob's Daughter, Dinah

If love is amusingly described as a temporary state of insanity that is cured by marriage, seduction in biblical legal sources brings with it a remedy that points the couple in the same direction. There are two laws that express what the cure might be.

> And if a man entice a maid that is not betrothed, and lie with her, he shall surely endow her to be his wife. If her father utterly refuse to give her unto him, he shall pay money according to the bride-price of virgins. (Exod 22:16, 17)

> If a man find a damsel that is a virgin, which is not betrothed, and lay hold on her, and lie with her, and they be found; then the man that lay with her shall give unto the damsel's father fifty shekels of silver, and she shall be his wife; because he hath humbled her, he may not put her away all his days. (Deut 22:28, 29)

The particular bias of the Exodus rule is the issue of a father who refuses to negotiate with his daughter's seducer about a bride-price. The resolution is that the seducer still pays one according to the price that is the going rate for virgin women. The Deuteronomic rule differs in that it leaves no scope for negotiation: the seducer pays a fixed price, marries the woman, and is refused any future right to divorce her.

Critics understandably, but wrongly in my view, see the two rules reflecting different historical periods in the life of the nation. Their contents may well mirror actual practices and be based on rules known to the Exodus and Deuteronomic writers, but the rules are even more interesting than any such assumptions about the historical realities of ancient Israel would suggest. Because the rules are integral to an ongoing narrative about legendary history (Gen–2 Kgs), we might look into that account to illumine them. After all, the tales incorporated in the larger narrative communicate ideas and issues that are important to the ancient Israelites, and, given the nature of storytelling, these tales are inevitably idiosyncratic in character. The subject matter of the rules, in turn, is frequently narrow in focus, and that narrowness alone suggests a close link between story and rule. The intent of the compilers of Genesis through 2 Kings, laws and narratives, is not to preserve a record of conventional practices but to relay the remarkable. As a case in point, the narrative in Genesis 34 about Shechem's seduction of Dinah explains why the two rules about seduction exist and why they differ markedly. The rules, in effect, constitute ideal judgments by a circle of scribes reflecting on the issues that arise in the story in Genesis 34. The contents of the rules differ because divergent judgments can arise depending on what aspect of the case is under review.

The story tells of Jacob's one and only daughter, Dinah. She is the first Israelite daughter, and no doubt partly because of that her experience comes under scrutiny by the writers who compile the legendary history of their nation. In terms of how a young, virginal girl properly conducted herself at the time, it has to be said that Dinah dubiously takes it upon herself to make a trip out of her circle unaccompanied by any male relative. She visits the women of a particular group, the Hivites, a Canaanite clan, who are settled in the region that her own people have just reached in their travels. Shechem, the son of the Hivite leader, Hamor, sees Dinah, "takes her, lies with her, and humbles ['*innah*] her" (Gen 34:2). It is almost certainly seduction (Shechem "speaks tenderly to her"), not rape, as so commonly claimed.

By reading force into the term '*innah*, translators and critics almost invariably speak of the rape of Dinah.[12] However, the verb '*innah* means to take a woman without observing the proper formalities, that is, without speaking to her father or guardian first to arrange a marriage. It is why her brothers say that Shechem treated her like a harlot (Gen 34:31). In a later narrative that does involve a rape, the victim, Tamar, after appealing to her half-brother Amnon not to humble her *('innah)*, asks him to speak to their father about marrying her. If force is involved, a verb like *ḥazaq* is added, as in Amnon's rape of Tamar (2 Sam 13:11, 12). In Deuteronomy 22:24, '*innah* is used of a betrothed woman who consents to intercourse, so force, in this instance, is out of the question. To be sure, '*innah* can come to mean forced appropriation, but that is because of a freer, nonlegal use of the term, as in the extended meaning in Lamentations 5:11 about conquerors ravishing the enemy's women. The reason, I think, why so many interpreters speak of the rape of Dinah is a need to lessen their horror at the extreme vengeance exacted by Jacob's sons on the entire Hivite male population. They slaughter every one of them.

Shechem's "soul cleaves to Dinah" (Gen 34:3), and he asks his father to negotiate a bride-price for her. Hamor then tells Jacob about his son's longing for Dinah and that his group and Jacob's should intermarry and enter into commercial arrangements. Shechem also involves himself in the negotiations and generously says, "Ask of me a bride-price ever so high" (Gen 34:12). Yet the negotiations break down in dramatic fashion. Two of Jacob's sons, not Jacob himself, express outrage that Shechem should have ravished their sister. They deceptively go along with the idea that the two collectives should enter into connubial and commercial arrangements, but they lay down a formidable condition. The Hivite males must first become circumcised. They agree, and "on the third day, when they were sore," the two sons of Jacob, Simeon and Levi, enter the Hivite city and slay every male there. Despite Jacob's protests about the fierceness of their action, these sons have the last word: "Should he deal with our sister as with a harlot?" (Gen 34:31).

The compilers of the rules about seduction in Exodus and Deuteronomy are, I submit, focused on this tale of seduction and its fierce outcome. The very wildness of the tale has them ask what rules might apply in later Israelite life when the problem of intermarriage is not the concern. They see two different ways of handling comparable if much less dramatic, and from their own inner Israelite perspective, undesirable developments. The Exodus rule focuses on the girl's father as the one normally involved with marital negotiations. It concentrates on that aspect of the story whereby Dinah is refused her suitor despite his offer of a very high bride-price. If for whatever reason the girl's family is unwilling to give their daughter in marriage to the man, even at a high bride-price, the outcome is that the failed suitor has to pay the going rate for virgins. The solution compensates the father for the seducer's having deprived him of a virginal daughter in any future marriage he may arrange for her.

Reflecting a stricter attitude toward a man's, or rather an Israelite's, sexual conduct, the Deuteronomic rule concentrates more directly on the dishonor done to the Israelite woman. The rule is against yielding to the wish of a father who might oppose giving his daughter to her seducer. Instead, the Deuteronomic rule maker requires the seducer to take the woman and support her for the rest of his life, as well as having him pay a fixed bride-price for her. There is no negotiating a bride-price as in Genesis 34, and, since we are dealing with internal Israelite relations and not the situation in Genesis 34, a family's refusal to let the woman marry the man is ruled out. The two rules differ markedly in that in one the father can refuse his daughter to her seducer, whereas in the other he cannot. The difference, however, reflects the tension in the story between Jacob genuinely entering into negotiations and the brothers only going through the motions of doing so, while being secretly intent on preventing any marriage. If we view the rules as hypothetical, scribal constructions—ancient Near Eastern laws in general appear to be of this nature—then both positions are intelligible in light of the events in Genesis 34.

Rules are designed to end disputes in as peaceable a way as possible. In the final resolution of the problem in Genesis 34, the refusal of Dinah's siblings to let Shechem marry her led to a fearful outcome, the death of all the male Hivites and the threat of vengeance from their fellow Canaanites against Jacob's family (Gen 34:30). One way to forestall unwelcome consequences should a girl's family not be inclined to give her over to her seducer is to deny the family any right to refuse her to him. The Deuteronomic rule reflects that solution. The Exodus rule, on the other hand, is less bothered by such a consequence and accepts a situation (within Israel) that has the head of the girl's family refuse. It is worth underlining that whereas Dinah's brothers are fiercely opposed to a marriage between Shechem and Dinah, Jacob seems not to be opposed and is willing enough to conclude a marital arrangement for his one and only daughter. The Exodus rule concentrates on a family's refusal, in the proper person of the father, but the Deuteronomic rule concentrates on the sole fact that a seduction has occurred. It takes the sensible position in light of the consequences of the refusal in Genesis 34 that the matter should proceed to a marital arrangement involving a fixed bride-price in the negotiations between the two parties. There is no room for someone like Shechem to say, "Ask of me a bride-price ever so high" (Gen 34:12). There would also be no scope for a situation like the one Jacob experiences earlier in his life. Recall that after he takes Leah sexually and finds himself mistakenly married to her, he seeks to be rid of her when he finds out that she is not the woman he wanted (Gen 29).

I already noted that idolatry in biblical sources is commonly expressed in the language of sexual seduction. "And the people began to commit whoredom with the daughters of Moab, for they called them unto the sacrifices of their gods" is one example of the problem (Num 25:1). Genesis 34 is clearly an account of an actual sexual seduction. Yet, so sophisticated are the biblical writers, the story's real intent may be to warn later Israelites against foreign marriages because of the problem of idolatry. Less obviously than in John's account of Jesus with the woman of Samaria (where in the end we are left in no doubt that the fundamental concern is with proper religious belief), the story in Genesis 34 may also be taken up with the religious issue of idolatry.

A feature of the narratives in the Book of Genesis is that they anticipate issues in the life of later Israel—which means that the narratives have been written at a much later date than the events described in them. One later issue that emerges in a major way is a concern with Israelite identity in the face of foreign cultural influences. S. R. Driver wonders whether the narrative in Genesis 34 about Jacob's encounter with the Canaanite group, the Shechemites, is one in which individual persons stand for tribes and whether the focus is really on the larger issue of national identity. He points out that, after the conquest of Canaan, Israelites and Canaanites dwelt in Shechem side by side (Judg 9). In that there is similar language in Genesis 33:19 and Judges 9:28 ("the sons of Hamor, Shechem's father"), the name Shechem that signifies a place in Judges may in the person Shechem in Genesis 34 really be a personification of the inhabitants of the place. Consequently, we may not be dealing so much with the sexual seduction of Dinah by Shechem as with the later religious seduction of Israel by a Canaanite group. Driver may be correct in his surmise.[13]

In the story in Genesis 34, Simeon and Levi exhibit the moral, religious zeal that opposes all Canaanite influence on the Israelites. The more prudent Jacob represents the wiser sociopolitical stance of a group accommodating itself to another that is perceived to possess values different or even alien to it. After all, the future Israelites are to live in Canaan, a land already inhabited by Hivites who are in a position of power and ownership of the land. The narrator's sympathy is with the zealous sons, because he lets them have the last word after Jacob complains that they have made the house of Jacob-Israel vulnerable to attack by other Canaanites: "Should he deal with our sister as with a harlot?" (Gen 34:30, 31).

Jacob's farewell address to his sons in Genesis 49:5–7 continues to express his anger at what the two sons did. They, he complains, had "slain a man" and "hamstrung an ox." Wordplays and comparisons of humans to animals characterize most of Jacob's farewell remarks to his sons in Genesis 49. In this example, Simeon and Levi slew a man Hamor (Hebrew for "ass"), who represents all the male Hivites, and hamstrung an ox (Jacob-Israel), who represents all the Israelites. The name Hamor is clearly a derogatory one.[14] An ox, wild or domestic, often refers to Israel's fighting capacity (Num 23:22, 24:8; Deut 33:7; Ps 132:5), the issue that confronted Jacob because of his two sons' ferocious treatment of the circumcised Hivites and the expected response from their allies. Hamstringing an animal is an action associated with warfare (Josh 11:6, 9; 2 Sam 8:4), and the allusion is to how these sons brought trouble on the house of Jacob by slaughtering all the male Hivites (Gen 34:30). The two words ʿiqqēr ("to hamstring," in Gen 49:6) and ʿakar ("to bring trouble," in Gen 34:30) are close in sound and meaning.[15]

A rule in Deuteronomy 22:10 also takes up Jacob's complaint in Genesis 49 and, consistent with the narrator's attitude in the story in Genesis 34, dismisses it on the grounds of ethnic purity. The figurative rule in Deuteronomy 22:10 against plowing with an ox and an ass together opposes Jacob's complacent attitude to the Canaanite Shechem's attempt to marry his daughter, Dinah (Gen 34:5). The Deuteronomic lawgiver is very much on the side of her brothers, Simeon and Levi, whom he views as praiseworthy in fiercely opposing the idea of intermarriage between the house of Jacob and any Canaanite group. Shechem, the son of the ass, Hamor, sexually "plowed" Dinah, the daughter of the ox, that is, the house of Jacob. Plowing is yet another example of an agricultural metaphor applied to human sexual activity. Jacob, we just noted, alludes to his house in Genesis 49:6 as the ox (*šor*, "ox," not *šur*, "wall," as in AV) when he refers back to the incident in Genesis 34. The rule against plowing with an ox and an ass together is but a figurative way of expressing what Deuteronomy 7:1–5 openly declaims against: no unions between Israelites and Hivites, no giving of an Israelite daughter to a Hivite son or taking a Hivite daughter for an Israelite son, "for they will turn away thy son from following me, that they may serve other gods." The resort to figurative language in Deuteronomy 22:10 is probably to be explained as a veiled attack on the complacent, if pragmatic, stance of Jacob, the father of the nation, to the issue of intermarriage with a Canaanite group. The later author of *Jubilees,* sensitive to such criticism of Jacob, removes it by having Jacob align himself with Simeon and Levi in their anger at Shechem's seduction of Dinah (Jub 30:3, 4).[16]

Is, then, the story of Dinah's seduction by Shechem really a warning against religious seduction, the practice of intermarriage being seen as the bridge that leads to such enticement? The view underlying the narrative would be in keeping with a frequent one in biblical sources, only in them it is foreign women who are seen as likely to persuade Israelite men to become adherents of foreign cults. "Now King Solomon had many strange women, and they turned away his heart after their gods" (1 Kgs 11:1); "Ahab took to wife Jezebel, the daughter of the king of the Zidonians, and went and served Baal" (1 Kgs 16:31); and "Jehoram walked in the way of the kings of Israel, for he had the daughter of Ahab to wife, and he did that which was evil" (2 Kgs 8:17). Yet in Genesis 34 the situation is rather different. It is not an Israelite male who goes among the Canaanites but a Canaanite male who wishes to marry an Israelite woman. We might note that when Deuteronomy 7:3 openly condemns Israelite-Hivite intermarriage, mention is first made of Israelite daughters marrying Hivite (and other Canaanite) men—Dinah's situation in Genesis 34. A unique aspect of the Dinah story is that the Hivites, by undergoing circumcision, show themselves willing to follow her into her religion, the opposite situation that constantly confronts the Israelites. From the perspective of the Hivites, they are seduced by a woman into a new religion away from their own, much to their detriment.

The story of Ruth carries no such negative overtones about the beguilement of foreign religious practice. Although the book later became a model for inculcating values a convert to Judaism should acquire (*b. Yeb.* 47b; *Ruth Rab.* on 1:16 f.), there is no sensitivity to religious issues in the original composition and certainly none in the section about Ruth the Moabitess seducing the Israelite worthy, Boaz. The book ends with an account of the lineage of David. A striking feature of the history of the kings in 1 and 2 Samuel and 1 and 2 Kings is the recurring praise of David for walking in the ways of God and observing his commandments (1 Kgs 3:14, 11:33, 38, 14:8). That is odd because David's offenses against Uriah, the husband of Bathsheba—adultery followed by callously bringing about Uriah's death in battle—should certainly exclude him from any such positive assessment. Yet these two offenses do not affect the judgment, although one text, 1 Kings 15:5, has the following stricture: "David did that which was right in the eyes of the Lord, and turned not aside from any thing that he commanded him all the days of his life, save only in the matter of Uriah the Hittite." The explanation for the positive assessment—with the one exception of 1 Kings 15:5, which critics commonly regard as a later addition—is that David never exhibits any temptation to idolatry. [17] No wife of his is singled out as a religious seducer. His positive rating derives wholly from his being free of idolatry. In the next chapter I turn to how sexual-genital contamination of a kind especially linked to David has left its mark on Israelite religious sensibility.

5

Contamination

Something hath befallen him, he is not clean; surely he is not clean.
—*1 Samuel 20:26*

The climax to the Book of Ruth informs us that King David is the descendant of Boaz and Ruth, a grandson in fact (Ruth 4:18). The lineage begins with Perez, the son born of Judah's intercourse with his daughter-in-law Tamar, who had disguised herself as a prostitute (Gen 38), and concludes with David. The much later genealogy of Jesus in Matthew 1 has David at its center because the concluding person in it, Jesus, is depicted as a new David. Of the many mothers who could have been mentioned in Jesus' lineage, puzzlingly only five are named. What is striking is that sexual impropriety attaches to each of these women (which I shall comment on in due course). Thus, in sequence, we have Tamar, a prostitute; Ruth, a seductress; Rahab, a prostitute; the wife of Uriah, that is, Bathsheba, an adulteress; and Mary, an adulteress (because her betrothed state is tantamount to a marital one). The fact that the author of the genealogy feels the need to single out these predecessors of Mary indicates much reflection on dubious sexual conduct. What I wish to show is that when we inquire further into David's lineage, an unexpected dimension turns up. The Book of Leviticus has rules about genital impurity. Whatever their prehistory, the rules found in Leviticus 15 are the product of reflection on his person and on persons, male and female, who are associated with David's lineage, either as belonging directly to it or as crucially involved in establishing David as king.

Leviticus 15 has, first, a rule about male bodily impurity, with the primary focus on a pathological genital discharge. The second rule curiously presents as a united text the two quite different topics of a male's seminal emission considered by itself and a male's discharge of semen with a woman. The third rule is about a woman's normal menstruation, and the fourth and final rule concerns pathological menstrual bleeding.

A number of questions arise. Why, after the topics of childbirth (Lev 12) and scale diseases (Lev 13, 14), does the subject of genital discharges appear at this point in Leviticus; and why is the subject matter of the first rule a pathological male genital condition? In regard to the rules themselves: why is the rule about male-female intercourse not set out separately—translations typically do not bring out the separation—from the preceding rule with its sole focus on a male's emission? Are translators and critics correct to affirm a rule of uncleanness any time a man has intercourse with a woman, or does such a rule come into play only when the man ejaculates outside of the woman or when he enters her during her monthly flow of blood (hence the rule in Lev 15:24)? The problems can be illuminated by seeing these rules as the lawgiver's response to events pertinent to the rise of King David.

A distinctive period in David's life is King Saul's hostility to him. One major episode begins when David fails to turn up at the sacred feast of the New Moon, which King Saul hosts. The king initially explains David's nonappearance by speculating that David is unclean: "Something hath befallen him, he is not clean; surely he is not clean" (1 Sam 20:26). When David fails to turn up again the next night, Saul inquires of his son Jonathan, who tells him that David had asked permission of him to attend a family sacrifice in his hometown of Bethlehem. Saul's response is one of intense anger, and he again brings up the topic of uncleanness—only this time he attributes it to Jonathan and Jonathan's mother. Viewing Jonathan's friendship with David as a betrayal of family loyalty and a threat to the prospect of establishing a royal line of descendants, Saul utters a curse that damns the genitalia both of his son and of Jonathan's mother (1 Sam 20:30).

David, in fact, has not gone to his family feast but to the sanctuary at Nob, where focus falls upon his genital uncleanness (1 Sam 21). In order that the high priest Ahimelech permit him to consume food that is reserved for the priests at the sanctuary, David claims that he and his companions have observed the military taboo against engaging sexually with women and are, therefore, ritually clean (1 Sam 21:4, 5; cf. 2 Sam 11:9). David tells two lies: his companions in combat do not exist, and he is not, as he also claimed, on the king's mission (1 Sam 21:2). The incident, tied as it is to the previous two developments (nonattendance at the feast and Saul's curse), also highlights the topic of impurity, particularly genital.

J. P. Fokkelman draws attention to David's previous involvement in sexual impurity when he takes to Saul two hundred foreskins of the uncircumcised Philistines as the bride-price that Saul required for his daughter, Michal. Fokkelman views Saul as deliberately seeking to contaminate David.[1] Indeed, throughout the accounts about Saul and David there is a good deal of interest in impurity of one kind or another. David regrets having cut off a piece of King Saul's cloak, because the king is the "Lord's anointed" (1 Sam 24:6, 7). Abner ("Am I a dog's head?") disassociates himself from canine uncleanness in response to Saul's son Ishbosheth, who does not like Abner's sexual involvement with his dead father's concubine, Rizpah (2 Sam 3:8). The dead body of Ishbosheth ends up defiled when his hands and feet are dismembered (2 Sam 4:12). The cart that carries the Ark of the Covenant is a new one that has not been contaminated by any previous use (2 Sam 6:3). Ahitophel's counsel that Absalom have sexual intercourse with his father's concubines results in Absalom so defiling them and, by extension, David too (2 Sam 16:21–23).

At this point, I turn again to the topic of genital impurity in the rules in Leviticus 15. The first rule about a pathological male discharge takes up, I submit, Saul's speculation about David's nonappearance at the sacred feast on account of uncleanness and also his attribution to Jonathan of a pathological genital state on account of Jonathan's tie to David. The fourth and last rule about pathological female discharge takes up the alleged state of Jonathan's mother. The reason for the hiatus before the mother's condition receives attention is that the second and third rules take up earlier developments relevant to the origins of David and Jonathan, respectively. There is a good reason for this look at previous generations. The lawgiver (like the narrator) is always intent on probing the beginnings of his nation. Equally significant in this instance, Saul's hostility to David and Jonathan comes from his recognition that his family will not be the one providing a line of kings. Hereditary succession is, in fact, at the center of the narrative developments.

The second rule, then, about a seminal emission takes under review Onan's spilling of his seed when he avoids his sacred duty to raise a child for his dead brother (Gen 38). The reason for the lawgiver's switch to the episode in Genesis 38 is that Onan's deed is relevant to the precarious beginning of David's lineage. If Judah's son Onan had not deliberately spilled his seed with Tamar, she would not have proceeded to engage sexually with Judah, and David's ancestor Perez would not have been born (Gen 38:29). The third rule, about a woman's menstrual period, examines a situation in the history of Jonathan's lineage that corresponds to the one in David's. Saul condemns his son's affiliation with David and curses Jonathan's birth. As in the preceding rule, where David's origins going back to Onan's action with his semen are under review, so too are Jonathan's origins going back to an equally precarious development involving the menstrual blood of his first ancestress Rachel. If Rachel had not avoided death by lying about her menstrual impurity when concealing her father's sacred objects (Gen 31), she would not have lived on to produce Jonathan's ancestor Benjamin (Gen 35).

The topic of bodily uncleanness, especially of the genital kind as it turns up in the lives of David, Jonathan, and their ancestors, prompts the lawgiver to take up the subject in his rules in Leviticus 15. His specific motivation for doing so is to explicate rules that the history raises regarding sexual impurity as it affects the sanctuary (Lev 15:31). To begin with, he asks about the incident of David's nonattendance at Saul's sacred feast (1 Sam 20), what infractions and consequently what rules of Moses (which we should probably think of as being formulated in writing for the first time) might be relevant to the question hanging over David's avoidance of a sacred occasion.

Before exploring the incident in David's life, however, it is worthwhile to ask why the lawgiver might turn to it at this point in his work (Lev 15). We have to inquire why he came to focus on the topic of genital uncleanness, initially of males and then of females. If the sequence of the rules in Leviticus 12–15 was based on the topics following logically one to the next, we might have expected the order: childbirth, female discharges, male discharges, and scale diseases (affecting the skin, for example). Instead we find: childbirth, scale diseases, male discharges, and then female discharges. I do not think that we can comprehend how the lawgiver went about his task by just looking at the contents of one law and then attempting to puzzle out how they relate to the contents of the previous law, as is the standard approach to the study of these laws.[2] We have instead to see the rules as responses to matters in biblical narratives, and once we uncover the topics we can plot exactly the movement of his thought.

If we assume that a sequence of incidents in 1 Samuel 2–6 determines the sequence of the rules in Leviticus 11–15, we can see why the order of the rules is as we find it. Before the incident about David's nonattendance at Saul's sacred feast in 1 Samuel 20, we have in 1 Samuel 2–6 the following series of events associated with the sanctuary at Shiloh. The sons of the high priest Eli die because, in abusing the people's animal sacrifices on account of their greed, they desecrate the Shiloh sanctuary (1 Sam 2:17). The Ark, which that sanctuary houses and which manifests a "virulent holiness," on being captured by the Philistines, becomes a terrifying force and causes the deaths of the offending priests.[3] At this time also one of their wives dies giving birth to her child. So do many Philistines when the Ark produces a plague of tumors. The lawgiver followed these events, linked as they are by the role of the sacred Ark, and responded with his rules regulating appetite for meat (Lev 11), impurity associated with childbirth (Lev 12), and repellent, mainly bodily growths (Lev 13, 14). Hence we have the sequence of topics in Leviticus 11–15: rules about food, about childbirth, and about scale diseases.[4] Why, then, do the rules about genital discharges appear next?

The explanation is that after the chaos caused among the Philistines by Israel's preeminent cultic object, the next related occasions when the topic of an Israelite's impurity arises *and affects his or her relationship to the sacred order* are indeed the incidents in 1 Samuel 20, 21. Thus, after

David fails to attend Saul's sacred feast and Saul curses Jonathan and his mother, David next appears at the Nob sanctuary, where the high priest raises the question of David's fitness to receive sacred food there. The question turns on the issue of genital impurity. The Leviticus 15 rules, in turn, address this very issue of a person's lack of fitness for the sanctuary on account of genital impurity.

Pathological Genital Discharges in Males

The first rule, about a male's pathological genital condition, reads (in part): "When any man hath a running issue out of his flesh,[5] because of his issue he is unclean. And this shall be his uncleanness in his issue: whether his flesh run with his issue, or his flesh be stopped from his issue, it is uncleanness. Every bed, whereon he lieth . . . and every thing on which he sitteth, shall be unclean. And whoever toucheth his bed shall wash his clothes . . . And he that toucheth the flesh of him that hath the issue . . . and be unclean until the even. And he that hath the issue spit upon him that is clean . . . and be unclean until the even. And what saddle soever he rideth upon that hath the issue shall be unclean . . . and the vessel of earth that he toucheth . . . shall be broken: and every vessel of wood . . . shall be rinsed in water . . . and the priest shall make an atonement for him before Yahweh for his issue" (Lev 15:2–15).

We do not learn what particular kind of uncleanness Saul has in mind when he speculates about David's failure to appear at the New Moon feast on its opening night. Most commentators suggest that it must be the nonpathological kind articulated in Leviticus 15:16, which they reckon refers to a nocturnal emission of semen. Since, however, David's presence is expected at the feast in the evening, it is difficult to see how a nonpathological emission from the previous night could account for his absence. By the time of the feast he should have been free from uncleanness attaching to a previous night's emission (assuming that there did exist a rule about uncleanness of the kind in question that lasted but one day).[6] P. Kyle McCarter is more circumspect. He refers to various bodily discharges, including emission of semen and contact with an animal carcass. He is not alert, however, to the remarkable role of genital impurity in the continuing narrative, which does indeed make it likely that Saul is thinking specifically of genital uncleanness.[7] But of what kind?

If we assume that the lawgiver sets out to commit to writing rules about genital impurity in the saga about Saul's problems with David and Jonathan, the first thing we might note is that on the second night when David again fails to turn up to the feast Saul realizes that it cannot be on account of the reason, albeit unstated, that he gave for the first night. David's absence from the sacred occasion for both nights is, in fact, attributable to his fear that if he does attend the feast Saul may turn out to be less than hospitable. But Saul does not know that this is David's concern. If the Leviticus lawgiver is indeed intent on pursuing his interest in unclean bodily discharges in the narrative, the question arises: what kind of genital discharge might prevent him from attending for two nights? The lawgiver, I submit, raises this very matter and duly describes the pathological one in the rule in Leviticus 15:2–15, one with which he would have been familiar in some shape or form. He would be especially inclined to raise the diseased type for the following reason. After speculating about David's absence the first night, Saul's next comment the second night is to ascribe a pathological condition, albeit of a highly peculiar kind, to his son Jonathan on account of his friendship with David. We must not forget that stories are about the unusual, and the lawgiver's task is to take up more commonly recognizable problems.

If the laws come from this kind of scrutiny of what occurs in the national record, then we can say about their contents that they contain hypothetical elements as well as customary practices known to the lawgiver in his own time. Hypothetical legal constructions characterize Near Eastern law codes. We cannot say if the biblical lawgivers were familiar with scribal, academic practices of neighboring cultures, but even if they were not, they too produced similar hypothetical rules. If they were familiar with the type of lawmaking found among their neighbors, the one major difference would be that the inspiration of the biblical lawgivers in producing their laws came from searching out topics and problems that arose in their own national history, that is, the history that lies before us in Genesis through 2 Kings.

Another reason why hypothetical rules are standard in biblical law is precisely the inevitably oblique, idiosyncratic character of the narrative incidents that inspire them. There is prevalent, for instance, the considerable role of lies and deception. David, in collusion with Jonathan, deceives Saul about David's nonappearance at the New Moon feast by falsely claiming that he had gone to Bethlehem for a family feast. David falsely claims at the Nob sanctuary that he has companions with him who need to be fed and that both they and he have kept themselves sexually pure. None of this is accurate. When he leaves the Nob sanctuary and takes refuge among the Philistines he feigns madness in order to deceive the King of Achish by letting "his spittle fall down upon his beard" and randomly marking the doors of a gate (1 Sam 21:13). Like the speculation on Saul's part about the reason why David has not come to the feast and the unusual kind of genital blemishes Saul attributes to Jonathan and his mother, these lies and deceptions can but invite exploration as to what central issues might be isolated from the conduct under review.

It is why particular features of the rule in Leviticus 15:2–13 may owe something to David's life at the time in question. The rule curiously singles out how the spittle of a male with the pathological discharge makes someone else unclean should that person come into contact with the spittle. To all appearances David did not suffer from any kind of discharge at the time of the feast. Saul's guess about his absence did not match the reality of David's fraught situation. Nonetheless the topic of spittle as indicating an abnormal condition does arise in David's life at this point in time, a condition that Robert Alter describes in terms like those appropriate to someone with a pathological condition: the King of Achish reacts with disgust and repulsion to David's state.[8] Just as David's uncleanness that Saul speculates about does not correspond to any actual state, so his spittle does not betoken one either. Yet spittle in relation to some peculiar mental condition when David is in the Philistine camp does present itself as a topic of interest. The lawgiver's move would then be to attach this fake symptom of David's to the fictitious one that the narrative nonetheless raises about his bodily state.

Another singular feature in the rule is the contamination of a saddle upon which the infected person sits. It is again perhaps worth noting that David's life at this time is one of a freebooter riding around the countryside to avoid Saul's homicidal intent. The question of the uncleanness of such objects does indeed turn up in the context of David at the Nob sanctuary (1 Sam 21:5). David journeys there in his flight from Saul. He assures the priest Ahimelech that "the *kelim* of the young men are holy" and will not consequently contaminate the sanctuary. These young men are also fictitious. The term *keli* (meaning "article," "vessel," "weapon") would certainly include saddles, which one imagines the men would remove from their mounts and place in the sanctuary. Frequently in Leviticus 15, the word is used of something on which one sits (vv. 4, 6, 22, 23, 26). The term is the same one the law employs for the vessels of earth and wood that become unclean because of the male's genital condition (Lev 15:12).

Nonpathological Seminal Fluid

The second rule reads: "And if a man's seed of copulation go out from him, then he shall wash all his flesh in water and be unclean until the even. And every garment and skin, whereon is the seed of copulation, shall be washed with water, and be unclean until even. The woman also with whom a man lies [with or whereon is] seed of copulation, they shall bathe in water, and be unclean until the even" (Lev 15:16–18).

Saul's speculation about David's unclean state could certainly be attributed to a seminal emission. In terms of the narrative, however, it is beside the point. Nonetheless, in the history relevant to the rise of David as king there is a real example of just such an emission. Onan's act of spilling his seed in Genesis 38 is crucially associated with the beginning of David's lineage and precisely because of this fact the lawgiver in his next rule in Leviticus 15:16, 17 turns to the episode. By turning back in time, he is doing what the narrator of Genesis through 2 Kings does, namely, taking stock of the history of the generations. The chief feature of biblical historiography is that narrator and lawgiver, whenever they can, pay particular attention to national beginnings and view what happens in the earliest times as having impact on later generations.

Moshe Garsiel is one critic who points to many links between the narratives in 1 Samuel and Genesis in particular; for example, 1 Samuel 18 and Genesis 29 about David's and Jacob's marriages involving two sisters; the nonmonetary bride-prices; the devious fathers-in-law; and the flight from them, which involves a wife, Michal, Rachel, each of whom makes use of household gods (*teraphim*) in escaping.[9] The role of Rachel's household gods will prove relevant to the rule in Levicitus 15:19–24 about menstruation. Another reason why the lawgiver might show interest in David's lineage when assessing the episode in 1 Samuel 20 is that David's failure to appear at the feast brings up Saul's deepest fear: David will usurp his son Jonathan from becoming the first king ever to be a hereditary ruler and thereby prevent Saul's family line from providing kings for the nation. Equally to the point is that Saul's cursing a mother's genitals is a universal mode of casting aspersions on a person's lineage.

The rule in Leviticus 15:16–18 starts out with a concentration on a male's emission, considers how the semen might come upon clothing or skins, and then turns to a sexual partner's contact with semen. Surprisingly, the sexual partner is not necessarily a wife. Only the Samaritan text reads "her husband," and critics rightly reject this reading in favor of the MT reading.[10] Most important, as Jacob Milgrom rightly emphasizes, verse 18 (about the woman) is "a continuation of vv 16–17 and still deals with semen." Verses 16–18 have to be evaluated together. It is unsatisfactory to make, as translators and commentators sometimes do, a separate rule of the third clause so that the latter stands apart to read, "If a man lies with a woman and has an emission of semen." The sentence about intercourse continues the preceding focus on semen in verses 16, 17. Why, then, is the one rule bound up with the other? To suggest, as most critics contend, that it has to do with form and not substance, that it effects the transition between the preceding topic of male genital discharges and the following topic of female discharges, is not a sufficient reason.[11] It is accurate so long as we recognize that the lawgiver goes from David's and Jonathan's genital uncleanness to Onan's in relation to David's lineage, to Rachel's in relation to Jonathan's lineage, and finally to Jonathan's mother's uncleanness.

Despite the curious combination of topics—focus on a male's emission, male's intercourse with female—critics still choose to consider the first part of the rule to be about male nocturnal emissions and persist in perceiving the second part as a separate injunction about ordinary male-female intercourse. I repeat, however, that we cannot separate the two rules, nor do I think that the focus is initially on nocturnal emissions. Milgrom thinks that the choice of the verb for the emission of seed, *yaṣa'*, "to go forth," is deliberately intended to include an involuntary act. Less cautiously, Nihan states that the emission is "uncontrolled and involuntary." As David Daube points out, however, "Lev 15:16f. primarily refers, not as is prevalently assumed to accidental pollution, but to intercourse.

74 Contamination

Verses 16f. deal with the man, 17 includes the woman." He further states, "The use of yaṣa', 'to go forth,' is no argument against this [that we are dealing with accidental pollution]: 'we will certainly do whatsoever thing goeth forth out of our mouth' (Jer 44:17) does not imply that they were speaking in their sleep."[12] A biblical event explains why the two rules are interrelated. If David's and Jonathan's alleged impurity comes into reckoning in the preceding rule, I suggest that we continue to take our cue from the topics that the narrative about them raises.

The problem Saul confronts is that of hereditary rule. As he sees it, his lineage experiences not just a political threat from his son's friendship with David, but genital contamination too. (I am aware that some scholars posit a homosexual relationship between David and Jonathan, but I am skeptical about any allusion to one.)[13] Attention to both Saul's and David's lineages is, we might note, a central feature of the larger narrative, even extending to details. For example, Saul frequently and probably disparagingly refers to David by his family name, the "son of Jesse" (1 Sam 20:27, 30, 31, 22:7, 8, 13, 25:10; 2 Sam 20:1), and Saul's own descent from his ancestor Benjamin is cited (1 Sam 9:1, 21, 10:2).[14] In response to the topics of contamination and hereditary succession in the narrative, the lawgiver looks at both David's and Jonathan's lineages for comparable examples of pollution. The result is striking and occasions the setting down of the remaining rules in Leviticus 15.

The remarkable feature of David's origin is that he would never have been born if it had not been for—certainly from a priestly perspective—an act of uncleanness. In Genesis 38, Onan ejaculates outside of Tamar to avoid a conception, an action that leads to his death. Tamar, in turn, is provoked into disguising herself as a "sacred prostitute" (*qedešah*), seduces the father Judah, and produces David's ancestor Perez, a lineage, we saw, spelled out in Ruth 4:18. Clearly, the author of Ruth, the Moabitess, is one ancient writer who is interested in the history that takes us from the birth of Perez to the appearance of David.[15] The Leviticus lawgiver has a similar interest.

What Onan does accounts for the curious combination of topics in Leviticus 15:16–18. The rule focuses on a male's emission of semen before turning, in the same context, to the effect of an emission on a woman. The spotlight is first on Onan's ejaculation outside of Tamar (Gen 38). She is not a wife in the regular sense, and the rule formulates accordingly: "the woman with whom a man lies." The details of the story tell how a member of the first family of Israel, Judah, has two sons, Er and Onan. Judah takes Tamar as a wife for Er, but Er does something displeasing to God and God strikes him dead. Judah then sends Onan into Tamar in accordance with the levirate custom. Onan, however, because he would like to acquire his dead brother's share of the family estate, deceives his father by only going so far in having sexual intercourse with her and then withdraws and ejaculates outside of her. God strikes him down too. Spilling his seed is a highly significant action. The name Onan, from 'ôn, "virility," is a mocking, made-up designation that incorporates his infamy and is intended to recall it. By not giving of his seed Onan attempts to take from his brother the latter's due claim to provide its future head. Saul, in turn, perceives David as removing from his line its rightful claim to provide the future ruler of the nation. It is why Saul chooses to curse his wife's genitals for having delivered Jonathan.

Onan's action (or nonaction) is the only one in any biblical narrative that focuses on a male's ejaculation of seed. The lawgiver's spotlight on it would explain why, in the double-part rule, attention first focuses on a male's emission aside from the presence of any woman. The same focus, however, would also account for the rule's joint concerns, because Onan is not, in fact, alone. He is with Tamar. Reflecting on and extrapolating from the incident, a lawgiver might dwell first on a male's emission of semen and where it might fall, and then on how the emission might affect the woman too. In other words, the rule may be focusing not primarily on a completed act of intercourse, but on an interrupted one, where semen falls outside of the woman. P. J. Budd comes close to this view when he suggests that sexual intercourse was only polluting "should the semen go astray."

In taking for granted that sexual intercourse is contaminating, Howard Eilberg-Schwartz and Meir Malul come up with complicated explanations that fit their respective theories. Eilberg-Schwartz speaks of how the emission of semen is mainly a controlled, conscious act, as against the discharge of a nonseminal fluid, like menstrual blood, which is a passive, involuntary occurrence. Insofar as the emission of semen even in intercourse is only partly under the man's control, it is mildly contaminating, whereas menstrual blood, which is uncontrolled, is a major pollutant. Levels of controllability account for different degrees of contamination.

Malul, in turn, with his emphasis on what is known and unknown—the latter is mysterious, dangerous and thus taboo—speaks of how semen issues from a known, visible source (the penis), and menstrual blood from an unknown source, the "invisible, hidden, and mysterious vagina." In intercourse, linking the known with the unknown, the mysteriousness of the woman's body is sufficient to render the act mildly contaminating. But, in my view, if the rule deals primarily with semen spilled outside the body, only that semen is contaminating.[16]

There is further evidence for the restricted meaning of the rule. In Leviticus 15:32 the lawgiver provides a summary of his rules—and, curiously, only for the rule about a male's emission, not for the other rules, does the MT explicitly state that impurity is involved. Milgrom rightly puzzles over what appears to be an unnecessary statement. He recommends that we not read the redundant reference to the male's impurity but take the Hebrew *leṭomʾa-bah* as the *piʿel* verbal form *leṭammeʾah-bah* to mean that the man contaminates the woman with his semen ("the one who has an emission of semen and contaminates her with it [not 'and becomes impure thereby']." The specific kind of uncleanness is spelled out. Instead of concluding, as Milgrom surprisingly does, that the rule in Leviticus 15:16–18 is really two separate rules, first about semen and then about sexual intercourse, we should indeed keep them together by thinking of intercourse where the male ejaculates *outside* of the woman and the semen then touches her external body and clothing.[17] A further indication that we are dealing with an incomplete act of intercourse is that in the concluding summary in Leviticus 15:32–33, although an emission of semen is cited, there is no mention of full sexual intercourse as a source of impurity. Christophe Nihan is struck by the omission but thinks it is because "sexuality as such plays a very minor role as a source of pollution." His position is contradictory. He too thinks that Leviticus 15:18 is about a regular, completed act of intercourse, and the entire point of the rule for him is to bring the matter under the category of pollution. If accurate, which I think it is not, then for Nihan sexuality and pollution are indeed given attention, and the topic on his interpretation is hardly minor.[18]

The problem of giving a precise interpretation to the double rule in Leviticus 15:16–18 is that while the incident with Tamar might prompt its formulation, we cannot say how far the lawgiver generalizes from the particular situation to include possibly any act of intercourse when the semen might not remain within the woman. In any event, the alleged uncleanness of David, which is under consideration in the preceding rule, can be linked to the uncleanness associated with Onan, because, if the latter had not misdirected his seed, David's birth would never have occurred.

Menstrual Blood

The third rule, about a woman's normal menstrual period, reads: "And if a woman have an issue and her issue in her flesh be blood, she shall be apart seven days: and whosoever toucheth her shall be unclean until the even. And every thing that she lieth upon in her separation shall be unclean: every thing also that she sitteth upon shall be unclean" (Lev 15:19, 20).

When David fails to turn up the second night of the New Moon feast and Saul learns that his son Jonathan is privy to David's affairs, as already noted, Saul curses Jonathan by attributing genital pollution to both him and his mother. "Do I not know that thou art a companion of the son of Jesse, to thine own shame and to the shame of thy mother's nakedness?" (1 Sam 20:36). It is well recognized that the terms *shame* and *nakedness* in 1 Sam 20:36 refer to the male and female genitalia, respectively. As McCarter states, "By calling Jonathan the *son of a perverse, rebellious woman* Saul means to brand Jonathan as genetically disloyal, but the choice of words points the insult at Jonathan's mother; his *mother's nakedness* refers euphemistically to her pudenda, which are shamed by his having entered the world thereby." Shimon Bar-Efrat's comment about 1 Samuel 20:30 is even more to the point. He states, "It is clear from Jonathan's answer that he sides with David. This infuriates Saul and causes him to use obscene language. Both *shame* (besides its usual meaning) and *nakedness* denote the genitals."[19] We might note that in reference to both David and Saul the attribution of pollution corresponds to no actual physical condition of their person. There is but speculation on Saul's part in regard to David, and in regard to Jonathan and his mother (Ahinoam), Saul's attribution of uncleanness is strikingly crude, albeit literally directed at their genitalia.

We might first ask why, when Saul attributes contamination to Jonathan and his mother, he does so in the context of condemning Jonathan's friendship with David? The answer is that from Saul's point of view Jonathan's fraternizing with David puts in jeopardy, as we already noted, the prospect of the throne passing from father to son in Saul's line.[20] Saul's response is to view retroactively Jonathan's birth from his mother as conferring on each genital impurity of a peculiarly pathological kind. The retrograde effect plainly carries a good deal of conscious or unconscious reflection extending back through at least a generation. One is reminded of the radical state of consciousness to be found in both biblical and Greek sources when a person (Hephaestus, Job, and Jeremiah, for example) expresses the wish never to have been born (*Odyssey* 8.312; Job 3; Jer 20:14–18). That wish involves much reflection on the person's overall past, and for the Leviticus lawgiver the backward-looking curse on Jonathan's birth takes in, we shall see, an even earlier event.

The two rules in Leviticus 15:19–30 concern female genital impurity and are to be linked to Saul's despair about Jonathan and the alleged contamination of their line of descent. Genealogical considerations prove to be paramount in the story. Saul traces his line back to Jacob's son Benjamin, who was born of Rachel (1 Sam 9:1, 21, 10:2). The lawgiver goes further by noting the following: in Judah's generation, Onan's misuse of his semen leads to his death; Tamar then goes to Judah, narrowly avoids death for doing so, and produces David's ancestor Perez. In the previous generation, Rachel's misuse of menstrual blood leads to her avoiding death for stealing her father's household gods and proceeding to produce the line of Benjamin, Saul, and Jonathan (Gen 31:32–35, 35:16–20). If Rachel had not made her claim about menstrual blood, Jonathan would never have been born, just as David would never have been born if Onan had not spilled his semen. In his anger, Saul can only view David and Jonathan's friendship as tied to their tainted origins.

One wonders if behind the biblical traditions there may have circulated taunts about such dubious origins. In any event, behind the rules lie stories about national beginnings, and these inspire the lawgiver to provide an account of the origin of Israel's laws in the person of Moses. Such a link between the laws and the narratives is spelled out in Deuteronomy 6:20, 21: "When thy son asketh thee in time to come, what mean the testimonies, and the statutes, and the judgments, which Yahweh our God hath commanded you, thou shalt say unto thy son, We were Pharaoh's bondmen in Egypt and Yahweh brought us out of Egypt." Every law, I might emphasize, relates back to a storyline with the Exodus at the center of the story, because Moses speaks out of his own experience of events. Stories about events leading up to the Exodus and those about events after it are equally relevant.

Rachel steals her father's household gods because she perceives that he is withholding her right to form an independent family with her husband, Jacob. When her father, Laban, pursues and catches up with the fleeing Jacob and his family, Rachel hides the sacred objects. Laban searches for them, but Rachel prevents him from entering the tent where they are hidden by claiming to be unclean because of her menstrual flow. She tells her father that she cannot arise from the camel's saddle on which she sits (Gen 31:34). Implicit in her statement is that he should touch neither her nor the object on which she sits because each is off-limits on account of the blood.

It is precisely such an event about the nation's beginnings that typically triggers the lawgiver's interest in any implicit rule that might be at stake, in this instance, the one underlying Rachel's attitude to her menstrual discharge. Thus we have the rule: "And if a woman have an issue and her issue in her flesh be blood, she shall be apart seven days: and whosoever toucheth her shall be unclean until the even. And every thing that she lieth upon in her separation shall be unclean: every thing also that she sitteth upon shall be unclean" (Lev 15:19, 20). What is remarkable, and links one Genesis event to the other, is that both Rachel and Onan make use of genital discharges—sacred life forces in the priestly scheme of things—to escape detection of their wrongdoing: Rachel's theft of a father's gods, and Onan's attempted theft of a birthright.

There is yet another striking parallel between the Judah-Onan-Tamar story and the story of Rachel and her father's gods. Each narrative has to do with another quite specific religious matter. In the Tamar story, because of Onan's spurning his sacred duty to grant her conception, Tamar proceeds to act the part of a "sacred woman" (*qedešah*) to become pregnant. Impregnation is her right because she is a member of Judah's family and her dead husband's line has to be perpetuated. In the story about the theft of the household gods, Rachel sits on divine objects, her father's domestic gods, to claim a right to establish her own independent family. Little wonder that, with his focus on priestly concerns, the author of Leviticus revealed an interest in sacrosanct matters arising within the first Israelite family. If, in truth, Rachel has her menstrual period, her sitting on these revered domestic objects is an offense against the hallowed order of her family's Aramean way of life. The incidents in question occur before there is a formal Israelite cult. They belong, however, to its prehistory. Had there been no family member who played the part of a sacred woman or who possessed household gods, David, Saul, and Jonathan would have had no part to play in later Israelite cultic life, never mind raising questions about genital impurity in their own time.

Pathological Female Discharges

The fourth and final rule, concerning pathological menstrual bleeding, reads: "And if a woman have an issue of her blood many days out of the time of her separation, or if it run beyond the time of her separation; all the days of the issue in her uncleanness shall be as the days of her separation: she shall be unclean ... and the priest shall make an atonement for her before Yahweh for the issue of her uncleanness" (Lev 15:25–30).

The lawgiver next takes up the topic of pathological female discharges (Lev 15:25–30). The interest could be viewed as an understandable extension of the preceding concern with natural discharges, especially since he scrutinizes both types of discharges among males. There is more to it, however. Saul had occasion to focus on his wife's genitals as unclean because of his son's disloyalty. The uncleanness in question is associated not with menstruation but with childbirth in an indirect and curiously retroactive way. Saul's wife's genitals have been rendered unclean by the fact that the disloyal Jonathan once emerged from them. The condition is such that contamination adheres to her long after birth. It is neither the expected, natural, and time-limited impurity of regular childbirth nor that of menstruation. The peculiar nature of the mother's impurity has, therefore, prompted the lawgiver to come up with more recognizable types of irregular, unnatural discharges, ones associated with neither childbirth nor menstruation, but pathological in nature.

I should point out that time and again in the history of law some exceptional matter prompts a rule formulating the wider problem. Alan Rodger provides a common enough example from Roman law. Where, as a result of construction on your neighbor's land, rainwater damages land belonging to you, a remedy in classical Roman law is available so long as the one who did the construction still owns the land. What could happen, however, is that the owner, anticipating the problem, resorted to a dodge and sold the land temporarily to avoid any action at law for damage done by the rainwater. In Justinian's *Digest* (D.50.17.167 pr.), a rule reads: "Things are not deemed to be given which do not become the property of the recipient at the time they are given." The general maxim gives no indication that the dodge to avoid liability for rainwater is what prompted the general formulation of the rule in the *Digest*.[21] In evaluating any rule in any body of legal material, a move from the particular to the general has frequently to be borne in mind.

Proverbs and parables function similarly in that their intent is often comparable to what we find for biblical laws in relation to the background stories that inspire their formulation. In Proverbs 6:6, a lazy man is sent to the ant to become wise by learning to imitate its commitment to disciplined labor. The ant does not articulate the rule for him, but the sluggard is meant to pick up from the ant's example a general rule of sensible conduct. In Luke 11:5–11, Jesus relays the parable about the Helper at Midnight, which describes a particular set of circumstances. A man in need of bread to serve to a late-arriving guest appeals to his neighbor for some. The neighbor, however, does not wish to be disturbed because it is midnight; nonetheless he responds, even if not for the most commendable of reasons. He acts because he does not want to lose face in the matter. The general message is doubtless that, whereas a neighbor might be reluctant to aid someone but in the event does so, God is always ready to heed a person's needs. In the matter of being of service God represents the perfect but unstated rule of conduct. Like parables, then, biblical laws are frequently the result of a progression from the peculiar developments in the narratives to the more generally recognizable topics in the laws. The move reflects a universal phenomenon. We are drawn to the idiosyncratic, but our tendency is then to impose on the captivating details some generalization, "to put things in a nutshell," "to get the point." To be sure, sometimes, as with the rule in Leviticus 15:2–15 about a pathological condition, the tendency of a lawgiver might be to select particulars from among many particulars in a case rather than wholly generalizing.

Jesus' Genealogy

The topic of impurity in the rise of David to kingship appears to be a longstanding one, turning up not just in narrative accounts about him but also in the Leviticus rules about genital discharges. It is consequently less of a surprise that the perception of impurity in David's line eventually comes to dramatic expression in Matthew's genealogy of Jesus (Matt 1).

The only women who are cited in the genealogy are all linked to David, and, as previously indicated, dubious sexuality is associated with each of their roles. In sequence, we have Tamar in the guise of a prostitute who produces Perez by Judah, David's tribal ancestor (Gen 38, Matt 1:3). The Canaanite prostitute Rahab, according to Matthew, produces Boaz, the great-grandfather of David (Josh 2; Matt 1:5). Ruth compromises herself by lying down beside the lone figure of Boaz at midnight, after he has eaten and drunk and slumbers next to his freshly threshed grain. It is Ruth who produces Obed, the grandfather of David (Ruth 3, 4, Matt 1:5). There is next the wife of Uriah, Bathsheba, with whom David commits adultery at a time when, whatever the meaning, she "is in a state of self-sanctifying" (2 Sam 11:4). We have, it would appear, another instance of impurity impacting the sacred.[22] After David has her husband killed, they marry and Solomon is born (2 Sam 11, 12, Matt 1:6). Climactically, there is Mary whose betrothed husband seeks to divorce her quietly because she is pregnant, although not by him (Matt 1:18, 19). The child Mary produces, the genealogy makes clear, is a "son of David" (Matt 1:20). The birth, we learn, turns out to be virginal.[23] I wonder whether one aim of telling the story with this slant was to sever Joseph's sexual (but not, incongruously, genealogical) link with the line of David and thereby remove Jesus from the impurity long associated with it.

After his rules in Leviticus 12–14, in which the sacred Ark of the Covenant plays a central role in prompting their formulation, the lawgiver continued to focus in Leviticus 15 on topics that concern uncleanness. The matters in question again turn up in certain narrative traditions. After the Ark settles back in the midst of Israel, the next two related occasions that bring up the topic of uncleanness in relation to the cult occur when Saul attributes uncleanness to David at the time of the New Moon festival and David asserts his sexual purity to the priest at the Nob sanctuary. On the occasion of the festival Saul attributes uncleanness to David, and to Jonathan and his mother. Noting the claims about David's and Jonathan's bodily state at this point in their life, the lawgiver pursued the problem of pathological male uncleanness.

The lawgiver further developed his interest in the topic of genital uncleanness by tracing David's lineage back to circumstances that prove crucial for its beginnings, namely, Onan's ejaculation outside of Tamar so as to avoid giving her conception. David's ancestor Perez is born when Tamar, disguised as a prostitute, irregularly seeks a child by her father-in-law, Judah. The related topic of female genital discharges appears next because, tracing back Jonathan's lineage, the lawgiver noted the claim that his first ancestress, Rachel, makes about her menstrual uncleanness. It enables her to conceal the theft of her father's household gods and to avoid death for doing so. Rachel then produces Benjamin, the head of Jonathan's lineage. The lawgiver has also expanded his reflection on the peculiar genital impurity imputed to Jonathan's mother by setting out a rule about genital uncleanness that is about neither normal menstruation nor normal childbirth but about a pathological state.

A climactic statement in Leviticus 15:31 warns that uncleanness impacting the cult brings death: "Thus shall ye separate the children of Israel from their uncleanness; that they die not in their uncleanness when they defile my tabernacle that is among them." Death or the threat of it plays, we saw, a remarkable role among the actors in the saga that constitutes the history of the lineages of David and Jonathan. Equally important is that these experiences all occur in contexts involving sacred matters. Onan dies for spurning his sacred duty to continue his brother's name, and Tamar, acting the part of a sacred prostitute, is involved in salvaging it. Rachel and Tamar nearly die, because the former conceals sacred objects under her and the latter almost burns to death for an alleged act of common prostitution at a time when legally bound to Judah's son, Shelah. David and Jonathan too almost die. Saul is intent on murdering David, and, immediately after cursing the genitals of Jonathan and his mother, he almost succeeds in killing Jonathan with a spear (1 Sam 20:33). Saul's evil intent against both David and Jonathan is exhibited at a sacred feast.

The precarious developments that show up in the lineages of David and Jonathan are duplicated again with David's descendant, Solomon. Uriah, the cuckolded husband of Bathsheba, declines David's inducements to return to his home and have intercourse with his wife. David then engineers Uriah's death in battle, and, without that death, David's son Solomon would never have been born (2 Sam 11, 12). Also noteworthy is that David and Bathsheba's son conceived in adultery had previously died. Little wonder that in his rules the Leviticus lawgiver focused on death-producing or death-threatening occasions all linked to genital or sexual uncleanness in the lives of David, Jonathan, and their ascendants. Even with the events that lead to Solomon's birth, the link between sexual purity and the sphere of the sacred is again prominent. The reason why Uriah resolutely refuses to have intercourse with his wife is because sexual activity is taboo on account of the sacred Ark dwelling among his fellow warriors in the open fields (2 Sam 11:11).

To claim, as the lawgiver does, that genital uncleanness of both a regular and irregular kind brings death because it offends against the sacred order seems rather extreme and reinforces the perception that holiness represents "an absolute lack of sense of proportion."[24] The background events that inspire the laws, however, render the view more comprehensible.

6

Adultery

Behold now, I know that thou art a fair woman to look upon.
—*Genesis 12:11*

Matthew's genealogy begins: "The book of the generation of Jesus Christ, the son of David, the son of Abraham. Abraham begat Isaac...." One famous woman not named in Matthew's genealogy is Sarah, Abraham's wife, even though like the other women mentioned she too can be cited for blatantly outrageous sexual conduct (Gen 12, 20).

A Case of Pimping

Recall how at one point Abraham is traveling in unfamiliar territory and is accompanied by his attractive spouse, Sarah: "Behold now, I know that thou art a fair woman to look upon" (Gen 12:11). Abraham has her agree to pass herself off as his sister so that the males of the place will be well disposed to the foreign couple, indeed that one of them will take a fancy to her and marry her. Such a development will ensure that Abraham, a brother from one perspective, a former or current husband from another, will be treated favorably as her family guardian. Their mutually agreed ploy does indeed turn out as they expected: no less a figure than the Pharaoh takes her as a wife, and Abraham, as her brother, receives largesse. Later, when Pharaoh discovers the true relationship between Abraham and Sarah, he says to Abraham, "Why did you say, 'She is my sister,' so that I took her for my wife?" (Gen 12:19). However sympathetic one might be to Abraham's concern for his safety in foreign territory, we are confronted with an instance of a husband pimping his good-looking wife and her willingness to go along with the scheme.

An inquiry into the episode could take us in many different directions. At least, in a case reported by Seneca (*On Providence* 3.10), although Terentia kept divorcing Maecenas (to get around the ban on gifts between spouses), he took her back without her marrying another man (a liaison with Augustus not counting). "He married a thousand times, all the while having one wife." In puzzling over the likely remote origin of the biblical stories, we might have to reckon with customs similar to the one reported of the ancient Persians by Herodotus (1.215–16). Darius created a law prohibiting adultery, but the Massagetae said that they could not obey it because of the custom of treating guests to their wives. We might speculate about the reverse: how honor could accrue to a man in Abraham's position by his giving over his wife to a high foreign dignitary. At some stage, a storyteller may have regarded the development as a great compliment to Sarah's beauty and, in a way, an honor to her husband. In Greek myth, we have the story of no less a figure than Zeus visiting Alcmene the night before her husband, Amphitryon, was about to return from war. In his retelling of the life of David, Stefan Heym has Uriah honored by the king lying with his wife, Bathsheba. Meir Malul draws attention to sexual hospitality of this kind, ancient and modern, with a wife given to a guest or to a host. E. A. Speiser sees another custom lurk in the distant background, namely, a legal practice among the upper-class members of the Hurrians, who existed around the time of the patriarchs. When a man concluded a marriage, the woman also became a sister to him.[1]

When visiting the territory belonging to Abimelech, the king of Gerar, Abraham and Sarah resort to the same ploy that was successful with the Pharaoh (Gen 20). Only this time, although Sarah is already lodged inside the palace, the king has a dream from God during the night in which he is warned not to touch her because she is a man's wife (Gen 20:3). The revelation puts an end to any prospect of sexual contact between them. To be sure, Abimelech's kingdom is afflicted by infertility because of the situation that has arisen, one that is condemned as adultery. Abraham himself, who initiated the untoward development, has to pray for relief to Abimelech's house.

Whoever is responsible for shaping the narratives about Abraham's use of his wife to benefit himself is clearly exercised by the morality of the arrangement. The introduction of the deity into both accounts indicates such disquiet. Plagues afflict the Pharaoh and his house in Genesis 12. More articulated views on the problem emerge in Genesis 20. In this narrative the deity characterizes Abimelech's taking Sarah as adultery, pronounces a capital sentence for the offense, and shows his displeasure by afflicting the women of Gerar with sterility. Abimelech justifiably protests the deity's judgment because he has been deceived about Sarah's true status. The deity relents, because, acknowledging Abimelech as a fundamentally decent type, he interferes just in time, by means of the dream, to prevent Abimelech from actually having Sarah. No such interference occurred in the comparable story in Genesis 12, when Sarah was taken as a wife by the Pharaoh. The deity's action in Genesis 20 is, we would have to judge, intended to communicate that Sarah is still seen as a married woman and that the married couple's machinations to have her go to another man are unacceptable. The story's outcome conveys the view that for Sarah to be restored as Abraham's wife she must remain untouched by another man. Presumably, if there had been union with Abimelech, it would have constituted a defilement of Sarah and consequently barred her restoration as Abraham's wife. In line with later Jewish law, until about the early third century CE, so long as the man's intent was to make the woman his wife and she consented, intercourse alone would have been sufficient to establish Sarah's status as Abimelech's wife—but only if she was no longer recognized as the wife of Abraham.[2]

The presentation of the story in Genesis 20 as part of the body of material that constitutes Genesis through 2 Kings is presumably intended to communicate, among other matters, a negative reaction to Sarah's sexual defilement by the Pharaoh in Genesis 12. The narrator responsible for setting out both stories does not remove one and keep the other. After all, the dubiousness of Abraham and Sarah's ploy is still very much to the fore in Genesis 20. The aim is certainly not to sanitize tradition about Abraham and Sarah but, it would appear, to present the later development in Genesis 20 by way of furthering ethical reflection about the conduct of the actors in the stories. There are parallels to this kind of reporting about Israelite tradition. The Chronicler often does not accept what is found in the Book of Kings: he does not record, for instance, David's adultery with Bathsheba (2 Sam 11) so as not to damage King David's reputation, and he also does not like the idea to be found in 1 Kings 3:12—that Solomon is superior to Moses ("there was none like to thee, neither after thee shall any arise like unto thee"). In 2 Chronicles 1:12, Solomon's wisdom is to surpass only that of the kings before and after him. Likewise adopting a critical stance, the biblical lawgivers take up tradition after tradition about the history of the ancestors, explore their doings, and make judgments on the issues that arise.

The ancient moralizer, who incorporates a role for the deity in the Genesis stories, concentrates on the consequences of Abraham's deception. There is no comment by the deity-narrator on the initial situation: a husband who feels pressured to give over his attractive wife to another, more powerful male. A story, after all, is directed toward an ending and can hardly stop just as it has begun.[3] A lawgiver, however, can choose to be more focused and pay attention to initial developments. This is precisely what Moses does in a Deuteronomic law attributed to him. That law reads: "If a man takes a wife, and marries her, and it come to pass that she find no favour in his eyes, because he hath found the nakedness of a thing ['ervat-dabar] in her: and he writes her a bill of divorcement, and gives it in her hand, and sends her out of his house, and she departs out of his house, and she goes and becomes another man's wife. And the latter husband hates her, and writes her a bill of divorcement, and gives it in her hand, and sends her out of his house; or the latter husband dies, which took her to be his wife; her former husband, which sent her away, cannot take her again to be his wife, after that she is defiled; for that is abomination before Yahweh: and thou shalt not cause the land to sin, which Yahweh thy God giveth thee for an inheritance" (Deut 24:1–4).

The woman can doubtless go to a husband number three after the divorce from husband number two or after he dies. She just cannot return to husband number one. But why should she not? And if he takes her back, why should it cause sin to the land? And in what sense has she been defiled should he take her back, when legally she is again a free woman? Also, why is the description of the first divorce different from and much milder than the one of the second divorce, which cites hatred of the spouse, the standard reason for divorce in ancient legal sources? Why in the first place do we need to be given reasons for the divorces? If a husband chooses to divorce a wife, there will be economic consequences, but he is free to proceed without justifying the grounds for his action. Little wonder that the law is unique in world legal literature.

In reaction to what transpires with Abraham and his spouse, Moses, anticipating some comparable future development in the life of the nation, takes up the matter of a wife's release from her marital bond, because it is to the benefit of the husband that another male seek to have her. The topic has a long history. E. P. Thompson writes, "The sale or exchange of a wife, for sexual or domestic services, appears to have taken place, on occasion, in most places and at most times. It may be only an aberrant transaction, with or without a pretended contractual basis—it is recorded sometimes today." In Roman history we have Cato's release of his wife, Marcia, to his wealthy friend Hortensius. After Hortensuis' death, Marcia returned to Cato considerably enriched from her second marriage.[4]

Moses proceeds to handle Abraham and Sarah's action not as the deity handles it with Abimelech—no law can prescribe a dream to warn a putative husband against consummating a union with a new wife—but in line with later Israelite life and institutions. The problem that might present itself among later Israelites is where a man divorces a wife not because he dislikes her—the usual reason for a divorce—but because he finds a vulnerability in her, namely, her attractiveness to another male that he chooses not to oppose and that is actually to his advantage. Even though the rule is not drafted to cover the Genesis story but, rather, some future Israelite development after Moses' time, its language nonetheless reflects Abraham's situation closely. When Abraham anticipates that the exposure of Sarah to other male eyes is a problem for him, the result for her is that *as his wife* she finds no favor in his eyes. The relatively mild and surprising language of the rule ("And she find no favor in his eyes because he hath found the nakedness of a thing in her") accurately conveys the situation in the Genesis narrative. What Abraham discovers about Sarah is not that she is desirable to look upon, but that having her looks on display to foreign males renders both of them vulnerable in face of these males' likely reaction to her appearance. The Hebrew word ʿervah ("nakedness") well conveys this notion of vulnerability.[5] In the Book of Esther, Queen Vashti's refusal of her husband's request to expose herself to a (drunken) male audience is cause for her dismissal from the matrimonial home. Unlike Abraham, King Ahasuerus need not fear the loss of his wife to another male. Indeed, his impregnable position is the very opposite of Abraham's and accounts for his audacious request.

When we turn to the descriptions of the two divorces in the law—the woman experiences hatred from the second husband, a loss of favor from the first—their negative aspects have misled interpreters assessing the first divorce to read into the puzzling phrase "the nakedness of a thing" (ʿervat-dabar) something unsatisfactory about the woman's character. The surprising mildness of the language about losing favor in the first husband's eyes should have made them more cautious. The term ʿervah ("nakedness") almost inevitably pulls in the notion of shame, but it is crucial to note that the emotion emerges only when the situation in question is public, when the focus is on the woman's role in a public setting and not on any private feature of hers that causes her husband to reject her.

Shame by its very nature comes into play only when the switch from private to public realm is made. The situation of Noah, lying naked in his tent in a drunken stupor, becomes shameful only when his son looks upon him and tells his two brothers about what he has seen (Gen 9:22). Human excrement is not shameful but becomes so if the deity, turning up in the Israelite army encampment, sees it within that area of ground. In that setting the expression ʿervat-dabar, used only one other time in the Bible in the law in Deuteronomy 23:15, takes on a negative connotation. Egyptian territory is open for all to see. There is nothing untoward about that, but if spies are taking stock of it, as the disguised Joseph claims his brothers are (Gen 42:9), then "the nakedness of the land" (ʿervat-haʾareṣ) depicts a negative development. Just as Joseph cannot protect the land against the inquisitive eyes of foreign visitors, so Abraham cannot protect his wife against the prying eyes of foreign males. In each instance the problem is neither the land itself nor the woman herself. The problem lies in wrongful looking on the part of others, as in the example of Noah's son looking upon his father's nakedness or Joseph's brothers taking in the land before them. Because of their alleged ulterior motives,

Joseph's brothers should not have been viewing the land, nor the foreign men in Gerar viewing Sarah's physical beauty.

Consistent with the use of ʿervah in other contexts, its use in regard to the woman in the rule points to an aspect of nature, specifically, how she looks. There is consequently no need to apply it to her conduct, as translators and commentators do—for example, they typically attribute indecency or improper conduct to her. No wonder they have difficulty in attempting to specify her offense: they make it fall short of adultery, and rightly so because of the rule in Deuteronomy 22:22 that demands a death sentence for an adulteress, but they insist on some kind of sexual offense. We cannot tell from a reading of the law itself what is going on. We have to assume that when Genesis through 2 Kings was created, the law was composed with the narrative about Abraham and Sarah specifically under review. We must constantly be alert to the fact that these laws are part of the longer narrative of Genesis through 2 Kings and fit into it.

The expression ʿervat-dabar ("the nakedness of a thing") as applied to the woman in the law refers, then, to a public situation, in particular, how she is viewed by someone outside her marriage.[6] Here it is crucial to note that when she leaves the first marriage she enters upon a second. The language of the law, contrary to what the RSV makes of it, is not conditional in character. The language is not "And *if* she goes and becomes," but "And she goes and becomes." It is one clue in the law that a second liaison may well have been anticipated for her. If this speculation has merit and we additionally bring in Abraham's and Sarah's situation in Genesis, we can readily understand the prohibition against the first husband taking her back should the second husband divorce her or even die. What is being condemned is the release of the woman from a marriage because, for whatever reason, the husband anticipates a favor by letting her go to another man. Different is the ritual of wife-selling in eighteenth- and nineteenth-century England, a procedure used by the poor, who had no access to the legal machinery of divorce, which involved an act of Parliament and could be used only by the rich and influential.[7] Different too is the transaction in Genesis 30:14–16 between the co-wives, Rachel and Leah, when Rachel hires out Jacob to Leah for a night's lovemaking.

When the law goes on to say that a woman would be defiled should she return to the first husband, we can understand why this language is used. The verb *tame'* ("to defile") refers, as often, to sexual defilement. She would be so regarded because the first husband encouraged her to seek a relationship with another man. No doubt, should she become free again, he would presumably be as willing to have her back as he was opportunistic in releasing her from the first marriage. Although the outward conduct is in order because of the machinery of divorce, its motivation is base, a common enough phenomenon. Jezebel uses witnesses in a proper way in order to throw a cloak of legality over her criminal move to be rid of Naboth (1 Kgs 21:10).[8] In ancient Rome, under the *lex Iulia de adulteriis* of Augustus (18 BCE), a husband who did not divorce a wife caught in the act of adultery was guilty of *lenocinium,* or pandering (D.48.5.30[29]).[9] The biblical lawgiver views the husband as pandering too, only the husband uses the institution of divorce as a cover for it. Correctly interpreting the law in my view, Philo attributes an adulterous motive to the woman and a pandering one to the man (*De Spec. Leg.* 3.30, 31). The biblical lawgiver's attitude is similar to the Roman legislator's: "A [husband] is seen as having made a profit out of his wife's adultery if he has accepted anything in return for her committing adultery" (D.48.5.30[29]). John Calvin's view of the prohibition in Deuteronomy 24:1-4 is that "by prostituting his wife, he [the husband] would be, as far as in him lay, acting like a procurer." Calvin's view comes from his reading back into the Deuteronomic law his understanding of Matthew 5:31 and 19:9: Jesus recognizes no divorce, and consequently a man who divorces his wife is indeed encouraging her to prostitute herself.[10]

A further puzzling feature of the Deuteronomic law is worth commenting on. Much of its language is unnecessary. The drafting of laws at this stage of legal development is typically to the point and not inclined to spell out what can be taken for granted.[11] There is consequently no need to set out the reasons for the two divorces or to mention how a written document of divorce is handed to the departing spouse. Only if such a written document constituted an innovation might we expect a reference to it, but nothing indicates that it is an innovation. Why, then, such unnecessary description? To highlight, I suggest, what can plausibly be legislated for in later Israelite life as against the impossibility of prohibiting what Abraham does with Sarah. The issue of a formal divorce does not arise when Abraham, Pharaoh, and Abimelech each in turn release Sarah from her ties to them. Only the deity could control the development that arises with them. The law, on the other hand, can have access to a comparable situation only if the development occurred among Israelites themselves and involved the legal machinery of divorce. The formulation of the law reflects the attempt by a human lawgiver to transform the unmanageable circumstances described in the Genesis tale into manageable ones that can be addressed by the law. Even with this transformation we can still observe the powerful influence of the story on the law.

There is, as I have already indicated, the encapsulation of Sarah's exposure to prying male eyes in the expression ʿervat-dabar. We can also explain a crucial aspect of the interpretation that I am arguing for in the law. Why, if it really is the case of a husband's encouraging his wife to seek another liaison, does the law not refer to a transaction between the first husband and the second?[12] Realistically, we would expect evidence of a deal struck between the two of them. Such an indication would have put the interpretation of the rule beyond doubt. The influence of the story on the rule has again to be reckoned with. Abraham knows only that some male will be attracted to his wife. He decides on his scheme before he knows the identity of the second husband. The law proceeds from a description of the first husband's release of his wife to a simple statement that she goes and becomes another man's wife. The statement leaves us wondering whether the second husband knows the woman while she is still married to the first husband, or only after she is divorced. The story has prompted the lawgiver to keep the matter open—hence the omission of any reference to collusion between the two men.

Even the double description of the woman's release from her second marriage—the husband divorces her because he hates her or he dies—owes much to Abimelech's position with Sarah after he realizes what her deception has done to him and his kingdom. He rightly protests to the deity that she claims to be Abraham's sister and not his wife. In consequence he has occasion to change his attitude to her, from attraction to aversion. After all, a plague of sterility has struck the women of Gerar because of his association with her. Worse, Abimelech has a death sentence placed upon him because of her presence in his house: "Behold, thou art a dead man, for the woman which thou hast taken; for she is married to an husband" (Gen 20:3). The law, in turn, contemplates two likely developments by which the woman may be released from her second marriage: the husband dislikes her, or he dies. The two possibilities can be read as the equivalent of the peculiar problems faced by Abimelech in the story, namely, his aversion to Sarah and the death sentence he is under.

The law has the odd reference that sin is caused to the land because of the woman's relationships with the two men. Again the story in Genesis 20 proves illuminating. Abimelech protests that sin has been brought upon him and his kingdom because of Sarah's previous marital bond with Abraham (Gen 20:9, 10). The law also states that should the divorcee return to her first husband after her marriage to the second, such an outcome would constitute an abomination to the deity. The characterization is in line with the depiction of the deity's outraged response in Genesis 20, as reflected by the sterility of the women and the sentence of death. The Deuteronomic lawgiver reveals the same sensibility to Sarah's near defilement as shows up in the story in Genesis 20 about Abimelech. Both its narrator and the lawgiver would have opposed Abraham's taking Sarah back after Pharaoh took her as a wife in Genesis 12.

We might conclude by noting the sequence of responses to a husband who encourages his wife to go to a second husband. The first incident, in Genesis 12, recognizes that the sin of adultery occurs, but the attitude is that, while the matter is cause for condemnation, the development does not bar the husband's taking back his wife. The second incident, in Genesis 20, declares the development to be adultery but then has it made clear that the deity actually prevents the offense from occurring. The message conveyed is that if sexual intercourse takes place, the woman cannot return to her husband who encouraged her to be with the new partner. A third incident, in Genesis 26, involving Abraham's son Isaac and his wife, Rebekah, has the development thwarted almost from the start, even though the husband again encourages his wife to be taken so that they both end up in the palace of King Abimelech of Gerar. The king, having seen Isaac embrace Rebekah and realizing that they are husband and wife, upbraids Isaac for what he has done. Focus falls on the initial phase of the man's letting his wife go to another man because it is to his advantage to do so. The spotlight on the initial move by the husband is sufficient to attend to the matter. The final response in the sequence, the law of Deuteronomy, also addresses the issue at the outset: any move by a husband to release a wife to another man, because it is advantageous for him to do so, will have a negative consequence. In that such a development is likely to involve the institution of divorce, the lawgiver makes it clear that any husband taking that route can forget about reclaiming his wife in the future should she become free from the second marriage into which she has entered, even if the second husband dies. Manifestly, the lawgiver wishes to nip in the bud any such eventuality.

Needless to say, the law is not enforceable. It is an ideal moral construction designed to appeal to the honor of future Israelites after the time of Moses. That is why the prophet Jeremiah can have the deity appeal to a law like it when he has occasion to remind his wife, Israel, that he wrote her a bill of divorce because she played the harlot with many lovers and shamed herself (Jer 3:1, 8). The deity need not adhere to the bar against taking back his spouse because of his love for her. Unlike Abraham, he certainly did not encourage her to go to another partner in the first place.

The nonenforceable character of the rule comes out in the use of language. If the woman has become free after her second marriage, her first husband "cannot take her again after that she is defiled, for that were abomination before Yahweh" (Deut 24:4). The use of "cannot" in the rule, as in a number of other laws in Deuteronomy and in some biblical narratives, expresses "a psychological inability because of respect for an accepted, compelling evaluation." It is an appeal to conscience, to the high standards of the group to whom the laws are addressed: "in view of our standards you cannot, he cannot [remarry]."[13]

Contrary to the universal understanding of the rule in Deuteronomy 24:1–4, I do not take it to mean that a marriage can never be renovated.[14] On the surface it appears to mean that. A man divorces his wife, she becomes the wife of another man, he in turn divorces her, or he dies—the first husband cannot take her again as his wife. Such an interpretation is too broad and is also contrary to common sense. The rule applies only where, with his wife's collaboration, there has been pimping by the husband. The remarriage of Richard Burton and Elizabeth Taylor would not have fallen under the rule (unless Burton had encouraged Taylor to go to another partner), and a recent development in Japan would not come under the rule either: "A decade after the appearance of *yamesaseya*, professional 'splitters' who specialised in ending relationships at the behest of an unhappy, but timid, partner, Japan is in the midst of a boom in services that promise the opposite: reuniting couples months, and sometimes years, after they have gone their separate ways [and often being with other partners]. Ladies Secret Service, a private detective agency in Tokyo's upmarket Ginza district, has successfully rekindled romances on behalf of hundreds of men and women who are prepared to spend huge sums on their quest to win back former lovers."[15]

A Wife's Sexual Pleasure

There is a surprising reference to such pleasure in the rule that follows the one prohibiting the renovation of a marriage should the husband collude with his wife in having her go to another partner. The rule reads: "When a man hath taken a new wife, he shall not go out to war, neither shall he be charged with any business: but he shall be free at home one year, and shall give joy to his wife which he hath taken" (Deut 24:5). The rule clearly wants a newly married man to be out of harm's way for a year so that, doubtless, he may produce a child to continue his lineage. But why do we not find a concise rule alone stated: a man is to be free for a year from military commitment when he has taken a wife (cf. the similar rule in Deut 20:7)? Why add the unnecessary comment that he "shall give joy to his wife?" Also, while military engagement will indeed take a man away from his wife and be obviously death threatening, why add some other activity that is viewed as similarly threatening?

The danger to Abraham, which prompts his plan to let Sarah be acquired by the king of Gerar, is also the inspiration for this rule about newlyweds. I am not denying that the rule may have had a basis in the real-life circumstances of the ancient Israelites. My intent is to explain why it has come to be written down as a particular law of Moses. Moses, we recall, delivers these rules as his death is approaching and life in the new land for his fellow Israelites, but not for him, beckons (Deut 1:1, 33:1–34:12). Incidents in which death is imminent, similar to the one confronting Moses, often engage the lawgiver's attention, a good example being the rule about the newlyweds. Moreover, in the situations he scrutinizes there is also a threat to the promise, so prominent elsewhere in Deuteronomy, of the blessing of fruitfulness and increase of numbers. The intent of the rule about the newlyweds is to give them time to conceive a child. When Abraham and Sarah go on their foreign trip, he perceives his life to be under threat on the grounds that they are strangers in a foreign land. At Gerar, Abraham and Sarah have not yet produced a child, even though they have been married a long time. The deity has promised them one (Gen 18:10), but at the time of their visit to Gerar Sarah is yet to conceive. Supernatural assistance to overcome Sarah's age barrier to pregnancy, as well as the removal of the threat to Abraham's life, is part of the history known to Moses.

Marriage and the birth of a child are very much bound together, especially in a society where the role of contraception is of marginal significance. Marriage followed by childbirth within a year will have been a common development. With newlyweds any barrier to childbirth will be revealed very soon. Characteristic of how a great many biblical rules come to be formulated, the lawgiver picks up a problem from a highly unusual situation in the history of his ancestors and then turns to a comparable problem in more normal circumstances. In this instance, the move is from an aged couple who, exceptionally, are going to have a first child, though the husband faces a threat to his life, to newlyweds who are likely to have a child but might be prevented from doing so if he is called to battle or has some other duty imposed on him.

Moses' task, precisely because his special relationship to the deity will not be found again, is to issue rules that further the deity's designs. The rule about the newly married couple reflects the concern with the threat to Abraham's life. Only the rule does so in the more conventional instance drawn from later Israelite events—that of death on the battlefield. Aside from exemption from military duty, the rule also permits a man to stay at home and be free of any other duty or business for a year. In the tradition, Abraham, as it happens, is engaged away from home in an unspecified business transaction in Gerar when he runs into danger (Gen 20:1). We might surmise that the lawgiver, in turn, thinks of a newly married man similarly engaged in a foreign trip that takes him away from his wife. In the comparable tradition in Genesis 12:10, Abraham is away from home in order to purchase food in Egypt. In Proverbs 7:19, 20, there is reference to the husband of an unfaithful wife who has gone on a distant journey and will not return until the middle of the month. Among the Sarakatsani, a Greek shepherding community in recent times, a man left his place of business for a number of months in order to establish his wife's pregnancy.[16]

The rule primarily incorporates the concern with the childlessness of Abraham and Sarah. The focus on children in the rule can be inferred from the man's exemption for one year and from the language about giving joy to his wife. The association between joy and the birth of a child is a standard one in biblical antiquity (Isa 66:10; Jer 20:15; John 3:29, 30; 15:11; 16:21; 17:13). Typically, in the formulation of a biblical rule, its language echoes the tradition that has inspired it. The surprising emphasis about giving pleasure to the woman comes from Sarah's speaking this way when she hears that she will be made pregnant: "After I am waxed old shall I have pleasure, my lord being old also" (Gen 18:12).

Sarah's participation in adultery in Genesis 12 and attempted adultery in Genesis 20 receives little or no attention in either account, when she and Abraham are in Egypt and Gerar, respectively. There is certainly no open recognition of her complicity in the scheme to deceive the foreign potentates. In his rule about adultery, however, the Deuteronomic lawgiver confronts the issue of her involvement. That rules reads: "If a man be found lying with a woman married to an husband, they shall die indeed *[gam]* both of them, both the man that lay with the woman, and the woman; so shalt thou put away evil from Israel" (Deut 22:22).

There are at least three striking features about the prohibition. One, it is unnecessarily detailed in its formulation. Why is its construction not along the lines of the formulation in the Decalogue: "Thou shalt not commit adultery"? Second, the statement that "they shall die indeed both of them" indicates a concern that both participants pay the penalty for their offense. What has prompted the clause in question? Third, the clause makes clear that whereas there is no question that the man is culpable, it is at pains to ensure that the woman is viewed as equally culpable: "both the man that lay with the woman, and the woman." What is behind the emphasis on the woman's culpability?

The rule, I submit, is also a response to the narrative incidents in Genesis 12 and 20, its particular focus being Sarah's role in her involvement with the Pharaoh and Abimelech, respectively. Her contribution to the offense is recognized, and the law ensures that any comparable occurrence in future Israelite life will make the woman as culpable as the man. To be sure, the future occurrence will also entail that someone like the Pharaoh or Abimelech be aware of the woman's married status, that she is *beʿulat-baʿal* ("a man's wife"), a legal designation to be found only in this particular Deuteronomic rule about adultery and in the incident involving Abimelech ("Behold, thou art a dead man, for the woman which thou hast taken; for she is a man's wife" [Gen 20:3]). Indeed, it is precisely because both men are innocent of the woman's status, yet each is unfairly treated as guilty of the offense, that the situation cries out for a plain ruling about adultery. The dramatic circumstances of a narrative prompt sober assessment by a lawgiver of any offense that is detailed.

The rule about adultery in Deuteronomy 22:22 follows after the rule about the slandered bride in Deuteronomy 22:13–21 (see Chap. 4). Both rules are the result of reflection on incidents about the patriarchs in Genesis. In the rule about the bride, the incident in the background is Jacob's being deceived about the woman with whom he has intercourse on his wedding night. All three incidents involve a man—Pharaoh, Abimelech, and Jacob—each of whom is deceived about the woman's status: Sarah's marital standing in the two incidents in Genesis 12 and 20 and Leah's lack of betrothed status in Genesis 29. There is also the confusion, which is then exploited, as to the precise status of the woman. Leah substitutes for her sister, Rachel, and thereby becomes Jacob's wife, and her father claims that the exchange is legitimate. Abraham's Sarah is both his wife and his sister, and he has her exchange one status for the other so that, as his sister, she becomes available for marriage to another man. Little wonder that these deceptions by the founding fathers evoked ethical responses such as we find in the rules in question.

Adultery and the Created Order

Biblical rules represent Moses' responses to issues arising in the history of his nation, responses that are critical of conduct in times past, present, and future, that invite adherence to his norms, and that set out ideal standards after he is gone. How does the rule against adultery in the Decalogue—it is the first formulation of the offense in Genesis through 2 Kings—fit into this scheme (Exod 20:14; Deut 5:18)? We might first take stock of the fact that the rules in the Decalogue are addressed to the sons of heads of household, not to daughters (a neighbor's wife is coveted) and not to the heads themselves (sons are to honor parents). A prime characteristic of all biblical rules is that the scribes responsible for their construction typically search out the first instance of a problem in the traditions available to them. We can see this process readily at work when we note that the first expression of a rule against murder in Genesis through 2 Kings targets the first son ever, Cain, who commits the first murder ever. The victim is his brother, Abel. Both have been born to their mother, Eve, with Yahweh's aid ("I have gotten a man from Yahweh" [Gen 4:1]).

The first humans' first encounter with God is in Eden. They are expelled from the place because of their refusal to desist from acquiring knowledge of good and evil. The acquisition of godlike knowledge contains the first indication of God's moral code, because, in interacting with the first family, God conveys certain ethical and legal standards, some articulated and some (the fundamental ones, in fact) not. Later at Sinai, in giving the Decalogue, God articulates the rules not made explicit in Eden. The event at Sinai is a symbolic return to the initial interaction in Eden. For instance, at Sinai there is nakedness, as there had been in Eden. The Israelites launder their clothes in the wilderness and do not, we might readily assume, have other garments to wear. There is also awareness of sexuality, for by separating from their spouses (Exod 19:15), like Adam and Eve the Israelites become conscious of sexual difference, maleness and femaleness. A threat of death hangs over humans and animals should they touch the sacred mountain (Exod 19:12, 13), just as a similar threat hangs over the two humans and the serpent should they encroach on the tree of the knowledge of good and evil (Gen 3:3).[17] In any event, the second tablet of the Decalogue gives voice to the unarticulated rules in the Genesis narrative.

To illustrate the process by which implicit rules in the Adam and Eve story are made explicit in the Decalogue, we might consider the following two examples involving Cain. The first humans, Adam and Eve, disobey the first commandment when they refuse to accept the distinction between the two kinds of food in Eden, trees from which they are permitted to eat and the tree of the knowledge of good and evil, whose fruit is forbidden. (As I indicated in Chap. 1, the words in Gen 1:28, "And God blessed them, and God said to them, Be fruitful and multiply," is not the first commandment. It is a blessing.) As a result of their disobedience, the naked pair in the garden acquires the capacity both to discriminate between good and evil and, concomitantly, to experience the emotion of shame. Further on in the narrative, the first instance of the exercise of this new human state of enlightenment occurs when their son Cain refuses, like his parents before him, to accept divinity's distinction between two kinds of food, Cain's vegetable offering and his brother Abel's animal offering. Despite God's counsel to Cain to exercise judgment and accept what is, in fact, a deliberately arbitrary act of discrimination to test that capacity (Gen 4:6, 7), Cain's anger overcomes him and he murders his brother. Anger is antithetical to the positive employment of discrimination and by destroying what his parents created, Cain commits the first act of dishonoring parents and the first murder. Philo and the rabbis are sensitive to God's unwarranted downgrading of Cain's offering (*Gen. Rab.* on Gen 4:3 ff., and *Sac.* 13.52 ff). It is unwarranted, but it is the means by which an ancient author probes a fundamental feature of human life, the handling of another's discriminating act.

Once we take into account the link between Eden and Sinai, the Decalogue's odd juxtaposition of the two rules about honoring parents and prohibiting murder becomes intelligible. We can also understand why the Decalogue is addressed to the sons of households, because Cain's actions are under scrutiny in some of the rules, Cain being the first son of the first parents to commit an offense. A clause attached to the rule about honoring parents promises long days upon the land if one honors them. Such a reward is hardly an obvious result of respect for one's progenitors. The link makes sense if the lawgiver has in focus Cain's punishment for his misdeed: his life as a tiller of the ground is cut short, and he is forced into the precarious life of a wanderer. The rule curiously speaks of living long upon the "ground" and not, as we might expect, upon the "land." The lawgiver's reflection upon the first murder by the first tiller of the ground explains the surprising choice of the word "ground" and not "land."

God's moral code is, then, detectable in his dealings with the first family, and at Sinai he gives voice to it. Why then, again seemingly haphazardly, does the rule about adultery come after a rule about murder? The clue lies in the next phase of Cain's life history. He marries a woman who does not exist in any historical sense. She is neither identified nor named in the text. But these ancient stories, we must constantly remind ourselves, are mythical in character, a means of reflecting on mysterious, fundamental aspects of human existence. Relaying the history of the generations, the narrator recounts Cain's marriage in terms identical to Adam's union with Eve: "And Cain knew his wife; and she conceived, and bare Enoch"

(Gen 4:17; cf. 4:1: "And Adam knew Eve his wife; and she conceived, and bare Cain"). The focus is on the origins of an institution embedded in human life, not on any supposed actual history of humankind.

The topic of marriage has already for Adam and Eve received explicit attention. Adam's wife comes from his own body: "And Adam said [of Eve coming from his rib], This is now bone of my bones, and flesh of my flesh: she shall be called Woman because she was taken out of man. Therefore shall a man leave his father and mother, and shall cleave unto his wife: and they shall be one flesh" (Gen 2:23, 24). In line with how marital union is depicted, Cain is in fact the first son ever to leave his father and mother and marry a woman. That is, Cain, too, when he marries, unites with part of his own body, because the idea of marriage is that a man unites with his original female bodily part. As a state in which a man cleaves to his wife (touching rib cages, so to speak) and becomes one flesh with her, an androgynous idea underlies the description of marriage in Genesis 2:23, 24. The married couple is male and female in one, a notion that links marriage to the original creation of man. A major implication is that any interference with this union constitutes an offense against the created order. It therefore follows, as the rabbis long ago saw (*b. San.* 58a), that a rule prohibiting adultery is implicit in Genesis 2:23, 24: adultery breaks the bond of the united male and female that God originally intended at creation. It is this rich background that accounts for the appearance of the prohibition of adultery in the Decalogue.[18]

The Woman Taken in Adultery

To understand the laws in the Pentateuch it is necessary to take account of their relationship to the overarching biblical narrative, Genesis through 2 Kings, in which they are embedded. To comprehend narratives such as those found in the New Testament, we often need knowledge of biblical laws as they have come to be interpreted in that later period. An example of how an understanding of such later interpretation illumines a narrative is found in the episode about the woman taken in adultery (John 8:1–11).

Generally speaking, it is not common to find a work of literature that has an impact on the law, but there are exceptions. One is A. P. Herbert's *Holy Deadlock*, which focused on the absurdity of the law of divorce in

England.[19] Herbert's book hastened the setting up of a Royal Commission, and its deliberations led to major reforms in the law. In the eighteenth century, Pierre Augustin Caron de Beaumarchais' *Mariage de Figaro* (1784) attacked the institution of the *jus primae noctis*, whereby the seigneur, a prince or lord of the manor, spent the wedding night with the bride of one of his retainers. Came the French Revolution and Beaumarchais' work influenced the decision to abolish the seigneur's right.

When it comes to links between law and literature, it is much easier to demonstrate how an understanding of law illumines a literary work. We cannot, for example, properly appreciate the Exodus story in the Bible without an awareness of the social laws pertaining to slavery in the ancient world. The role of the curse in Greek literature is better understood in light of ancient notions of individual and communal responsibility. The dramatic character of Shakespeare's *The Merchant of Venice* is enhanced through knowledge of the Ciceronian proverb *Summum jus, summa iniuria* ("utmost law, utmost injustice"), the notion that by keeping the law, all of it, you can break the law.

Many problems in New Testament literature yield a solution only by taking into account legal background of the time. The prohibition against divorce on the part of Jesus makes no sense without a comprehension of prevailing notions about the institution of marriage. His counsel to turn the other cheek is bewildering unless we take into account a contemporary development in the law pertaining to insult. Without awareness of rabbinic law as it applies to converts, we can make no sense of a situation described in the Pauline epistle to the Corinthians. The community to whom Paul writes boasts about a couple in its midst who have contracted a union that even the surrounding heathen cultures regard as incestuous—a man is living with his stepmother (see Chap. 8).

There is a manifest problem in the famous story in John's Gospel about the woman taken in adultery.[20] Recall that she is indeed taken in the act. She, but not her male partner, is brought before Jesus by the authorities in the form of scribes and Pharisees—an all-male crowd because only males could act as witnesses and executioners in any trial. The legal authorities remind Jesus that the Law of Moses lays down that she be stoned. What has he to say in the matter? He pronounces words that have become proverbial: "Let him who is without sin among you be the first to throw a stone at her." The scribes and Pharisees go their way, the clear implication being that they accept his judgment. He then speaks to her, and he too does not condemn her but tells her to sin no more, a stance involving the distinction between a sin and a punishable deed.

Here is the problem. It is inconceivable that Jesus could have gone against sacred legislation that clearly laid down a capital sentence for her offense. Yet from our point of view he does just that. Moreover, those who are seen to support the bindingness of their sacred constitution, those who quote the very law in question, do not consider that he has in any way abrogated it. Otherwise they would not have left the scene so readily. How can this be?

It cannot be that Jesus gets round the scriptural rule by an appeal to the conscience of the authorities. That would not have sufficed to overturn the rule, certainly not in terms of how the law is understood in first-century Palestine. The statement about casting the first stone, it has long been noticed, is of a type familiar to all cultures: "Judge not that you be not judged"; "The pot calls the kettle black"; "Don't throw stones from a glass house"; and "Sweep before your own door." To bring a legal judgment to an end by bowing out with this sort of appeal would be bewildering. This is especially so when we recall that the written law is so clear in the matter of the offense of adultery. In an offense involving the murder of an orphan and the embezzlement of his money, it is unlikely in the extreme that Jesus' response would have been the same, that he would not have approved of an appropriate punishment for the offender.

It is important to know what the saying about casting the first stone actually communicates. "Let him who is without sin" is not general in scope. It has come to take on a general character, but that was not its original import. It would not include, for example, someone involved in a shady business deal. Nor is the saying so specific that it refers only to males who have not committed adultery. The saying refers to sexual licentiousness in all its forms: a serious infraction by deed or intent of sexual morality. The Greek term *anamartetos* ("sinless") readily connotes such a meaning.

The puzzle cannot be solved without awareness of a legal development roughly contemporaneous with Jesus. In biblical law, the Law of Moses, there is the procedure of the bitter water test, whereby a husband who suspects his wife of adultery has her subjected to a particularly unpleasant ordeal. She is brought before the priests and made to take a potion which, she is told, will do terrible harm to her if she has committed adultery but have no effect if she is innocent. There is no comparable ordeal to which a husband has to submit. We have as flagrant an example of a double standard as we can find anywhere. We might ask in passing why such a double standard should exist in this area. There is, for example, no comparable ordeal for a woman or a man who is suspected of having committed theft or murder. Why, then, the ordeal for the suspected adulteress? A major consideration is that a woman's adultery is different from a man's in that she might bear another man's child. Indications are that for a man to have a child where there is some doubt as to paternity is just too difficult for him, worse even than a wife's proven affair.

The institution of the bitter water test for a suspected adulteress still existed in first-century Palestine. We know of a woman convert to Judaism, Queen Helena of Adiabene, who gave the gift of a plaque to the Temple in Jerusalem; on it were inscribed the fearful words of this biblical law (*m. Yom.* 3:10). Her gesture illustrates how the oppressed often collaborate with their oppressors.

At some point in the first century, however, the rabbinic authorities become sensitive to the double standard involved in the application of the ordeal with the consequence that, from our point of view, they abolish the institution. However, and this is a crucial point, from the rabbinic stance there is no way in which a hallowed scriptural institution can be set aside. Someway, somehow, the law has to remain as a divine commandment. What to do? Well, they proceeded in a manner familiar to us from many a decision that comes out of the U. S. Supreme Court. Like the justices with the American Constitution, the rabbis look at their biblical constitution and read it in a way that we never would. The concluding text of the biblical law about the ordeal states: "If the spirit of jealousy comes upon a man, then shall he set the woman before the Lord and the priest shall execute upon her all this law; and the man shall be clear from iniquity and that woman shall bear her iniquity" (Num 5:30, 31). The rabbis divide the text by using a hermeneutical rule, *collocatio,* that is borrowed from the Hellenistic rhetorical schools and read the Hebrew text as follows: "If the spirit of jealousy comes upon a man and if he sets the woman before the Lord and if the priest executes upon her all this law and [this is the point] *if the man is clear from iniquity,* then shall that woman bear her iniquity." It is certain that this way of reading the text is not original to the biblical text in Numbers. Although the Hebrew can just about be read in the way the rabbis take it, there can be no doubt that they do not just reinterpret a biblical institution but, in our terms, misinterpret it. For them, however, it is, to repeat, the only way to read it. Moreover, when they take into account, as they must, the rest of scripture, their reading has to be the correct one. They choose a text from the prophet Hosea, and, as it turns out, it is an apt text to quote in support of their position. God says to the men of Israel, "I will not punish your daughters when they commit whoredom, nor your spouses when they commit adultery: for you yourselves make off with whores and sacrifice with harlots" (Hos 4:14).

The only way to resolve the puzzle about the woman taken in adultery is to assume that a similar line of reasoning is being applied to her. In light of all that scripture says, the argument runs, she cannot be convicted by a male court because every one of them is given to sexual licentiousness. The absence of her male partner suggests that the biblical law of adultery has already fallen into disuse. But if so, why, then, is the woman brought for judgment? We are probably witnessing a phenomenon common in both New Testament and Talmudic literature: the attempt by one party to trap another in matters of legal interpretation. Each party fundamentally shares the same set of beliefs, but for one reason or another (for example, jockeying among themselves for greater authority), they joust with each other. Presumably the new way of looking at the bitter water test for the suspected adulteress is in the air, so to speak, and there is, in fact, general acceptance about how to interpret it. Jesus cleverly squares the circle in regard to the adulteress by showing that he knows his way around the law too. The text from the prophet Hosea about proven offenders readily lends itself to a woman caught in the act. In the contemporary United States, adultery is illegal in most states but is rarely prosecuted. The constitutionality of these laws is nonetheless upheld because a compelling state interest is thought to be at stake. In *Oliverson v. West Valley City,* 875 F. Supp. 1465 (D. Utah 1995), the court stated, "Even the most recent case law on this issue belies the notion that the Constitution precludes reasonable state regulation of sexual behavior."

Legal argumentation in ancient New Testament society should occasion little surprise. A healthy process of conciliation, compromise, argument, and debate between diverse groups prevails because knowledge of law and legal reasoning is much more widespread at a time before law is institutionalized and a professional class of lawyers emerges.

7

The Suspected Adulteress

She hath been more righteous than I because that I gave her not to Shelah my son.

—*Genesis 38:26*

To understand Jesus' argument opposing capital punishment for the woman caught in the act of adultery in John 8, I indicated in the previous chapter that the biblical law of the suspected adulteress is relevant because of the interpretation put on it at the time. I turn now to addressing the original significance of that much discussed law.

There are many reasons why the law of the suspected adulteress receives so much attention. First, the topic of sexual wrongdoing is always likely to attract interest; a husband suspecting his wife of adultery makes us curious as to the grounds of his suspicion, and, as I mentioned, there is a blatant double standard when we consider that no corresponding rule exists for a man under a similar cloud of suspicion. The husband's fears cause the woman to be subjected to a trial, the only one of its kind in the Bible, and its unfolding—she is guilty or innocent judging by the reaction of her body—is quite dramatic. Second, with no witness available to testify against her, the trial involves self-incrimination, no small matter from a legal point of view. Third, little or no light has been forthcoming to account for what prompted the lawgiver to present the law in the first place and why he set it down at the point he does in Numbers 5.

Fourth, from the perspective of comparative law it is of some interest to find a rule in the Code of Hammurabi in which a husband accuses his wife of adultery but lacks evidence (CH 131). She swears an oath to clear herself. In CH 132 someone else accuses the man's wife, and in this instance she is subject to an ordeal comparable to the biblical procedure: she is cast into a river to determine her guilt (she drowns) or her innocence (she survives).[1] In Numbers 5 water also plays a role. There, however, the woman has to drink a concoction that is part water, part dust taken from the floor of the sanctuary, and part an inky residue from a parchment on which a curse has been written. The imprecation is to the effect that if she is guilty her belly will swell and her thigh will rot. The reference is almost certainly to her uterus and genital area. By and large, critics and translators assume, rightly in my view, that she is pregnant and that the effect of the curse is supposed to cause a miscarriage. Numbers 5:28 is about her innocence: "she shall be free, and retain seed," that is, her conscience being clear, she will carry her child to term.[2] Fifth, the Near Eastern parallels that critics point to are rather thin, one critic bluntly stating: "This ordeal of bitter waters has no analogy in the ancient East."[3]

The narrative in Genesis 38 about Tamar's illicit union with Judah, which in the event turns out to have tremendous consequences (the line of David and the Messiah), is vital, I shall argue, for understanding why the rule attributed to Moses is set down in writing in Numbers 5. Just as the stories in Genesis point to significant events in the future, so also they contain matters that the future Moses will issue judgments on. The Tamar story also proves crucial for addressing the issues set out in the law that precedes it, about a breach of trust, and the law that follows it, about the sacred mission of a male or female Nazirite. We shall touch on matters that bring out how the sacred and the sexual often overlap.

Any narrative contains norms. The story of Cain and Abel, for instance, contains implicit rules against murder and against the dishonor of parents. If we find similar rules in biblical law codes, how do we judge whether they are later or earlier than the ones presupposed in a biblical narrative? More likely than not, the rules set down in each source will have a history behind them. The question is then, how do we judge whether the norms presupposed in the narrative are later or earlier than the rules formulated in the codes of law?

Biblical law codes obviously contain rules, but, surprisingly, they sometimes explicitly refer to biblical narratives, for example, the story of the Exodus: "Thou shalt not oppress a stranger: for ye know the heart of a stranger, seeing ye were strangers in the land of Egypt" (Exod 23:9). We must also take seriously the fact that the law codes in the Pentateuch interrupt at certain points a continuous narrative history that stretches from Genesis to 2 Kings. The relationship between the legal and the literary components is, then, of a rather special kind, and because the codes interrupt the flow of the narrative, their placement suggests that they complement it. In my view, the explanation for their placement is that each and every law turns out to be a response to some issue in a particular narrative. I repeat that the rules in the codes have a history behind them, only we have no means of knowing that history. At some point in the past an implicit or explicit rule in a narrative may well predate some earlier form of a rule in a code. But, as formulated in the biblical text, the contents of any rule owe a great deal to what goes on in a narrative. Excellent examples are the ones cited in the previous chapter: the three rules with a puzzling sequence—honoring parents, prohibiting murder, and prohibiting adultery—appear in this order in the Decalogue because of events occurring in the first family ever (Gen 2–4).

Another narrative that has inspired a puzzling sequence of laws is the story of Judah and Tamar, in Genesis 38. The story contains many legal issues, three of which, I suggest, are taken up in three successive laws in Numbers 5 and 6: breach of faith in some matter, a suspected adulteress, and the temporary vocation of a Nazirite who devotes herself or himself to a sacred task for a period of time.[4] Why at this point in the Book of Numbers is there a return to the tradition in Genesis 38?

Numbers 2–4 focus on the tribe of Levi, whose special destiny is to play the role of God's firstborn. It substitutes for the other tribes of Israel, who, as a collective constituting God's firstborn son, experience redemption from enslavement in Egypt at the expense of the Egyptian firstborn sons and animals (Num 3:12, 13). The Levites serve at the camp sanctuary and have a perpetual inheritance there. The sanctuary is holy and spells danger to those who wrongfully approach it or are unclean. Numbers 5:1–4 has a rule about the expulsion of unclean persons from the camp because their state threatens its holiness. In Genesis 38 God kills Judah's firstborn, Er, and Onan replaces him for the purpose of providing a firstborn for his brother in accord with the levirate custom. Onan, however, dies for discharging his seed, so both Er and Onan die at the hands of God because of an offense that, certainly in the case of Onan, involves uncleanness of the kind cited in Numbers 5:2, namely, a genital discharge. The story of Judah's family thus provides the first example in the nation's history of the death of an Israelite firstborn at the hands of God. God's holiness is asserted and he claims a firstborn directly by death. The lawgiver explores facets of the development in Genesis 38 by viewing them from the perspective of the cult, because God is localized in the established Israelite sanctuary. It is not so much that a lawgiver returns to the history in Genesis as that an issue there awaits attention in the most appropriate context, in this instance, that of cleanliness in the newly established camp.

In the narrative, Judah promises to give his son Shelah to the widowed and childless Tamar in order that she acquire a child by him in fulfillment of the levirate custom. But Judah fails to deliver on the promise. There is a breach of faith here, as in the law in Numbers 5:5–10 (which I shall discuss shortly). Second, in the narrative, Judah's broken promise results in Tamar so arranging matters that she acquires Judah instead of Shelah, not as a husband in the usual sense, but as a levirate husband. Judah is not aware of what she is doing because she disguises herself in order to obtain seed from him. A consequence of her ruse is that he accuses her of adultery, because, as the levirate custom requires, she is betrothed to his son Shelah and betrothal in Hebrew law is equivalent to marriage. Judah orders her to be burned, but on further inquiry he finds that he is the one who has made her pregnant. However bizarrely—it is the exceptionalism that characterizes storytelling—Judah turns out to be a husband of a certain kind who suspects a wife of adultery, subjects her to a death-threatening experience but discovers that she is not in the wrong. This is precisely the subject of the next law of the suspected adulteress in Numbers 5:11–31. A third issue in the narrative is the tenacity of Tamar in her commitment to acquiring a child for her dead husband in fulfillment of what would have been regarded as a sacred custom. To accomplish her aim she becomes a *qedešah* ("a consecrated woman"). The sacred task to which she is committed, for a brief period, has its analogue in the temporary dedication of the Nazirite in the subsequent law in Numbers 6.

In sum, the narrative has a betrayal of trust resulting in an apparent act of adultery, but on inquiry the act is perceived as justified because it is in a sacred cause, the preservation of a family line. The sequence of topics is natural to the story line. The same sequence shows up in the law code—a broken promise, a suspected case of adultery, and a temporary dedication to a sacred task. In the case of the law code, however, the three rules appear to bear little or no relation to one another. The seemingly unsatisfactory sequence can be accounted for by assuming that the lawgiver responded to specific events in the Tamar-Judah narrative. The same sequence of topics, I submit, is a strong indicator, even if not conclusive, of the connection between narrative and law code.

One might argue that the lawgiver could have produced, for other reasons not obvious to us, three such laws with no thought of the events of Genesis 38 in mind. What proves decisive, I will argue, in revealing a major link between the story and the law code are details in the laws that connect to particularities in the story. In other words, while the laws will have come from the lawgiver's acquaintance with previously existing laws, he shaped those preserved in the text in light of the narrative. What kind of relationship might we expect? A lawgiver chooses those subjects that are most capable of regulation. He is not going to rule on the extraordinary situation where a man, Judah, does not know that the woman he has lain with has become a wife to him. It is in narrative literature that we encounter such sensational developments, as when the count in the *Marriage of Figaro* does not know that the woman he is committing adultery with is his own wife, or when, as we saw, Jacob acquires a wife he did not want (Gen 29:21–23). What the lawgiver does is to consider a comparable, less unusual situation. Topics such as breach of trust, suspected adultery, and sacred commitment to a cause will be familiar enough to him, and their presence in some form in a narrative is what challenges him to formulate rules about them. I will detail a considerable number of features in the Tamar narrative that show up, sometimes by way of contrast because of the lawgiver's opposition to what is going on in the narrative, in the three laws that are formulated for proper Israelite conduct in such matters.

Breach of Trust

The law concerns a man or a woman who breaks faith (*ma'al*) in some matter: "When a man or a woman shall commit any sin toward a fellow human, thereby also trespassing *[ma'al]* against Yahweh, and that person feels guilty; then they shall confess their sin which they have done: and shall recompense the trespass with the principal thereof, and add unto it the fifth part thereof, and give it to the person against whom the trespass was committed. If that person has no kinsman to recompense the trespass unto, let the trespass be recompensed unto Yahweh, even to the priest; beside the ram of the sin-offering whereby a sin-offering shall be made for him. And every offering of all the holy things of the sons of Israel, which they bring unto the priest, shall be his. And every man's hallowed things shall be his: whatsoever any man giveth the priest, it shall be his" (Num 5:6–10).

At least two particularities of the story pertain to elements in the first law about a breach of trust. First, Judah explicitly confesses that he failed to keep his promise to give Shelah to Tamar for the purpose of producing an heir for her dead husband (Gen 38:26). The rule in Numbers 5:5–10, but not the comparable rule in Leviticus 5:20–26 [6:1–7] (similar rules are inspired by different narratives or by different facets of them), calls for a promisor to confess his failure to deliver a promised benefit.

Anticipating life in the land of Canaan, the law in Numbers 5:6–10 concerns an Israelite man or woman who breaks a promise about some sacred trust. Should the person acknowledge guilt, he or she is to confess the offense, make good the promise, and pay a measure of gain.[5] If, remarkably, the wronged person is not only dead but has no relative to whom restoration can be rendered, compensation goes to the sanctuary. As Gray accurately states: "Provision is now made that if the rightful owner be dead, and there also be no next-of-kin (*goel*) to whom the property can be restored, it is to become the priest's."[6] In addition, the offender has to give an '*asham* ("sin-offering") because there is a sacred dimension to the betrayal.

If we turn to Judah's conduct with Tamar, we find, taking into account the uniqueness of the situation, parallels that are most suggestive. Judah leads Tamar to believe that he will send his youngest son, Shelah, to her to fulfill the duty of continuing the line of Tamar's dead husband, Er, thereby granting him the benefit of a son and heir (Gen 38:11). In material terms, the benefit is the dead man's part of the patrimony. The sum *(ro'š)* referred to in the rule is its equivalent. But Judah breaks faith in the matter by failing to send Shelah to Tamar, and hence, just as in the law the wronged person is dead, so the dead kinsman (Judah's own son, Er) is wronged. The verb in the law, *ma'al,* although used in regard to that aspect that offends the deity, can mean "to act counter to one's duty, to be unfaithful, to deprive, take away something due to a person." It accurately describes the wrong done to Tamar and hence to Er (or, more precisely, to equivalent Israelite players in the future land).[7]

Why is the verb *ma'al,* which has sacred overtones, employed in the rule? If we assume that the narrative has inspired the rule, we might note that the seed in a levirate situation is something deposited in trust with a surviving male family member. It is precisely in matters of human trust that the notion of the sacred comes to prominence, because, absent any legal instrument, trust is not enforceable. The very weakness of the depositee's remedy calls for reliance on divine protection, on Yahweh. In biblical rules about deposit, where one must rely on the good faith of the depositee not to act badly, the only quasi-legal remedy is resort to an oath (Exod 22:7–13; Lev 5:21–26 [6:2–7]).[8]

Second, Tamar is motivated to obtain seed from her father-in-law because she fears that her dead husband's name is otherwise going to die out. If no child is born to her husband, no heir inherits his estate. The Numbers rule takes into account the exceptional circumstances in which not only is the victim of the wrong dead, but a beneficiary to receive a promised property settlement is lacking; indeed, the main concern of the law is to address the consequences of the absence of an heir.

The story raises the distinct possibility that Tamar's husband might not (through a legal fiction) produce an heir. Onan, who should redeem the situation, dies when he offends against the levirate custom by spilling his seed during intercourse with Tamar. His death leads Judah deliberately to hold back Shelah from taking Onan's place. The lawgiver would unquestionably have opposed Tamar's next move. To produce an heir to reestablish her deceased husband's share of the patrimony, she acts the part of a prostitute in order to seduce her father-in-law into impregnating her. As Tamar views the matter, should she fail to produce an heir, the line and the inheritance that goes with it will be forfeited to Yahweh. Although the narrator of Genesis 38 is aware of the wrongfulness of sexual relations between father-in-law and daughter-in-law (Gen 38:26; Lev 18:15), he understandably does not bring the story to an end on this account. He does recognize, however, the effect of a sacred sphere of influence. Thus Yahweh causes the deaths of Er and Onan (Gen 38:7, 10), and Judah fears that if he gives Shelah to Tamar, Shelah too may die. Yahweh's extreme position is attributable to an anti-Canaanite bias in the narrative: Judah's sons are the product of a Canaanite mother (Gen 38:2).

The situation does not, in fact, result in failure to produce a firstborn, although it very much looked as if it would. The Numbers lawgiver, moreover, as just noted, would have opposed Tamar's deceptive act of prostitution to acquire an heir. He therefore proceeds to take up the question of what would happen to a benefit in the absence of a beneficiary. If an heir is not available to whom compensation can be given, it is consigned to the sanctuary. The law's levied donations—they are equivalent to the share of the patrimony that would have gone to Er's firstborn—go to a particular priest who is Yahweh's firstborn. The priest becomes the stand-in to receive the goods because Yahweh has a claim on a firstborn. Levine comments on how the text has it that (in his translation and punctuation) "the liability that is to be repaid belongs to YHWH, [credited] to the priest."[9] The language, with Yahweh cited first, is a response to a situation that occurs in pre-Israelite times as described in Genesis 38. Yahweh alone is active in the saga, and the lawgiver works out the equivalent situation in normal, later Israelite life when the deity's intervention comes to expression in the context of the cult.

Levine is puzzled by the role of expiation in the law because the kind in question seems available only for an inadvertent offense, as the rule in Numbers 15:30–31 makes clear. Yet the law in Numbers 5:6–10 assumes an intentional offense. The puzzle may be solved by noting that Judah deliberately holds back Shelah from giving conception, but Judah is not aware that he lies with Tamar and impregnates her. Judah's role involves both witting and unwitting misdeeds, a combination that the law appears to take into account.[10]

Looking at the unique and complicated aspects of a problem in the history of an important Israelite ancestor, Judah, the lawgiver has pursued more general matters pertinent to any significant kind of promised benefit. The complexity and ambiguity of the Judah-Tamar story is what inspires the lawgiver to tease out the issues in it. He references, for example, both a "man or a woman" breaking faith in some matter. Although Judah is clearly a culprit, it is also true from Judah's initial perspective that Tamar gives the appearance of being unfaithful to her dead husband when she becomes pregnant by prostitution. She appears to be breaking the bond that ties her to Judah's family and hence, like Judah's failure to keep his promise, jeopardizing Er's claim from beyond the grave.

A Woman's Suspected Adultery

The law reads:

If any man's wife go aside, and commit a trespass against him, and a man lie with her carnally, and it be hid from the eyes of her husband, and be kept close, and she be defiled, and there be no witness against her, neither she be taken with the manner; And the spirit of jealousy come upon him, and he be jealous of his wife, and she be defiled: or if the spirit of jealousy come upon him, and he be jealous of his wife, and she be not defiled: Then shall the man bring his wife unto the priest, and he shall bring her offering for her, the tenth part of an ephah of barley meal; he shall pour no oil upon it, nor put frankincense thereon; for it is an offering of jealousy, an offering of memorial, bringing iniquity to remembrance. And the priest shall bring her near, and set her before Yahweh: And the priest shall take holy water in an earthen vessel; and of the dust that is on the floor of the tabernacle shall the priest take, and put it into the water: And the priest shall set the woman before Yahweh, and uncover the woman's head, and put the offering of memorial in her hands, which is the jealousy offering: and the priest shall have in his hand the bitter water that causeth the curse: And the priest shall charge her by an oath, and say unto the woman, If no man hast lain with thee, and if thou hast not gone aside to uncleanness with another instead of thy husband, be thou free from this bitter water that causeth the curse. But if thou hast gone aside to another instead of thy husband, and if thou be defiled, and some man have lain with thee beside thine husband: Then the priest shall charge the woman with an oath of cursing, and the priest shall say unto the woman, Yahweh make thee a curse and an oath among thy people, when Yahweh doth make thy thigh to rot, and thy belly to swell; And this water that causeth the curse shall go into thy bowels, to make thy belly to swell, and thy thigh to rot: And the woman shall say, Amen, amen. And the priest shall write these curses in a book, and he shall blot them out with [into] the bitter water: And he shall cause the woman to drink the bitter water that causeth the curse: and the water that causeth the curse shall enter into her, and become bitter. Then the priest shall take the jealousy offering ... And when he hath made her to drink the water, then it shall come to pass that, if she be defiled, and have done trespass against her husband, that the water that causeth the curse shall enter into her, and become bitter, and her belly shall swell, and her thigh shall rot: and the woman shall be a curse among her people. And if the woman be not defiled, but be clean; then she shall be free, and retain seed. This is the law of jealousies, when a wife goeth aside to another instead of her husband, and is defiled; Or when the spirit of jealousy cometh upon him, and he be jealous over his wife, and shall set the woman before Yahweh, and the priest shall execute upon her all this law. Then shall the man be guiltless from iniquity, and this woman shall bear her iniquity. (Num 5:12–31)

At least six features of the story of Tamar relate to the law about the suspected adulteress.[11] First, in both narrative and law, a woman stands accused of adultery. We have to ask why it is proper to speak of Tamar's offense as adultery. Genesis 38 concerns the complicated custom of levirate marriage, complicated because of the legal fiction it seeks to enact. Judah's oldest son, Er, dies childless after marrying Tamar and, in keeping with the custom, Judah instructs his son Onan to impregnate her in order to raise a child to his dead brother. Alert, however, to the fact that should a child be born he stands to lose that part of the patrimony belonging to his deceased sibling, Onan scorns the duty and only goes through the motions of intercourse with Tamar. He withdraws from her and spills his seed outside her. His punishment is extreme. Heaven fells him. Fearing that if he directs his third and only remaining son, Shelah, to fulfill the levirate duty he will lose him too, Judah bows out of the responsibility to ensure the continuation of his and Er's family line and does not send Shelah to Tamar. Only when Tamar takes the initiative of dressing as a prostitute to conceal her identity and seducing Judah himself when he is on his way to a sheep-shearing festival do intercourse and conception take place for the purpose of the custom.

The childless Tamar is bound to Judah's family by what came to be called in later Jewish sources the *ziqah* bond, the interim state between the husband's death and union with a relative who acts as the dead man's surrogate to produce a child for him. She is not free during that period to marry any man outside of her dead husband's family (Deut 25:5), and certainly not free to engage in prostitution.[12] To all appearances, then, Tamar's pregnant state suggests that she had committed an offense against her special marital bond within Judah's family and that she can be rightly accused of adultery.

Second, in both narrative and law, it is the husband who suspects his wife of adultery, straightforwardly so in the law, quite exceptionally so in the story. By convention, a member of Judah's family automatically becomes Tamar's substitute husband for the purpose of continuing the family line of her childless, dead spouse, which in Tamar's case is the line of her father-in-law, Judah, and his own father's line of Jacob-Israel. Because of the peculiar character of the levirate institution, Judah, once he has lain with her, is Tamar's husband in some legal sense at the point in time when he accuses her of adultery. Although it seems strange to emphasize a husband-wife relationship between Judah and Tamar, we must bear in mind not only the curious character of the levirate institution but also the highly idiosyncratic matters of the story. A lawgiver seeking a more mundane parallel to the Judah-Tamar entanglement will think of a husband who, even if mistaken, has justifiable reasons to suspect his wife of adultery. Basically, it is the false but quite understandable accusation against Tamar that has prompted the lawgiver to pursue the surprising topic he describes in his rule.

Third, in the narrative, Tamar faces a fearful consequence when brought before the domestic jurisdiction of Judah's household for her suspected sexual impropriety. In the law, the suspected adulteress also faces the prospect of a terrible ordeal. When Judah learns that Tamar is pregnant, he is as yet unaware that he is the one who has impregnated her and proceeds to accuse her of harlotry. Bringing her before the *iudicium domesticum*, he condemns her to death by burning.[13] She saves herself by producing Judah's pledges—the seal, cord, and staff—to remind him of his promise to pay her for their sexual transaction. The law's "offering of memorial, bringing iniquity to remembrance" plays a similar role in recalling sexual wrongdoing. Tamar obtains Judah's personal items because she anticipates that she will be subjected to an accusation of sexual misconduct and face a dreadful consequence. Once Judah learns of his role as her sexual partner, he acknowledges that she has been "more righteous than I because that I gave her not to Shelah my son" (Gen 38:26). So Judah accepts that he is the father of her children (she is carrying twins) and when declaring that she is justified in doing what she did, he declares, in effect, that she is innocent of any essential wrongdoing. The outcome is that instead of the children dying with her they come to fruition.

The law considers how a woman may have committed an act of betrayal against her husband and the expression used, *limʿol maʿal* ("act unfaithfully"), has sacred overtones (Num 5:12). Notably, its use is the only instance in biblical legal sources to indicate a sacred character for the marriage bond, precisely because trust, being central to the institution of marriage, is the overriding consideration when the issue of unfaithfulness arises. In the story in Genesis 38, the idea of the sacred is central to the marital union that Tamar seeks. The levirate custom plainly goes against the incest taboo, against a union between a brother-in-law and a brother's wife, and, in Tamar's case, against a union between a daughter-in-law and a father-in-law (Lev 18:15, 16, 20:12, 21). As a "holy woman," however, at the time when she has intercourse with Judah, her sacred status enables her to transcend the taboo. On account of the uniqueness of the situation the idea of a sacred union powerfully emerges.

It is only during the much later period of the compilation of the Mishnah that the sacramental nature of the regular marriage bond clearly emerges. Hebrew *qiddeš* came to mean "to consecrate to wife," and the tractate *qiddushin* in the Mishnah means "consecrations." Tamar seeks a levirate union as a *qedešah*, and it is conceivable that the designation has contributed to the later use of the verb *qiddeš* for the regular marriage bond. Language often gives the remarkable a word before it is applied more generally. The word *heterosexual* first appears in regard to someone with an unhealthy interest in a spouse's sexuality before it comes to have the sense of regular male-female sexual relations. Even the word *regular* was first applied to something very special: compliance with a norm, as in "bound by a religious rule."[14]

The description in the law of what is to befall the woman should she be guilty of adultery very much implies that, as Levine rightly emphasizes, she will lose her fetus.[15] Needless to say, the fetuses in Tamar's womb would certainly have been destroyed if Judah's sanction had been carried out. I wonder too if the dust that goes into the concoction the woman in the law has to drink reflects Tamar's potential fate as dust and ashes, just as the water into which it is put can symbolize seed in the sense of offspring (Num 24:7; 2 Bar 57:1; Rev 17:15). It is made clear in the law that the curse the priest "writes" into the water concerns a woman's sexual offense. Other critics suggest similar symbolic meanings for the dust and water.[16] As for the effect of the curse, it is designed to suggest that there will be supernatural intervention. In reality, a woman wracked by guilt might well waste away from psychological distress. The workings of a bad conscience often lead to an offender being struck by sickness or death: Miriam's leprosy (Num 12), Jeroboam's withered arm (1 Kgs 13:4), Gehazi's leprosy (2 Kgs 5), and the death of the couple Ananias and Sapphira (Acts 5).

Fourth, both story and law address the topic of freedom from guilt. In the story, Judah declares Tamar free of guilt when he acknowledges that her sexual engagement with him is justified. In the law, the husband who mistakenly accuses his wife is declared to be free of guilt. Why, we might ask, does the rule bother to go to the length of making explicit mention of his innocence? In Genesis 38, Judah has good reason to suspect Tamar of an adulterous relationship. She is bound by a legal tie to Judah's family and has been sent to her father's home to await summons from Judah to receive Shelah, who never goes into her. Her pregnant state has all the appearance of indicating a wrongful liaison. At the conclusion of her trial, however, she produces reliable evidence proving Judah to be the father of the children in her womb. In most instances, solid evidence that a husband has in fact been the one who impregnated his wife would be lacking. It is this uncertain situation that invites recourse to a test of the kind we find in Numbers 5. Judah could not have expected to encounter Tamar disguised as a prostitute. His later justified suspicion of her conduct is pertinent to the surprising, seemingly unnecessary declaration in the law's concluding statement. An accusing husband whose allegation turns out to be wrong is declared to be free of guilt himself. The statement makes sense only if his motivation for accusing her is, in fact, genuine.

Here, then, is a rare situation in which a husband—in an abnormal, even frowned upon, but valid legal sense (from the perspective of the story)—understandably proceeds against a (levirate) wife on the grounds of her adultery, only to find that he is indeed the father of the children she carries. In line with how biblical laws and institutions come to be written down, the narrative, because it is about the history of the nation's origins, has invited reflection as to what recourse is open to a male Israelite in a regular situation of marriage who finds himself justifiably puzzled by his wife's pregnancy. The idiosyncracy of the story has its analogue in the situation depicted in Numbers 5.

As just noted, it is wholly exceptional to find that a wife who is suspected by her husband of being unfaithful can come up with a sure indication that he had (three months earlier in the case of Tamar) impregnated her. Such a state of affairs is likely only in Tamar's out-of-the-ordinary circumstances, which Judah acknowledges: she was denied the means of becoming pregnant until such time as she was able to seduce him as a prostitute. We might ask why in Numbers 5, as in the Code of Hammurabi 131, an oath by her was not sufficient to deal with the matter. Why the test and all the details about it? These elements are introduced, I suggest, as contributing some measure of fairness to a trial that is less arbitrary than the one to which Judah subjects Tamar. The woman in the law is afforded some means of controlling her fate in a way that is less fortuitous than Tamar's luck in having Judah's identifying emblems in her possession.[17]

The exceptional nature of the law hardly contributes to Frymer-Kensky's view that the law is dealing with "the societal problem posed by suspicion of adultery." Milgrom notes that "there is no other attestation in Scripture that the ordeal was applied or effective," a statement that acknowledges the surprising character of the institution.[18] The law is probably not depicting some actual ancient Israelite practice. After all, it is unrealistic to think that a virtuous husband would resort to it and even more unrealistic to view the law as catering to a paranoid or villainous husband. More likely, the law is a hypothetical exercise designed to construct an idealized institution that is inspired by reflection on the Israelite ancestor's procedure with Tamar.

C. E. Hayes points out how the Targums Pseudo-Jonathan and Neofiti imaginatively transform Tamar's trial in Genesis 38:25, 26, into a very public courtroom. The later Midrashim continue this emphasis, as Hayes demonstrates in a second study. In other words, all these sources illustrate how Judah's dealings with Tamar inspired a legal expansion of the issues, a process that I claim showed up in Numbers 5 long before the Midrash was set down. Targum Onkelos discusses Tamar's righteousness (Gen 38:26) in terms of her innocence of sexual transgression and uses the Aramaic *zk'/y* ("righteous") to translate both the Hebrew *ṣdq* ("righteous") and *nqh* ("innocent"). Without awareness of how close the link is between Numbers 5 and Genesis 38, Hayes notes the striking parallel between the Targum's treatment of Tamar and the treatment of the suspected adulteress in Numbers 5:19, 28, when the latter is declared innocent (*nqh*) of similar sexual sinning.[19]

Fifth, in the narrative, thinking that Tamar is a prostitute, Judah "turned unto her" (*yaṭah*) by the way (Gen 38:16). In the law, it is said of the accused wife (Num 5:12, 19, 20) that she has strayed (*śaṭah*). In Proverbs 7:25 (cf. 4:15) the same verb is employed in warning a man not to go aside to a prostitute.[20]

Sixth, in the narrative, because Tamar seeks out not just any client but her own father-in-law, she very much needs to conceal her identity by covering her face. In the law, emphasis is placed on the fact that the errant wife took pains to conceal herself from being found out. Numbers 5:13 employs not one but two verbs, *ne'elam* and *nisterah*, about her doing so.

In sum, the overlapping details of the law and Genesis 38 suggest a connection between them. Essentially, the woman in each instance stands accused of adultery, there are grounds for proceeding against her, but she can be cleared of the charge and her accuser, too, cleared of any blame for bringing her to trial. Tamar's situation is remarkable because there exists evidence as good as one can ever expect for an initial judgment against her. Yet on inquiry there emerge reasons to find her guiltless, her accuser likewise not being at fault for initially suspecting her.

The Vocation of a Temporary Male or Female Nazirite

The law reads:

When either man or woman shall separate themselves to vow a vow of a nazirite, to separate themselves unto Yahweh. He shall separate himself from wine and strong drink, and shall drink no vinegar of wine, or vinegar of strong drink, neither shall he drink any liquor of grapes, nor eat moist grapes, or dried. All the days of his separation shall he eat nothing that is made of the vine tree, from the kernels even to the husk. All the days of the vow of his separation there shall no razor come upon his head: until the days be fulfilled, in the which he separateth himself unto Yahweh, he shall be holy, and shall let the locks of the hair of his head grow. All the days that he separateth himself unto Yahweh he shall come at no dead body. He shall not make himself unclean for his father, or for his mother, for his brother, or for his sister, when they die: because the consecration of his God is upon his head. All the days of his separation he is holy unto Yahweh.

And if any man die very suddenly by him, and he hath defiled the head of his consecration; then he shall shave his head in the day of his cleansing, on the seventh day shall he shave it. And on the eighth day he shall bring . . . and the priest shall offer . . . and make an atonement for him, for that he sinned by the dead, and shall hallow his head that same day. And he shall consecrate unto Yahweh the days of his separation, and shall bring a lamb of the first year for a trespass offering: but the days that were before shall be lost, because his separation was defiled.

And this is the law of the nazirite, when the days of his separation are fulfilled: he shall be brought unto the door of the tabernacle of the congregation: And he shall offer his offering unto Yahweh . . . And the nazirite shall shave the head of his separation at the door of the tabernacle of the congregation, and shall take the hair of the head of his separation, and put it in the fire which is under the sacrifice of the peace offerings. And the priest shall take . . . and shall put them upon the hands of the nazirite, after the hair of his separation is shaven: and the priest shall wave them . . . and after that the nazirite may drink wine. This is the law of the nazirite who hath vowed, and of his offering unto Yahweh for his separation, beside that that his hand shall get: according to the vow which he vowed, so he must do after the law of his separation." (Num 6:2–21)

The law about this hitherto obscure figure, a man or a woman who chooses temporarily to dedicate himself or herself (*nazar*) to some sacred purpose, comes after the law of the suspected adulteress and also reveals tantalizing links with the Judah-Tamar saga. In fact, the connections between the narrative and the law open up new ways of viewing an institution that has been shrouded in mystery and also illuminates that most puzzling aspect of the saga in Genesis 38, Tamar as a *qedešah*, literally "sacred woman." The two laws about the suspected adulteress and the Nazirite—one follows the other, though only minor links in language and structure between them have been observed—have long proved notoriously difficult to interpret. About the vocation of the Nazirite, Levine writes, "A fascinating, albeit elusive, aspect of Israelite religion." Finding no indication that temporary Nazirites were even known in early Israel, Gray concludes: "Nazirites of this type had but little public significance." He may be correct, but how does he know about public life in ancient Israel? We might note the typical approach to the laws—they must have primary application to the daily life of a people. It is this assumption that I reject. A. R. Radcliffe-Brown's comment is apt: "My objection to conjectural history is not that it is historical, but that it is conjectural."[21]

About the Nazirite law, we would want to ask the following questions. Why are both genders included, because, as Baruch Levine points out, the "formulation *'iš 'o 'iššah* [man or woman] is actually quite rare in biblical law"? Karel Van Der Toorn further notes: "In a context that usually speaks of men only, this detail [reference to a woman also] is striking indeed." Why is there so much focus at the law's outset on refraining from wine and any product associated with the grape? To date, the despairing judgment is that "it is not possible to recapture the rationale behind the prohibition of grape products." Why does the rule confine itself to a temporary state of consecration? The two Nazirites we encounter elsewhere in biblical sources are lifelong dedicatees (Samson in Judg 13:1–7 and Samuel in 1 Sam 1:1–11). Why should the person's head signify his or her separated state? Why also is contact with the dead the only medium of uncleanness that disrupts the person's consecrated circumstances? Jacob Milgrom correctly asks why other types of uncleanness, such as skin ailments, sexual disease, or a female Nazirite's menstrual blood, do not disrupt the Nazirite's state.[22] Why is a wife or a husband not included in the close family members for whom the Nazirite becomes unclean if they die?

At least five features of the story can shed new light on the law of the Nazirite. First, in response to a time-hallowed custom, Tamar dedicates herself to the task of acquiring a child on behalf of her dead husband and chooses, quite unknown to Judah, to make him her co-dedicatee. Her role as a consecrated woman—she is explicitly called a *qedešah*—is solely for the period during which she can conceive through Judah. When she singles him out to give her conception, she draws him into the sacred sphere of the custom. Her extraordinary role enables her to transcend the taboo on incest with a father-in-law (Lev 18:15; 20:12). The Nazirite rule, in turn, has regard to either a woman or a man. Like Tamar, but unlike the examples of lifelong Nazirites in other biblical stories, the Nazirite considered in the rule is committed to some dedicated task for a period of time only. A focus on her mission would explain the contrast between the lawgiver's interest in temporary Nazirites as against the depiction of permanent ones in other biblical narratives.

From one perspective, however deplorable it might be to the lawgiver, Tamar's resort to prostitution is a temporary separation from her life as a widow. She opts for this temporary status in order to produce a child for her dead husband, Er, the continuation of his lineage being, in the context of the Genesis story, a sacred duty that is laid upon the surviving members of his family. Acting on behalf of the male members, the very ones who should be initiating its fulfillment but are not, Tamar's intent explains why she is portrayed in the narrative as a *qedešah*. Although Judah "thought her to be a harlot [*zonah*]," an ordinary prostitute (Gen 38:15), it turned out that she is, in fact, a sacred one (Gen 38:21, 22), possibly along the lines of those we hear about in two other texts (Deut 23:18; Hos 4:14). The curious switch in language points to the fact that, unknown to him at this point in time, Judah—not Shelah, as we might have expected—is drawn into the sacred intent of her mission. The dual character of her exploit—prostitution in appearance, sacred mission in reality—explains down to the narrowest detail the peculiar features of the law of the Nazirite, at least as that law is formulated in Numbers 6:2–21.

In his own society the lawgiver was presumably familiar in some form or another with a practice whereby a person opts out of regular life to consecrate himself or herself to some task. Or, more particularly perhaps, he noted that behind the description of Tamar as a "holy woman" or sacred prostitute lurked some foreign, Canaanite institution of temporary dedication to a deity (cf. Judg 8:33 and Ezek 16). After all, Judah is living in Canaan at this point.[23] The lawgiver then took the troubling character of how she proceeds and shaped it into the kind of office that he thinks would be appropriate in an Israelite setting. In doing so, he imitates in order to oppose the foreign example: "After the doings of the land of Canaan . . . shall ye not do" (Lev 18:3). However the law came to be understood in later Jewish life, its original formulation in Numbers 6 is likely to be a hypothetical scribal exercise that is largely inspired by Tamar's example. The failure of any male in the narrative to fulfill a sacred obligation points to the need to focus on his role in a dedicated task as well as on the woman's.

Second, in the story it is clear that Tamar takes advantage of Judah on his way to a sheep-shearing festival because she can anticipate that he will be in a state of merriment induced by wine. The scene is one bordering on debauchery, the very opposite of a consecrated state, and yet a sacred intent is its motivation. It is as explicit an example as one can find of how the sacred and the obscene can overlap. In this light, the rule's remarkable initial concern with anything to do with the produce of the grape becomes intelligible.

Jacob alludes to his son's drinking in his farewell address in Genesis 49:12, and the later Testament of Judah is very open about it. The biblical lawgiver would be opposed to the stratagem Tamar adopted to become pregnant, and we should read his rule as countering features in the story to which he objects. Hence in the Numbers rule, the Nazirite is to refrain from any association with the products of the vine. The rule even bans the consumption of dried products derived from grapes, and because other biblical texts refer to such products in contexts associated with lovemaking, we can relate this part of the rule as well to Tamar's sexual encounter with Judah.

Much in the law connects with the story, as if the lawgiver read into it his antithetical priestly concerns. The extraordinary emphasis on how the Nazirite must refrain from any association with the vine evokes features of Tamar's seduction of Judah at the place Enaim, where she conceived a son for her dead husband (Gen 38:21). The vine is one of the commonest metaphors for speaking of reproduction: Psalm 128:3 (a man's wife is a fruitful vine); Ezekial 19:10–14 (the vine has been destroyed and there is no stem remaining to provide a ruler of Israel); and Psalm 80:9–20 [8–19] (Israel as a luxurious vine has been ruined). The importance accorded to the vine and its products in the law reflects the lawgiver's negative reaction to the licentious character of the progeny-producing event at Enaim. *Post vinum Venus,* drinking and lovemaking go together, a combination well brought out, as I shall note, in Proverbs 23:26–35; 31:3–7.[24] It is a combination also made much of in Hosea 4:11: "Whoredom and wine and new wine take away the heart." The context is one that, as already observed, also brings out the same switching back and forth between actual harlotry and religious attachment: Yahweh will not punish daughters and spouses who play the harlot, because the men are unfaithful to him in a manner involving the libertinism of heathen fertility cults.

In Jacob's farewell comments to his son in Genesis 49:12, he cites Judah's drunkenness at Enaim (*'enayim*) in a play upon words so characteristic of these sayings: "Dull were the eyes ['*enayim*] from wine."[25] The rare word *ḥaklili* in reference to dullness or redness of eyes from drinking occurs only in Genesis 49:12 (about Judah) and Proverbs 23:29 (about drinking and lovemaking). The latter text also refers to inebriated males who fall for harlots. In the second-century BCE Testament of Judah, the patriarch recounts how he encountered Tamar on his way to shear his sheep; how she was adorned in bridal array and was sitting "in the city Enaim by the gate." "For," he adds, "it was a law of the Amorites, that she who was about to marry should sit in fornication seven days by the gate. Therefore, being drunk from wine, I did not recognize her; and her beauty deceived me, through the fashion of her adorning" (12:2, 3).[26] I find it interesting that in this later interpretation Tamar awaits marriage with someone when Judah has intercourse with her. In Genesis 38, Tamar awaits Shelah in marriage, but it is Judah who has intercourse with her. As the two other biblical references to it testify, sheep shearing was indeed an occasion of merriment and licentiousness (1 Sam 25; 2 Sam 13:23–28).

Tamar's situation has a revealing reference in Ruth 4:12. Both women, childless and in need of the remedy provided by the levirate custom, conceive by a man belonging to the previous generation, both are sexually experienced, and each in the boldest of ways seeks out the man to impregnate her. Similar to Tamar's ploy, Ruth waits until Boaz is merry from wine before making a seductive approach to him at midnight on his threshing floor (Ruth 4:7).

The Nazirite is not even permitted to eat food that is made from grapes and raisins (Num 6:3). The tidbits appear to be the raisin or grape cakes cited in Hosea 3:1 that an adulteress enjoys receiving from her paramour. In Hosea they symbolize the seductive attractions of idolatry (adultery) and in Jeremiah 7:18; 44:19 (cf. Isa 16:7) they are offered to a Canaanite goddess. In Cant 2:5, the lovesick maiden yearns for her lover's raisins.[27] Wine and the enjoyment of sex provide heightened states of temporary attachment. The lawgiver judges that the consecrated person in a temporary state of devotion to a sacred cause must avoid not sexual relations—involvement in them may be the intent of the sacred task at hand—but any products of the vine. Such thinking seems to belong to this aspect of the law and represents a reaction to Judah's enjoyment of Tamar, with its striking combination of worldly, foreign, and sacred features. In the Mishnah, mention is made of a man becoming a Nazirite for the purpose of producing a son (*Nazir* 2:7). A daughter does not count—a fact reminiscent of the levirate custom requiring a son to be born.

Third, in the narrative, Tamar acts the part of a prostitute, a profession that advertises itself by some external mark: "When Judah saw her, he thought her to be a harlot; because she had covered her face" (Gen 38:15). Tamar's disguise as a harlot relates to her head: she covers it with a veil (or as Judah describes the situation in the Testament of Judah 12:3, "her beauty deceived me, through the fashion of her adorning"). In the law in Numbers 6:5, an external mark signals the dedicated state of the Nazirite: long, loose, untrimmed hair is obligatory. According to Milgrom, "The Nazirite could always be recognized by his [her] appearance and it is no wonder that the term for Nazirite can also refer to his [her] hair." Levine rightly states that "throughout the present legislation, 'head' is a way of referring to 'hair.' "[28] Tamar's covered head signifies that she is a "holy woman." In contrast to Tamar's apparent intent (servicing a client) but comparable to her true intent (performing a religious duty), the Nazirite sanctifies her or his head (Num 6:11). Keil and Delitzsch are perhaps overstating the case, but are basically correct, when they declare that the role of hair in the law is a sign that the Nazirite's sanctified head is "an ornament in which his [her] whole strength and fullness of vitality were exhibited, and which the nazirite wore in honor of the Lord."[29]

The unloosening of the suspected adulteress' hair by removing her headdress (Num 5:18) and the withholding of a razor from the Nazirite's head so that her (his) hair continues to grow (Num 6:5) is not just a coincidental link between the two laws. Critics see the connection only in terms of how one law has come to be set down after what is to them a quite unrelated law.[30] In the narrative, the significance of Tamar's covered head relates both to the concern with her harlotry, for which Judah intends to burn her, and to her dedicated state for the purpose of fulfilling the levirate duty, for which Judah proceeds to commend her. Both these aspects emerge in the two laws.

In the law of the suspected adulteress, unbinding the woman's hair is a preliminary to the test determining whether she has played the harlot, and in the law of the Nazirite, growing the hair long indicates a dedicated state. Levine points out that all usages of the verb *para‛* "somehow connote dishevelment or disarray, but the phenomenology of the *nazir* differs from that pertaining to mourning or shaming."[31] This is not quite accurate. The loose hair in the law of the suspected adulteress relates to the shaming role of Tamar as a prostitute and the uncut hair in the Nazirite law relates to Tamar's covered head as a sacred woman. Each law, then, takes up a different facet of Tamar's activities. When the Nazirite's hair requires cutting because of contact with a corpse or because the period of dedication has come to an end, the hair is burnt. Burning in both narrative (Tamar is to be burnt for her offense) and law creates a boundary between the sacred and the profane. Another link between the two laws is the placing of sacrificial materials in the palms of the suspected adulteress in Numbers 5:18 and in the palms of the Nazirite in Numbers 6:19. The context in the former is when the woman has her head unbound to reveal her hair and in the latter when the Nazirite has her or his hair shaven off.

The description of the "holy woman" Tamar is, then, the inspiration for the focus on the hair and head of the Nazirite. Tamar's covered face signifies her intent to bring forth new life in the form of a child, and, as both Gray and Levine emphasize, the Nazirite's head–uncut hair communicates "vitality." Tamar is a *qedešah* for the duration of her task, and the term *qadoš* in the law signifies the Nazirite's holiness for the duration of her or his sacred commitment (Num 6:5). That the law focuses on some external sign to indicate the Nazirite's dedication might also reflect the fact that in the Genesis narrative Judah's outward identifying symbols, his signet, cord, and staff, are crucial in signaling that he is the father of Tamar's child. Tamar made sure that she acquired them because they turn out to be the evidence establishing that he has been drawn into fulfilling the levirate custom. The Nazirite in the law, we should remind ourselves, is female or male (Num 6:2). Both Gray and Levine draw attention to the text in Amos 2:11–12, with its reference to Nazirites and drinking. It might be noted that in the same context (Amos 2:7, 9) we have a reference to the destruction of the Canaanites and to a father and son going into the same woman, exactly the situation in Genesis 38.[32]

Fourth, the subject of the dead is central to both story and law. It is on behalf of her dead husband that Tamar carries out her sacred vocation when she dresses as a *qedešah*. It is he who makes a postmortem appeal, and it is she who answers it in the absence of a willing male relative. She remains a widow in her father's house, and after her sexual encounter with Judah she returns there until he summons her to condemn her supposed wrongdoing. Death comes into the law in that the Nazirite must avoid contact with a dead person, even if that person is a close family member. Should someone die suddenly beside or near the Nazirite, the consecrated state is actually disrupted but then resumed after a proper ritual has been carried out.

The lawgiver has probably taken his cue about a Nazirite and the dead from the events of Genesis 38. Tamar, for one, lives the life of a widow in an enhanced sense. She is the spouse of a deceased husband, but she is also subject to a claim from beyond the grave that requires her to seek new life in the form of a child by a family member. Incorporated into the law may be the reflection that death should not interfere with a sacred commitment to pursue new life. The first expression of mortality in the law concerns the death of a close family member, a father, mother, brother, or sister. So long as the Nazirite does not come into contact with the corpse, the sacred commitment is not affected.

The law does not spell out what kind of vow it has in focus, but it may be the specific one of producing a child (as with the births of Samson and Samuel), just as the preceding law about the suspected adulteress centers on the woman's pregnant state. The notice about close family members who die does not, puzzlingly, include a spouse, an indication perhaps that the law centers on a widow or widower intent on producing a child.

Quite different is the second kind of death the law takes up, namely, when someone dies "very suddenly by him [her]," in the translation of the AV. Why did the lawgiver not simply include this possibility when expressing his previous concern with the death of family members, and why does this particular death cause a temporary suspension of the vow? Why even bring up sudden death at all? It does not seem satisfactory to suggest that it is the unexpectedness of the event that puts it into a category different from the one of corpses of close relatives.[33] These relatives would themselves have died but recently, even suddenly.

The Genesis narrative is particularly illuminating in accounting for the special attention accorded the kind of death in question. Right at the beginning of the story, Onan unites with Tamar in order to fulfill the levirate custom. However, because he is disloyal to his deceased brother for having ejaculated outside of her, he dies, presumably at that very moment. The consequence is that the commitment to the levirate duty is put in jeopardy, because the next brother in line, Shelah, has not attained puberty. The interruption has Tamar take up residence in her father's house until such time as Shelah is ready to fulfill the family duty. When Tamar finds that Judah is not making Shelah available to her, she embarks on her mission to become pregnant by Judah in the guise of a "sacred woman." She is thus the one who resumes the sacred task.

In both narrative and rule, then, we have temporary suspension of the sacred task on account of a sudden death. The details are telling. In the rule, the Nazirite's consecrated state is interrupted "if any man die suddenly on [*'al*] him [on her]" (Num 6:9). Why should sudden death be singled out? The lawgiver, I suggest, thinks of the sudden death of Onan. To repeat, the disruption of the sacred task is common to both story and law. And so too is its resumption. As I already indicated, Milgrom is puzzled why other types of uncleanness—skin ailments, sexual disease, a female Nazirite's menstrual blood—do not interfere with the Nazirite's state. He accounts for the sole interest in corpse contamination by claiming that there exists in the law a residual hint of ancestor worship for the purpose of exorcising the fear of corpses. Why this concern should exclude the other manifestations of uncleanness is not clear. Again, however, the single focus on the Judah-Tamar story is so much closer to the lawgiver's concerns.

Fifth, after Tamar obtains seed from Judah, she changes out of the garments that convey her sacred state as a *qedešah*. She casts aside her veil and puts back on her widow's clothes. The change of garments signals the end of her sacred mission. The law, in turn, has the Nazirite shave the head to signal the end of his or her temporary consecrated state.

Critics express puzzlement about the curious notice that when a Nazirite's period of separation comes to an end, "he [she] shall be brought unto the door of the tabernacle" (Num 6:13). Gray states, "Why the nazirite should need to be brought instead of coming by himself [herself] it is not easy to see."[34] I would point out that the pregnant Tamar is brought before Judah's household jurisdiction, possibly even before his household gods (cf. Gen 31:30, 34). She does not come herself and announce her pregnancy. The judgment on her is that during the past three months she was not in fact covering up her harlotry but was indeed devoting herself to the sacred task of producing a child for her dead husband. There is thus acknowledgment of her commitment to a dedicated task, and from the viewpoint of the law in Numbers 6 she provides the earliest example of a Nazirite.

Nazirites in the Narratives

There are two narratives in which the Nazirite appears, the births of Samson and Samuel. Each contains features that take on added significance once we observe the link between the Judah-Tamar narrative and the Numbers Nazirite law. As in the law, each episode shares a focus on both male and female commitment to a sacred task and on the role of wine. As in the Judah-Tamar story, each shares a focus on the woman's conception of a firstborn child and on prostitution.

A barren mother, Manoah's wife, is told that she will conceive a son who will be a Nazirite. In the meantime she is not to consume wine or strong drink (Judg 13:2–5). When Samson is born and does live the life of a Nazirite, he involves himself with a prostitute (Judg 16:1). No doubt, the account is geared to showing the disorderly nature of the times: "In these days there was no king in Israel: every man did that which was right in his own eyes" (Judg 17:6; 18:1; 21:25). It is also the case, however, that Samson's involvement with the prostitute has a positive outcome, because, however precarious his situation, it enables Yahweh to visit death upon Israel's enemies and decrease their numbers. We recall that in the most precarious of ways Judah's involvement with a prostitute enables his future line to receive Yahweh's blessing of offspring.

In the other episode, Samuel's mother, Hannah, promises that if she conceives she will dedicate her son as a Nazirite to the sanctuary (1 Sam 1:11, especially emphasized in the Septuagint). She makes her vow at the sanctuary in Shiloh, where the priest Eli falsely accuses her of drunkenness and, equally interesting, views her as a loose woman of the kind that Eli's own sons promiscuously engaged with at the sanctuary (1 Sam 1:11, 13, 15, 16). Like Tamar, she has in fact dedicated herself to a sacred task, and, appearances to the contrary, she too is no prostitute.

In sum, the topics of prostitution and drinking in both the Samson and Samuel stories become more significant in light of Tamar's role as a prostitute on the occasion of Judah's trip to a festival. That the topics turn up in each story is not accidental but typical of biblical narrative, because aspects of what occur in one generation are seen to repeat themselves in another.

Aaron's Benediction

The climax to the law in Numbers 6:22–27 is the celebrated blessing upon the sons of Israel: "The Lord bless thee, and keep thee: the Lord make his face shine upon thee, and be gracious unto thee: The Lord lift up his countenance upon thee, and give thee peace." Critics invariably see no connection between this blessing and the preceding rule about the Nazirite. They have long expressed bafflement as to why it comes at this point in the Book of Numbers. A. H. McNeile states, "This fragment of priestly tradition has no connexion with what precedes or follows it."[35] If, however, the law has been formulated against the background of the troubles faced by Judah, a son of the original Israel, then the benediction is most apt.

Judah's troubles include strife (on account of Joseph) among the first sons of Israel, infertility, loss of posterity and possessions (Er's inheritance), and the potential disappearance of Judah's name (no offspring to perpetuate his line). The fate of this son of Israel constitutes the opposite of the typical content of biblical blessings for the collective sons of Israel. Coming on the back of laws that address salient issues among the first generation of these sons, the benediction wishes for future sons of Israel a destiny different from the one Judah faced. His very name was threatened with extinction because the continuity of his line was at risk owing to his marriage to a Canaanite woman. In the saga, Yahweh's role is a destructive one, causing the deaths of two of Judah's half-Canaanite sons (Er and Onan) and extinguishing the name of the third (Shelah). Three times the benediction in Numbers 6:22–27 repeats the divine name over the sons of Israel, and its climactic statement expresses the wish that Yahweh's name remain on them: "And they [Aaron and his sons] shall put my name upon the sons of Israel; and I will bless them." Upholding the name of the Israelite god preserves the purity of an Israelite's line of descent from Canaanite infusion of the kind that almost wiped out Judah's. Acknowledging Yahweh's name also guarantees future blessings on each generation of Israelites. It cannot surprise that what occurs in the Judah-Tamar story evoked so much interest, because it is about the genealogical history of David (Gen 38:29 and Ruth 4:18–22), whose own story is such a dominant one in Genesis through 2 Kings.

8

Incest

> *After the doings of the land of Egypt, wherein ye dwelt, shall ye not do: and after the doings of the land of Canaan, whither I bring you, shall ye not do.*
>
> —*Leviticus 18:1–3*

The topic of incest readily commands attention. In Roman Egypt, for at least two hundred years, we have detailed evidence of marriages between full brothers and sisters—publicly celebrated, with wedding invitations, and entailing marriage contracts, dowries, children, and divorce.[1] In the Bible, Paul cites the case in 1 Corinthians 5 of a man who is living with his stepmother, the father having died or divorced her. Paul does condemn the union in question, but it has to be pointed out that in doing so he has to counter a fundamental Christian doctrine that is very much associated with him, namely, re-creation.[2] His condemnation is remarkable because of the religious belief that has prompted the couple's relationship. Two features of the situation cause one to pause.[3] First, Paul says that not even the pagan world permits marriage to a stepmother, and, second and most remarkable, the Corinthian community he is writing to is very proud of the couple's union. They are "puffed up," boasting about it. One must wonder, why should they be so?

The belief in question is that a person who becomes Christian undergoes a passage from death to life. He or she is such a new creation as to no longer be the same person. All old relationships are dissolved. So, for example, if a brother and his sister convert, they are no longer brother and sister. They are free to marry.

The belief in rebirth is one that Paul takes over from the Judaism of his time. Someone converting to Judaism is considered newly born. It is a rising from the dead. According to the School of Hillel, "He who separates himself from the uncircumcision [heathendom] is like one who separates himself from the grave" (*m. Eduy.* 5:2); just as Paul says, "And you, being dead in the uncircumcision of your flesh, hath he quickened" (Col 2:13). The new birth is taken so seriously that the law of inheritance, for example, is affected. If a Gentile and his children become Jews, in strict Jewish law a debt owing to the Gentile need not, on the Gentile's death, be paid to his children (*m. Shebi.* 10:9). The convert and his children all count as newly born, and consequently are no longer related. In regard to marriage, the rabbis introduce not a watering down of the supernatural nature of the miracle of new birth—that is how they regarded it—but a concession to the outside world that disallows such unions. The result is that a variety of incestuous unions are banned because they are contrary to Gentile law and morality. The rabbis' reasoning is that the outside world is not likely to appreciate the miracle of new birth and would therefore judge Jews to be lax in sexual matters if unions prohibited by the surrounding culture are permitted. The Jewish leadership did not want that kind of Gentile response.

When Paul says that not even Gentiles permit the union that the couple in the Corinthian church has contracted—it is unlikely that Paul was familiar with, for example, full brother–full sister marriage among ordinary people in Roman Egypt—he is applying the same restriction. Paul's position is that the church has to put up with a second best: having become new creations, and are therefore no longer considered stepmother and son, the couple nonetheless has to avoid marriage. Theoretically, they are free to marry, but consideration for the milieu in which they find themselves, the dictates of public policy, and public relations on the part of their community rule it out. The Corinthian community's failure to understand the limitations on their newfound freedom proves to be as damnable as incestuous intercourse under the old law. Paul excommunicates the offending couple.[4]

In the Old Testament one finds traditions that might well have been viewed at some point as potentially offering a license for incestuous unions. I refer to the remarkable number of liaisons between close kin in the early narratives of the Bible. For example, Nahor marries his niece, that is, his brother's daughter (Gen 11:29); the daughters of Lot produce sons by their father (Gen 19:30–38); Abraham marries his half-sister Sarah (Gen 20:12); Jacob marries two of his first cousins, who are sisters (Gen 29); Judah's daughter-in-law Tamar remedies her childless state by having intercourse with her father-in-law (Gen 38:18); Moses' father marries his aunt, that is, his father's sister (Exod 6:20; Num 26:59). In the Book of Samuel, David's daughter, Tamar, tells her half-brother, Amnon, who is sexually harassing her, that he should go to their father, and he, King David, will consent to a proper way by which he can marry her (2 Sam 13:13).

Abraham, Jacob, Judah, Moses, and David are outstanding figures in Israelite tradition. It surely mattered that, given the power of storytelling and the status of these figures, the issue of incest arises with them. My contention is that it mattered very much. The patriarchs' incestuous involvements are the key to understanding how the incest rules of Leviticus 18 and 20 came to be formulated. Let us note right away that these rules treat the relationship that Abraham has with Sarah, union of brother and half-sister, as incestuous and problematic, and hence the relationship that Tamar discusses with Amnon as well. A relationship with a daughter-in-law is ruled out. So too is marriage to two sisters while both are alive. These Levitical rules, which are attributed to Moses, also prohibit the union that Moses' own parents contracted, namely, a man and his aunt. On the other hand, the lists do not contain any prohibition of a union between first cousins, or a union between a man and his niece.

A pressing question is: How do we relate the rules about incest in the legal sections of Genesis through 2 Kings to what occurred among the founding fathers of the nation? When we look at the reasons given by the biblical lawgiver to justify these rules, we are told that the Israelites must not imitate the practices of the Egyptians and the Canaanites. All later commentators readily accept these reasons. One must wonder, however, was the compiler of the rules and all later commentators, in turn, not aware of the conduct of some of the revered ancestors of the Israelite nation? I shall return to this question.

I first raise the general question: Why does one find rules barring incest at all? Alas, there are no ready answers, especially in light of brother-sister marriages in Roman Egypt. Montesquieu, the eighteenth-century political philosopher, thought that incestuous unions were not contrary to natural law, "nor, by their nature, are they contrary to civil and political law, like arson, robbery and murder. They even offend against divine law only in the sense that it prohibits them, like impiety and blasphemy. So all that can be said about them is that they are prohibited because they are prohibited." Montesquieu's view is certainly less surprising in light of these ancient Egyptian census documents. Even today, Sweden permits a marriage between a brother and his half-sister on application of a special license from the government.[5] One common view in our culture is that incest leads to defective offspring. No ancient source and no anthropological evidence support this view. If the ancients had known of such a causal connection between incest and defective children, they would have used it in support of their rules. I think we can exclude any awareness of a genetic factor as relevant to the origin of incest rules.

The verse 2 Samuel 21:20 (= 1 Chron 20:6) tells of a Philistine warrior who had six fingers on each hand and six toes on each foot. Jacob's experiment with cattle, sheep, and goats (Gen 30:25–43) indicates that these ancients were aware of the effects of breeding in animal husbandry. Exactly what they knew is impossible to judge. The medical geneticist L. B. Jorde stresses how difficult it is to reach firm conclusions about the deleterious effects of inbreeding. His unexamined assumption, nonetheless, is that at all periods incest rules testify to such effects. He wrongly thinks that all the relationships laid out in Levicitus 18:6–18 are consanguineous (a marriage to a woman and her mother, to a brother's wife, to an uncle's wife, and to two sisters are not). He suggests that in ancient Egypt brother-sister marriages among the upper classes resulted in reproductive problems: "Cleopatra VII was the product of a brother-sister mating, and she in turn married her two younger brothers but produced no children by these marriages (her relations with Mark Anthony and Julius Caesar were both fertile, however)." Jorde is not familiar with the long history of brother-sister marriages among other classes of Egyptians in the Roman period. We do not have figures about the fertility of these marriages.[6]

Biblical sources provide some indication as to why incest laws might exist. Consider again the story of Amnon's violation of his half-sister Tamar (2 Sam 13). His deed so enrages Tamar's full brother, Absalom, that Absalom has Amnon slain. What motivates Absalom to take such extreme revenge for his brother's misdeed? After all, it appears that Amnon could have married his sister had he gone about it in the proper way, namely, by speaking to their father, King David.

One major reason for the existence of some incest rules is to ensure that family life is as sexually unimpassioned as possible. If it is not, violence of the kind that Absalom has inflicted on Amnon is the likely outcome. The potential problem of violence is well brought out if we reflect on an incident in the Book of Genesis. Jacob's oldest son, Reuben, lies with one of his father's wives. His example draws to our attention the peculiar problems that may arise when polygamy is practiced. In a polygamous setup, when a father takes a new wife, a son by a previous wife may be about the same age as the new wife (though this consideration does not apply with Reuben). In ancient Mediterranean society, where there was little social mixing of the sexes, it cannot surprise that a son might conceive a desire for his father's new wife. To permit father and son to compete for her sexual favors is a recipe for violence. We can be fairly sure that the prevention of such conflicts constitutes one powerful reason for some incest rules. One has to be careful, however, not to generalize for every society. Among the Manchus group marriage existed in which younger brothers had the right of physical access to the wives of elder brothers.[7]

I return to the question of incest and the fathers of the nation Israel. How do we square the biblical incest rules with some of the relationships that existed among these revered ancestors? The view generally adhered to is that we have to reckon with historical development. Over time a relationship that is acceptable at one period is not acceptable at a later time.

My view is different. I argue that there is a direct link between patriarchal sexual conduct and the presentation of the incest rules in Leviticus 18 and 20. The reason for the link is that the lawgivers disapproved of what they found in some of their nation's traditions because the narratives condoned relationships that the lawgiver judged to be incestuous. I do not hold that biblical laws necessarily reflect the social history of the times when they were formulated. That unexamined assumption is the standard one among biblical scholars when they interpret biblical laws.[8] It has also been the assumption among so many thinkers, anthropologists, ethnographers, historians, lawyers, novelists, philosophers, sociologists, and theologians down through the centuries. Sybil Wolfram cites such figures as Philo, Plutarch, St. Augustine, Maimonides, Jeremy Taylor, Grotius, Hume, Hutcheson, Montesquieu, Bentham, McLennan, Morgan, Tylor, Durkheim, Fraser, Freud, Malinowski, Radcliffe-Brown, Evans-Pritchard, and Lévi-Strauss. Two of her major findings are, first, that twentieth-century anthropologists revived most of the theories devised by seventeenth- and eighteenth-century lawyers and theologians; and, second, that in the elaboration of and the disputes about these various theories, the thinking revolved around the question as to whether the positions adopted were in accord with the prohibitions set out in Leviticus. For these thinkers the biblical incest rules as reflecting actual practice in ancient times were central to their theorizing about the topic of incest.[9]

An approach to these laws as mirroring social realities is not a fruitful one. The laws were not set down to govern society, even though some of them may in fact have governed society. In my view, to see the incest rules in relation to social history is a wrong approach, because, as I have repeatedly argued, the laws take up issues that we come upon in the stories and legends in, for example, the Book of Genesis. Biblical laws consequently constitute commentary on matters arising in the national folklore, not on the real world of ancient Israel. These matters are almost always unusual and idiosyncratic. It is why they are recorded. I shall come back to the notable fact that the lawgivers lash out at the Egyptians and the Canaanites for their supposed incestuous practices, and apparently not at the ancestors' individual histories.

I first turn to the lists of incest rules in Leviticus 18 and 20 to draw attention to some of their peculiar features. It is puzzling, for example, to find that a prohibition—it is the first in the list—against a son's violation of his father or his intercourse with his mother should be set down at all. By and large, if lawgivers are addressing societal problems, they are not motivated to set down in writing what no one questions, just as no university has written rules stating that those giving lectures are not to dress in space suits or deliver them in a monotonous plainsong. Silence about fundamental matters is a characteristic aspect of ancient law codes in particular, and language in general—for instance, there are no words for those who do not murder or who tell lies.[10] Everyone takes for granted such forbidden relationships as a son with his father or a son with his mother. They are so taboo that they will not even come to consciousness, except, for effect, to a modern filmmaker or writer of fiction. In contemporary culture, it is not much matter for comment to find the topic turning up with increasing frequency in film and fiction, because to entertain is to break boundaries in pursuit of the unusual and the idiosyncratic (precisely what characterizes biblical reporting). James Twitchell argues that even in advertisements by such well-known companies as PepsiCo and the Metropolitan Insurance Company there are undertones of father-daughter incest.[11] Yet, I repeat, we find the peculiar formulation about a son's sexual relation with a parent at the head of a list of incest prohibitions.

Again, the list contains no express prohibition against intercourse with a full sister. Nor is there a prohibition against intercourse with a son or a daughter, that is, where the father, not the child, is the target of the prohibition. We must take seriously and ask why the initial rule is addressed to the child of a family, as though he or she would be the instigator of an incestuous liaison.[12] After all, the sexual abuse of a son or daughter by a parent (or a sister by a brother) is much more likely in the world of experience. No one, so far as I am aware, has raised the problem of why the child and not the parent is the target of this particular rule. The concern with a child who initiates an incestuous liaison and the lack of any rule about more commonly occurring liaisons within a family suggest that the standard approach of reading these rules against the social practice of ancient Israel is not helpful in understanding them.

Yet another problem in studying the biblical incest rules is that mixed in with them are rules that have nothing to do with incest, for example, rules about marriages to two sisters while both are alive, sex with a menstruating woman, adultery, child sacrifice, homosexuality, and bestiality.

Another puzzle is the arrangement of topics in the rules, for example, the ones in the preceding sequence. We have to ask whether it really is the case that to account for the seemingly disorganized arrangement of the rules in Leviticus 18, we should reckon on additions over time. One can understand why this view has become so embedded in scholarly approaches. Thus there are two rules about intercourse with a half-sister, one rule more general than the other and separated from it by a rule prohibiting intercourse with a granddaughter. Can we solve these problems without resort to the assumption that biblical scribes went in for redactions of existing lists of rules apparently unaware that their insertions and additions were so badly done? I believe we can, if we bear in mind the process of legal formulation that I have described in accounting for the unique integration of law and narrative in Genesis through 2 Kings.

Light is shed on the puzzling structure and formulations of the rules in Leviticus 18 once we draw a link between the rules there and certain narratives in the Book of Genesis. The reason why the prohibition about sexual relations with parents is the first in the series in Leviticus 18, and why it is formulated at all, is because legends in the Book of Genesis determine the lawgiver's concerns. Moreover, because the Levitical rules were formulated as a reaction to what goes on in these legends, and not to what goes on in ordinary life, it becomes understandable why many of the rules strike us as strange.

Interpreters do draw attention to the fact that patriarchal history provides examples of unions that are prohibited in the incest laws of Leviticus 18 and 20.[13] They have not gone far enough in their observations, however. If, as is universally agreed, a writer not only knew but worked with the ancient traditions of his people that are contained in other biblical sources, it can occasion no surprise that much of the behavior he found objectionable became the focus of his concern. It is this kind of critical response to his sources—largely Genesis, but also Exodus—that accounts for both his setting down the rules in Leviticus 18 and the order in which he arranged them. After all, so many of the relationships cited in Genesis and Exodus involve kinship ties.

Leviticus 18 first takes up three examples of incestuous, or nearly incestuous, conduct in primeval and patriarchal times by responding to both actual and hypothetical situations involving incest, or related sexual matters, that the stories about Abraham, Isaac, Jacob, and Judah pose. Although he gives no reasons for his assessment, Malcolm Clark is correct to characterize Leviticus 18–20 as "a purely ideal literary construct without institutional realization."[14] I turn to the analysis of the first rule.

Intercourse with a Father or a Mother

The two earliest incidents of incestuous conduct in the Book of Genesis involve drunkenness, first Noah's and then Lot's. The two incidents have much in common: the role of wine, the initiative toward the parent that comes from the son or daughter taking advantage of the drunken father, and the concern with future generations. The lawgiver looked at the two incidents together and used them to set down the first of his series of rules on incest: "None of you shall approach to any that is near of kin to him, to uncover their nakedness: I am Yahweh. The nakedness of thy father, or the nakedness of thy mother, shalt thou not uncover; she is thy mother; thou shalt not uncover her nakedness" (Lev 18:6, 7). The first incident in the Bible that raises the issue of incestuous conduct is Ham's offense against his father, Noah (Gen 9:20–27). The account is confusing. Ham is the offender, but his son Canaan is cited in Noah's condemnation. It is as if there is a reversal of stances. Ham, who is explicitly cited as the father of Canaan, offends against his father, Noah, and Noah in turn acts against Ham's son Canaan. The lawgiver concentrates on Ham's offence. Ham looks upon Noah's nakedness, informs his two brothers, Shem and Japheth, who carefully walk backward and cover their father with a garment. When Noah finds out that his son has humiliated him in some way, he curses Canaan to a life of enslavement to his brothers. Whatever the precise nature of the offense, the lawgiver uses the incident to reflect on the potential sexual offense of a son against his father. It is safe to assume that sexuality is involved, that Ham is looking at his father's genitals. In light of the punishment—his son Canaan loses his status as a member of Noah's line and also becomes a slave to his brothers—the offense seems to be disrespect of a progenitor's status and consists in wrongful looking.[15] Noah's drunkenness is not considered relevant to his role in the matter. Herodotus (1.10) states, "For among the Lydians, and indeed among the generality of the barbarians, for even a man to be seen naked is an occasion of great shame." Anthropologists report that in many cultures fathers make every effort to ensure that they do not reveal their genitals to their sons.[16]

We should not at any time underestimate the powerful idea of a wrongful sight. Oedipus says that his self-blinding was necessary because he could not have gone to Hades and looked at his parents, against whom he had sinned (*Oedipus the King*, 1310). Some Deuteronomic rules are taken up with the repellent look of things: for example, the slain body on the new land, which requires a special ceremony of removal so that God will not look away and withhold the land's bounty; also God's looking away from excrement within the military camp and consequentially withdrawing his military support to the Israelites (Deut 21:1–9, 23:10–15). Today we also remove the blemish left by a crime. Recent examples are the tearing down of Abu Ghraib prison in Baghdad; of the school building in Soham in the United Kingdom, where two schoolgirls were murdered; and of the building where students were shot and killed at Northern Illinois University.

The second incident pertinent to the rule is that of Lot's daughters getting their father drunk and lying with him in order to produce offspring by him (Gen 19:30–38). Addressing males, the lawgiver sets down the equivalent male offense, a son's intercourse with his mother. This move on the part of the lawgiver is an example of how the link between a rule and a narrative can be of a sensible, indirect nature. I am claiming that the lawgiver moves from Noah's situation, where a son offends against his father, to Lot's situation, where daughters offend against their father. The language of the law about uncovering nakedness would be most appropriate if the lawgiver considered the two offenses in the legends together. Ham looks upon a father's nakedness, and Lot's daughters uncover their father's. In expressing an offense against a father in terms of nakedness, the lawgiver encapsulates both offenses well. I think it likely that the use of the expression "to uncover nakedness" in the sense of sexual relations first comes from the Leviticus lawgiver's focus on these two incidents.

Recent translations, for example, the RSV and JSB, interpret the rule as solely about intercourse with a mother. They choose to read not the literal "the nakedness of thy father and the nakedness of thy mother shalt thou not uncover" but place upon the connecting particle *waw* ("and") the weight of a circumstantial clause: "The nakedness of thy father which is [=*waw explicative*] the nakedness of thy mother." Although this is a possible, if a rather free translation, it is an awkward one that badly overloads the sentence, as interpreters who accept the translation point out.[17] Usually the lawgiver is more explicit when he makes the point that uncovering the nakedness of one person uncovers a related person's nakedness. For example, in the immediately following rule in Leviticus 18:8, we have: "The nakedness of thy father's wife shalt thou not uncover: it is thy father's nakedness." In Leviticus 18:14 ("Thou shalt not uncover the nakedness of thy father's brother, thou shalt not approach to his wife") uncovering an uncle's nakedness does indeed mean intercourse, not with him, but with his wife. There is no connecting particle *waw* between the two parts of the rule. Anthony Phillips also opposes the transferred meaning: "It is much more natural to understand Lev xviii 7a in its present form as prohibiting sexual relations with either of one's parents."[18]

Intercourse with a Father's Wife

The lawgiver takes up another offense that occurred in patriarchal history. Reuben, Jacob's oldest son, lies with his father's concubine Bilhah. Again, as in the legends about Noah and Lot, the child offends against a parent, in this instance a stepmother. Leah is Reuben's mother, not Bilhah. The lawgiver generalizes from this patriarchal incident to include any wife of the father: "The nakedness of thy father's wife shalt thou not uncover: it is thy father's nakedness" (Lev 18:8). Either the father has divorced his wife or he has died. If he was still alive, the offense would be adultery. The rule readily follows the previous one, because in the latter the focus is also a father's wife, specifically, a man's own mother. Another reason why the lawgiver would address the offense even though Reuben's misdeed is explicitly cited in Genesis 35:22 ("Reuben went and lay with Bilhah his father's concubine") is that he finds Jacob's condemnation too mild. All the text says is that Jacob heard about it. Only at the end of his life does Reuben learn of a negative consequence, namely, that he loses the right of the firstborn (Gen 49:4). The comparable rule in Lev 20:11 lays down a death sentence, as does Jubilees (33:1–17) in the Pseudepigrapha, whose author, linking rule and story, raises the issue of Reuben not receiving a capital sentence.

The rule describes the son's intercourse with the wife of the father as an uncovering of the father's nakedness, not the stepmother's. This focus on him and not on her may well come from Reuben's father's own description of the incident. When, at the end of Jacob's life, he assembles his sons and addresses each in turn, he tells Reuben that the offense is against him, his own father. In speaking to Reuben, he takes up the matter of the sexual offense, but, interestingly, he states it in such a way as to make it appear that Reuben has violated him. Thus Jacob says, "Thou wentest up to thy father's bed; then defiledst thou it: he [not thou, as in LXX] went up to my couch" (Gen 49:4). From his formulation we would not know that a woman is involved. A major reason why intercourse with a father's wife is thought of as uncovering the father's nakedness has to do with the near universal use of clothing to indicate the marital relation. As well illustrated in Deuteronomy 22:30 ("A man shall not take his father's wife, nor shall he uncover his father's skirt"), a husband and wife, for both protective and sexual purposes, cover each other as if each is a garment. The Koranic statement that wives are "raiment for you and ye are raiment for them" (Q.2:187) well describes the biblical position also (see Chap. 9).

In switching from the earliest history of the biblical ancestors to Reuben's escapade, the lawgiver typically ranges over the history of the generations. Where he finds an example in a later generation that is comparable to an earlier one, he will take that up. He then returns to the chronological sequence of events involving incest in the history of the ancestors.

Intercourse with a Half-Sister, a Granddaughter, and (Again) a Half-Sister

The next three rules pose an obvious puzzle. There is first a prohibition against intercourse with a half-sister, where she is either a daughter by the same father from another wife or a daughter by the same mother from her previous marriage. There is next a prohibition against a man's relationship with a granddaughter. The third prohibition is again intercourse with a half-sister, this time more narrowly defined: she and her brother have the same father, but a different mother. "The nakedness of thy sister, the daughter of thy father, or daughter of thy mother, whether she be born at home, or born abroad, even their nakedness thou shalt not uncover. The nakedness of thy son's daughter, or of thy daughter's daughter, even their nakedness thou shalt not uncover: for theirs is thine own nakedness.

The nakedness of thy father's wife's daughter, begotten of thy father, she is thy sister, thou shalt not uncover her nakedness" (Lev 18:9–11).

Why would a lawgiver set down the same prohibition about a brother and a half-sister almost side by side? Why too, for that matter, does a prohibition about a man and his granddaughter come between these two almost identical rules about a half-sister? The conventional view again is that we have to reckon with a code of laws patched together from different sources at some time in the history of ancient Israel. There is another, more interesting solution, one, I might add, that is more complimentary to the ability of ancient authors to set out rules in a way that made good sense to them.

The focus of these three rules continues to be patriarchal history. In the first, a man must not have intercourse with the daughter of his father's wife—a father's wife was the focus of the preceding law—nor a daughter by his mother's previous marriage. This rule and the two following ones about grandfather-granddaughter and the half-sister look at actual and hypothetical aspects of the history of Abraham.[19]

The lawgiver first focuses on Abraham's marriage to Sarah, when Abraham encounters problems during a sojourn in Egypt (Gen 12:10–20). On the occasion Abram (his name at this time) says to his wife: "Say, I pray thee, thou art my sister" (v. 13). Abram attempts to deceive the Pharaoh in order to conceal that Sarai (her name at this time) is in fact his wife. He is motivated to do so because he fears the Egyptians will kill him and appropriate her. The hypothetical issue of a man's marriage to his sister arises from the story in the sense that a man who can say that his wife is his sister, even if she is not, at least points to the question, can a man marry his sister? The lawgiver must have been all the more impelled to address the issue of brother–half-sister marriage because a similar incident occurs in the generation after Abraham. To protect himself from the men of Gerar, Isaac falsely claims that the woman (Rebekah) to whom he is married is his sister (Gen 26:6–11).

The issue of marriage to a sister arises even if we did not know from a later notice in Genesis 20:12 that Sarai is indeed Abram's half-sister, the daughter of his father. In the first of his rules about the half-sister, the lawgiver generalizes from Abram's remark to the Pharaoh, and he thinks of both the half-sister from the father as well as the half-sister from the mother. August Dillmann points out that the statement in Genesis 12:13

about Sarai as Abram's sister does not necessarily imply what we are told in Genesis 20:12, namely, that Sarah is the daughter of Abraham's father, but not of his mother.[20] Nor does the genealogical notice in Genesis 11:29 about Abraham's father's lineage give this information. In other words, the lawgiver has the statement in Genesis 12:13 in focus, and he simply covers the two possibilities: marriage to a sister who is the daughter of one's father, or marriage to a sister who is the daughter of one's mother. Of the daughter by the mother the lawgiver states that the prohibition applies to a daughter who has been born to the mother at home or abroad. Genesis 11:31 indicates that Abram's father, Terah, moves with Abram and Sarai from his home in Ur of the Chaldees to go abroad. Since we learn in Genesis 20:12 that Sarah's father is also Terah, her mother would presumably have been from Ur. The point, however, is not Sarah's possible genealogy. It is the contrast between home and abroad, brought out in the Genesis narrative, that has prompted the geographical distinction in the rule.

Why do we find the additional rule about the half-sister, in the instance where she is solely the daughter of a father's wife? Why this prohibition again, which the lawgiver has included in the preceding rule but one? The answer is that he has under scrutiny the specific, later notice in Genesis 20:12 about Abraham's relationship to Sarah. Abraham (his name and Sarah's have been altered by this time) is again sojourning in foreign parts, the kingdom of Gerar, and again he fears that he will be killed on account of his wife. He resorts to the same ruse he tries in his previous visit to Egypt. Again the ploy becomes undone. The foreign king, Abimelech, finds out that Sarah is in fact Abraham's wife. In response to the king's discovery, Abraham informs Abimelech that Sarah is indeed his sister as well as his wife: "the daughter of my father, not the daughter of my mother, and she became my wife." It is precisely this relationship that the lawgiver prohibits, having laid out in his previous law but one the more general prohibition against marriage to a daughter of one's father or a daughter of one's mother.[21]

The Granddaughter

The incident about Lot's daughters lying with their father is recounted between the two episodes about Sarah's sexual history with other men, the Pharaoh and the king of Gerar. The incident was pertinent to the first rule prohibiting intercourse with a parent. The lawgiver looks at the incident again and uses it to derive his prohibition against a sexual relationship between a man and his granddaughter. This time he scrutinizes the incident in its wider context as part of the history of Abraham.

Lot is Abraham's nephew, the son of his brother Haran. Lot's daughters are Abraham's grandnieces. Lot and his daughters are saved from the destruction of Sodom and Gomorrah because of Abraham's good standing with the deity (Gen 19:29). Their future husbands are not so fortunate, because they refuse to depart the threatened city. As a consequence of the destruction wrought on Sodom, the daughters reckon that for procreative purposes, "Our father is old, and there is no man in the earth to come in unto us after the manner of all the earth" (Gen 19:31).

The lawgiver has reflected on the reasoning of Lot's daughters. There is no man on earth to impregnate them, they reason. That is not true. If they mean that men from their kinship group are not available, that is not true either. There is their granduncle Abraham. To be sure, he is even more aged than their father, but as we learn from the account of Abraham's life at this point (Gen 18:10–15), Abraham is perfectly capable of performing sexually at an advanced age. In their old age he and Sarah produce their son Isaac. Abraham, then, could have come in to these daughters of Lot "after the manner of all the earth."

The lawgiver condemns out of hand the action of the daughters in resorting to sex with their father. The very fact that they get him drunk is an indication that they know their action is improper. For the lawgiver, on the other hand, intercourse with their granduncle Abraham would presumably have been acceptable. Just as the lawgiver does not prohibit a union between a man and his niece—a relationship Abraham's brother Nahor had with his niece Milcah (Gen 11:27, 29)—so he would not prohibit a union between a man and his grandniece. As in Roman law the relationship is too distant for it to prompt a prohibition.[22]

My submission is that the lawgiver derives his prohibition against a man having a relationship with a granddaughter from his examination of the episode of Lot's daughters. He has made the following move. He condemns a relationship of a daughter with a father but would not condemn one between a man and a grandniece. He does, however, consider the question, what about the relationship that is in between these two relationships? Can a man have a sexual relationship with his granddaughter? The lawgiver, prohibiting daughter and father, likewise prohibits grandfather and granddaughter. We might note that whereas the child is the focus of the prohibition against incest between son and father or daughter and father in Leviticus 18:7, it is the reverse in Leviticus 18:10, the grandfather being the focus of the prohibition. In the tradition recorded in Genesis, Abraham's sexual activity stands out because of his age and would explain why the lawgiver has even raised a grandfather's sexual relationship with a granddaughter.

Two other features of the material may also have been suggestive of a relationship between a man and his granddaughter. One, Lot is very old when the incident with his daughters occurs. Two, Lot's own father, Haran, died before Abraham and Lot migrated to Canaan. Abraham, as Lot's uncle, took on the role of father to Lot as a result. In this light Abraham is even closer to being a grandfather to these daughters.

Intercourse with a Daughter-in-Law and a Brother's Wife

These two rules have been formulated in response to the story of Judah and Tamar in Genesis 38. Recall that he marries the first of his sons, Er, to Tamar, but God strikes Er down before a child comes of the union. Onan is then obliged to give conception to Tamar to raise up a child to his dead brother but the deity also strikes down Onan. The obligation next falls upon the youngest son, Shelah. Shelah, however, has not yet reached puberty. Moreover, from Judah's vantage point it appears that Tamar is the sinister force that causes the deaths of his sons. Therefore when Shelah reaches sexual maturity, Judah, fearing for Shelah's life, does not involve him with Tamar and by withholding him fails to fulfill the duty to his dead son. Tamar takes the matter into her own hands and becomes pregnant by Judah. When he discovers Tamar's pregnancy, Judah pronounces a sentence of death on her. In her own defense, Tamar produces the objects that Judah gave to her at the time of their sexual transaction. Judah then acknowledges the rightness of her action, namely, producing an heir to her dead husband through a member of his family.

The lawgiver sets down his rule against a sexual relationship with a daughter-in-law in response to Judah's dealings with Tamar, his daughter-in-law. "Thou shalt not uncover the nakedness of thy daughter-in-law: she is thy son's wife: thou shalt not uncover her nakedness" (Lev 18:15). At the time of Tamar's ploy she is not actually married to any of Judah's sons, two of whom are dead by then. The point, however, is that whether Judah permits Shelah to consummate a marriage with her or not, Tamar's situation is such that she is affianced to Shelah by the custom of levirate marriage. That is why she can be accused of harlotry and, therefore, of adultery.

The story itself brings out the taboo inherent in a relationship between a man and his daughter-in-law. Tamar does not approach Judah openly to obtain seed from him but has to disguise herself and play the harlot. The story, moreover, tells us that after their one sexual encounter Judah "knew her not again" (Gen 38:6). There is, then, a sense in which all the lawgiver does is to spell out a rule, a father-in-law with a daughter-in-law, which is implicit in the narrative. After all, the narrative itself contains ethical and legal judgments. The lawgiver is simply extending this process of judgment. He is further encouraged to do so because the story gives an ambiguous message. Because Judah fails to have his one remaining son, Shelah, give Tamar conception, Judah states how Tamar, in getting seed from him, is "more righteous than I, inasmuch as I did not give her to my son Shelah." Judah's statement might imply that in some circumstances it is acceptable for a father-in-law to have a sexual relationship with his daughter-in-law. The lawgiver opposes any such inference.

The next rule against a sexual relationship with a brother's wife also comes from reflection on the story. "Thou shalt not uncover the nakedness of thy brother's wife: it is thy brother's nakedness" (Lev 18:16). The story presupposes the honorable custom of levirate marriage by which a man in certain circumstances is obliged to have a sexual relationship with his dead brother's widow. Onan is unwilling to meet his obligation and conceals his unwillingness in an offensive way. Either the lawgiver opposes any union between a man and his brother's wife no matter the circumstances, thereby canceling the levirate custom; or the lawgiver views Onan's example of unwillingness as wholly appropriate for all Israelite men, except in regard to the levirate custom. I think the former may be the case: rejection of the levirate custom.

Marriage with Two Sisters in Their Lifetime

The lawgiver sets down a rule that is not about incest. A man must not marry two sisters while both are alive: "Neither shalt thou take a woman as a rival wife to her sister, to uncover her nakedness, beside the other in her life time" (Lev 18:18).[23] It is easy to relate this rule to patriarchal history. Jacob is married to two sisters, Rachel and Leah. The rule uses the verb *laqaḥ*, "to take [as wife]." These women are also his first cousins, but that particular degree of consanguinity is plainly not the reason for the prohibition. Presumably the lawgiver permits a marriage between first cousins. The reason for the rule is the problem of rivalry. The notable feature of Jacob's marriages to Rachel and Leah is the contention between the sisters in competing for his sexual services. On one occasion Rachel even hires Jacob out to Leah for a night's lovemaking so that she can conceive a child (Gen 30:14–18).

The lawgiver has gone from the story of Tamar's marital history to the story of Jacob's. That is, he has gone from a woman's marriages to two brothers to a man's marriages to two sisters.[24] How do we account for this switch from one story to another? A fundamental procedure of the lawgiver is that he moves back and forth between the histories of the generations. What prompts him to do so is that time and again he finds that what occurs in a particular generation also occurs in a later or earlier one. His procedure is exactly in line with how the biblical narrators themselves proceed in setting out their narrative traditions. These narrators typically record similar developments in the lifetime of each patriarch; for example, how each of them, beginning with Abraham, has a problem involving his firstborn son.

The history of patriarchal sexual relationships accounts, I contend, for the setting down of the series of rules in Leviticus 18:6–18. Where these relationships raise issues of incest, the lawgiver duly records his judgment. Where the stories raise allied issues about marital relationships, but not ones that involve incest, the lawgiver also proceeds to give his judgment. His method, then, accounts for the mixing together of laws having to do with incest and laws not having to do with incest. Any hypothesis about the nature of these rules has to account for such combinations of topics.

Tamar is married first to one brother and then, after he dies, to another brother. The lawgiver logically turns to a comparable marital setup in the preceding generation, namely, Jacob's. Jacob is married to two sisters. Unlike Tamar's consecutive marital unions to two brothers, Jacob is married to each sister during the lifetime of the other. There are other features shared by the two stories. Tamar's marriages to the two brothers are disastrous. Jacob's marriages founder—he hates the elder sister, Leah, because he was tricked into marrying her, and Rachel, the one he loves, is barren. The fraught situation leads to contention between the two wives. In the generation after Jacob's, Onan's father instructs him, because of levirate custom, to take Tamar as a wife. Onan spurns her because, we might note, there is a sense in which he is in contention with his dead, childless, elder brother over the proceeds of an estate. The situation is comparable to how Leah's father instructs her, because of the custom to marry off the elder daughter before the younger, to become Jacob's wife. Jacob spurns her. Onan would never voluntarily have taken Tamar, just as Jacob never wanted Leah.

Non-Incest Rules

Finally, I wish to examine briefly why mixed in with the incest rules in Leviticus 18 are rules that have nothing to do with incest. These non-incest–related rules follow the one about a marriage to two sisters while both are alive. In sequence, the rules are: sex with a menstruating woman, adultery, child sacrifice, homosexuality, and bestiality (Lev 18:18–23). It is truly a motley collection of rules and exemplifies the unlikelihood that these rules come from unknown biblical legislators, who, in a rather chaotic fashion, directly addressed societal problems. What we have instead is a scribe who sets down rules by addressing issues from the beginnings of the nation's history according to the order and presentation of events in the Book of Genesis. The rules, following the one prohibiting marriage to two sisters, are: "Also thou shalt not approach unto a woman to uncover her nakedness, as long as she is put apart for her uncleanness. Moreover thou shalt not lie carnally with thy neighbour's wife, to defile thyself with her. And thou shalt not let any of thy seed pass through the fire to Molech, neither shalt thou profane the name of thy God: I am Yahweh. Thou shalt not lie with mankind, as with womankind: it is abomination. Neither shalt thou lie with any beast to defile thyself therewith: neither shall any woman stand before a beast to lie down thereto: it is confusion" (Lev 18:19–23).

The last rule in the incest series in Leviticus 18:7–17 focused on Tamar's burdened unions with two brothers. The lawgiver now turns his attention to problems in earlier marriages. He first turns back, as I have just indicated, to Jacob's marriages to two sisters. The tensions between

Rachel and Leah concern rivalry over their husband, Jacob, and Rachel's desire to overcome her barrenness. Her remedy involves heightened sexuality in the form of acquiring love apples and prompts the rule prohibiting unions to two sisters while both are alive. Continuing to move back through the generations, the lawgiver has the problem of Abraham's marriage to Sarah. That marriage too experiences barrenness and a remedy that also involves enhanced sexual awareness. Two dramatic, coincidental new things are to happen to Sarah in her old age. She is to resume menstruation, which will ultimately cease due this time not to old age but to pregnancy, and she will experience sexual pleasure again. The two happenings, because of their miraculous character, overlap (Gen 18). On account of the juxtaposition of the two topics in the story, the lawgiver raises the question of whether it is acceptable for a man to have sexual contact with a woman during her menses. His rule on the subject forbids it. (I am not suggesting that we can infer that the ancient author assumed that postmenopausal women did not experience sexual pleasure.)

The lawgiver stays with Sarah's sexual history and notes that events depicted in Genesis 20 intervene between her anticipation of sexual pleasure with her husband and its realization (Gen 21). The tradition recounts that Sarah came very close indeed to committing adultery with Abimelech. A prohibition about adultery is set down. Sexual intercourse between Abraham and Sarah then occurs, Isaac is born (Gen 21), and God requires Abraham, at the time living in the land of Canaan, to offer the child as a burnt sacrifice (Gen 22). In the event, Isaac is not sacrificed, and God promises Abraham that his descendants will overcome the Canaanites (Gen 22:17). The incident nonetheless brings up for the lawgiver that later time when the Canaanites actually sacrifice their children by fire to the god Molech (2 Kgs 16:3, 17:17, 21:6, 23:10; Jer 32:35); as a result, he sets down a rule prohibiting such a practice.

What occurs in Abraham's generation takes us from the topic of marriage to the birth of a child and a dramatic divine intervention in the form of fire that almost consumes the child. Attention becomes fixed on how the Canaanite god Molech does consume children by fire. If in the end the Israelite god desists from taking Isaac as an offering by fire, he nonetheless at this same time consumes all of the Canaanite inhabitants of Sodom by fire because the homosexual mob in that city seeks to abuse two visitors (Gen 19). The lawgiver next sets down a rule condemning homosexuality.

From wholesale destruction of one Canaanite city because of an intended sexual offense against visitors, the lawgiver turns to the mass destruction of another Canaanite city because of a sexual offense against a visitor. Lot offers his two daughters to the men of Sodom that they might be sexually abused instead of the two male visitors. The entire city is wiped out. In a later generation Jacob's daughter Dinah visits a Canaanite city belonging to the Hivites, and the Canaanite Shechem, the son of its ruler, Hamor, sexually violates her (Gen 34). All the males of that city are slaughtered. The name Hamor means "ass." Jacob later comments on the incident and refers to his own family's involvement: his sons' extermination of all the male Canaanites on account of Shechem's violation of Dinah weakens his house, the house of the Ox (as Jacob comments on the matter in Gen 49:6), because other Canaanite clans will seek vengeance (Gen 34:30). The suggestion that Shechem's violation of Dinah is that of an ass sexually violating an ox raises for the lawgiver the topic of human-animal intercourse. He sets down a rule against bestiality.[25]

I conclude with the problem that in introducing his incest and non-incest rules in Leviticus 18 the lawgiver expressly condemns not the conduct of the ancestors but the conduct of the Egyptians and the Canaanites (Lev 18:1–3): "After the doings of the land of Egypt, wherein ye dwelt, shall ye not do: and after the doings of the land of Canaan, whither I bring you, shall ye not do." In the warnings that follow the presentation of the rules, the lawgiver again returns to the unacceptable conduct of the Canaanite inhabitants of the land and insists that the Israelites should not imitate it when they occupy the land of Canaan (Lev 18:24–30). One problem about these warnings is the difficulty of finding any evidence in the pertinent Near Eastern sources that the liaisons prohibited in Leviticus constituted a major feature of Egyptian and Canaanite life.[26] Another problem is that it is hard to believe that Canaanite and Egyptian children were known for initiating sexual encounters with their parents. I know of no scholar who addresses the discrepancy between vices that Moses attributes to Egypt and Canaan and their prevalence in those cultures. Presumably the tacit view is that if we knew more about these societies, revelations of their outrageous ways would be forthcoming. I am skeptical, however, about the common assumption that these nations were indeed notorious for decadent behaviors, with the Israelites reacting against them in the regulation of their own social life.

In every time and place, a typical phenomenon is for one group to blame another for sexuality that is deemed damnable. Syphilis was initially called the "disease of Naples" or "Napolitan disease," but it rapidly became the "French pox" or "Morbus Gallicus." It was then given many names, with one nation or another being branded the cause of it: the "Spanish disease" in Holland, the "Polish disease" in Russia, the "Russian disease" in Siberia, the "Christian disease" in Turkey, and the "Portuguese disease" in India and Japan. In the years 1728–29, Captain James Cook, exploring the Pacific, heard the Tahitians call syphilis "Apa no Britannia"—the British disease (Cook thought that they had caught it from the French). Homosexuality has been termed the English disease; the term *bugger* means that it was the Bulgarians who engaged in homosexuality; and a Sodomite refers to the homosexual activity of the Canaanite natives of Sodom. AIDS has been blamed on Africa. In a pre-Socratic Greek source we are told that the "Persians think it seemly that not only women but men should adorn themselves, and that men should have intercourse with their daughters, mothers and sisters, but the Greeks regard these things as disgraceful and against the law."[27] According to the Bible (sexual) harlotry starts with foreigners, the Canaanites (Gen 34).

A scrutiny of incest rules suggests that it is the behavior of the ancestors of the Israelites, not Egyptian or Canaanite behavior, that the lawgiver condemned.[28] This conclusion should not be so unexpected when we recall that a fair number of the rules do prohibit relationships that are found among the patriarchs. Why, then, does the lawgiver point the finger at the Egyptians and the Canaanites instead of at them? The answer is that the lawgiver viewed the behavior of the ancestors in light of their milieu. It is a universal phenomenon. Conduct barely passable in one part of the United States (Denver) is considered good enough in another part (San Francisco). Philonic, New Testament, and Talmudic ethical judgments frequently take into account the influence of harmful milieu. For example, the reference in Genesis 6:9 that Noah was "just and perfect in his generation" occasioned much debate as to whether Noah possessed absolute virtue or whether he stood out only among his contemporaries (Philo, *De Abr.* 7.36 ff.; *Gen. Rab.* 6:9).[29] The patriarchs did not have the laws of Moses to live by, but instead were influenced by their Canaanite or Egyptian environment.[30] That milieu had to be taken into account in assessing their behavior. It is the lawgiver who infers in a way typical of all times and places that Canaanite and Egyptian practices were beyond the pale and that the activities of the ancestors were more understandable as a consequence.

Abraham marries his half-sister. The lawgiver probably inferred that such a union, offensive to him, simply reflected Abraham's deficient social and cultural setting, Mesopotamian in this particular instance. He and Sarah marry before they migrate to Canaan. Abraham himself sees the need to avoid a Canaanite marriage for his son Isaac (Gen 24:3). Abraham's awareness of such an undesirable union would be evidence for the lawgiver that already in Abraham's time the Canaanites represent harmful influence. Judah's relationship with his daughter-in-law occurs in Canaan, after he himself marries a Canaanite in Canaan. Moses prohibited the very union that his own parents have contracted. They contract it in Egypt (Num 26:59). For the lawgiver, then, it was the host cultures in which the ancestors lived, not the ancestors themselves, about which he had to warn.[31]

The consensus of scholarly opinion is that the Leviticus lawgiver was himself living in a host culture, namely, Babylon. If this is so, it may be significant that he does not cite Mesopotamia as one of the cultures he deplores. To have done so would have been unwise. At the same time, however, if this social historical context is relevant to the rules, the lawgiver is in a coded way telling his fellow Israelites to avoid Babylonian (Mesopotamian) ways. The reference to the Egyptians and the Canaanites would have directed attention to the Babylonians just as, later, when the Jews lived under the Romans, "Edom" was a code word for Rome.[32]

9

Desexing

And the eyes of them both were opened, and they knew that they were naked; and they sewed fig leaves together, and made themselves aprons.

—*Genesis 3:7*

A matter is sometimes sexualized in order to impress its nonsexual message on an audience. For instance, a spiritual idea such as God's love for a religiously unfaithful Israel is discussed in terms of a husband who is married to a scandalously promiscuous wife (Hos 1:2, 3, 2:2–13). Or, the search for wisdom is the pursuit of an attractive woman whose qualities, while the opposite of those of a loose woman, are yet similar—*imitation par opposition* (Prov 9). The Qumran Psalms Scroll (in Hebrew) on Sir 51:13–30 eroticizes the quest for Wisdom to an extraordinary degree. So eager is the young student to embrace Wisdom that he is told there is to be "no lolling on her heights." J. A. Sanders points out that the corresponding Greek version of Sir 51:13–30 "presents essentially pious ideas in lieu of those phrases in the Hebrew which suggest erotic figures and nuances."[1] In 1 Esdras 3:1–4:41 there is a convocation that has contestants articulate different opinions as to what is the strongest force in the world. The victor is to receive valuable prizes and high office. The first of the contestants accords preeminence to wine, depriving even the king of his judgment. The second accords preeminence to the king, since men rule over sea and land and he rules over them. The third gives the distinction to women, who give birth to the king as well as to "all the people that bear rule by sea and land" (1 Esd 4:15), and who, by their beauty, proceed to subjugate them both, king and male subjects alike. However, this third contestant, having made his case for women, goes on to praise truth as even mightier, forever directing earth and heaven righteously and steadfastly under God. He wins by unanimous acclamation. The move from the wiles of women to the attractiveness of truth is regarded as an addition to a common folk story in the ancient world, but it is in keeping with biblical precedents about the attraction of women and the pursuit of wisdom.[2]

Later, in Western tradition, the same link between the appeal of wisdom and the appeal of women showed up. The figures of Faust and Don Juan underwent mutual influence with the result that each ended up sharing a desire for knowledge and a desire for sexual success. It is the same connection that Proverbs 9, for example, has between sexual awareness and the pursuit of knowledge.[3] The Adam and Eve story also brilliantly brings out the link. Their awareness of sexual difference is tied to their quest for knowledge of good and evil. The result of consuming the forbidden nourishment is consciousness of sexuality, and that awareness is followed not by intercourse but by a particular intelligence. "And the eyes of both were opened and they knew that they were naked and they sewed fig leaves together"; and, when on trial, "I [Adam] was afraid because I was naked . . . Who *told* you that you were naked? Hast thou eaten of the tree?" (Gen 3:7, 10, 11). Later Jewish and Christian interpreters, Augustine, in particular, failed to appreciate the positive awareness of sexuality and its tie to knowledge in the Adam and Eve story. The result has been that because religion inclines typically to be interested not in enjoyable things but in sin, suffering, death, and the like, sexuality too tends to fall into the negative category.

The opposite phenomenon of desexualization, or desexing, of language, lore, and custom is also around at all times.[4] A sexual matter is defanged.

The earliest example of desexing in a biblical context is when God clothes the first human couple in Eden because they have become sexually alert. The couple's initial act of covering their nakedness is a response to their awareness of it. The deity's later act of clothing them in durable skins anticipates future life outside Eden when sexual desire has to be curbed and nakedness confined to the private relationship between a husband and a wife. God's action in the Adam and Eve story, in turn, inspires the particular formulation in the Decalogue of the rule against coveting a neighbor's wife.[5] Dress, to be sure, frequently has the opposite potential, but that is because, being so closely tied to nakedness, dress exploits the very awareness to which Adam and Eve become alert. Robert Herrick's "Delight in Disorder" expresses the matter well:

> A Sweet disorder in the dresse
> Kindles in cloathes a wantonnesse.

Commenting on Trajan's law prohibiting women from bathing with men, Montesquieu writes, "He obliged them in spite of themselves to hide those charms which, if modesty would not keep them secret, prudence alone would conceal from the eyes, the better to reveal them to the imagination."[6]

Last century, during the Mao era in China, the drab austerity of unisex suits proclaimed opposition to the perceived sexual decadence of the Western world. A biblical instance in which some facet of dress is intended to suppress sexuality is the placement of tassels on an Israelite male's garment (Deut 22:12; cf. Num 15:37–41; Prov 1:9, 3:3). The law requiring them is inspired by Joseph's resistance to the attempt of Potiphar's wife to have sexual congress with him (Gen 39). Recall that to conceal her wrongdoing she removes a garment from him in order to indicate that he tried to seduce her. The intent of the positive injunction in Deuteronomy is to advertise that, like the exemplary Joseph with Potiphar's wife, an Israelite's clothing should declare the opposite of wrongful sexual desire.[7] The Talmud records the story of a disciple whose tassels (those of the law in Deut 22:12) miraculously strike him on his face when he is about to have intercourse with a harlot. So impressed is she that she converts to Judaism and marries him (*b. Men.* 44a).[8] In Chapter 4 (and to be further commented on shortly), I draw attention to a garment as symbolic of a man or a woman in a sexual relationship. It is therefore not surprising that something attached to a garment, such as the tassels of the Deuteronomic law, is given symbolic sexual significance and that Joseph's restraint in the face of a foreign woman's boldness inspired the particular Israelite rule in Deuteronomy 22:12.

A readily recognizable example of the desexing of a piece of literature is the Song of Songs. It began life as a eulogy of earthly love, but only as an allegory of God's love for Israel did it come into the orbit of books fit for inclusion in the canon of biblical literature.[9] Jewish and Christian interpreters used allegory to derive a deeper layer of meaning from the surface meaning. Crucial to the enterprise was the belief that the biblical text had a supernatural origin. It is clear, however, that the mask of allegory is something imposed on the original composition and that without the mask the material remains decidedly erotic. Not appreciating the original mind-set of Jewish and Christian interpreters, Marvin Pope states, "The trouble has been that interpreters who dared acknowledge the plain sense of the Song were assailed as enemies of truth and decency. The allegorical charade thus persisted for centuries with only sporadic protests."[10]

Something of a parallel to the development that overtook the Song of Songs is the treatment of certain nursery rhymes, two of which I shall discuss below (and one of which is actually about desexing). These have a sexual content but have ended up in the nursery, though not originally intended for children. Like the Song of Songs, their contents too remain unchanged but are not, even by most adults, understood for what they are.[11] Social setting, a place of worship or the nursery, seems to be crucial for sanitizing the original language. At all times, in ordinary social circumstances, common speech contains sexual allusions that are heard but go unnoticed. Examples are "she is screwed up" in American English and a *Schlappschwanz* ("coward," literally "limp-tail") in German.[12]

If not exactly desexed, texts translated from the original Hebrew Bible into English often end up losing their specific rough or unrefined meaning. The word ʿ*arelim*, "those who have foreskins," becomes "the uncircumcised." The Hebrew of Isaiah 57:8 most likely means "you [feminine] have gazed on an erection [*yad*]."[13] The RSV translates it thus: "you have gazed on their nakedness," and the NEB emends it to read "in the heat of your lust." The AV has "where thou sawest it," leaving the reader to wonder what "it" refers to. Even in the textual history of the Hebrew Bible a word such as *šagal*, close to the vulgar "to fuck" (Deut 28:30; Isa 13:16; Zec 14:2; Jer 3:2), is changed to the less direct *šakhab*, "to lie with," because the Masoretes (those who handed down the codices of the Hebrew Bible) thought the former verb too obscene.[14] We also find in the original texts of the Old and New Testaments an avoidance of too direct a reference to indelicate matters. In Luke's Gospel there is the parable about the man who is requested to provide food for his neighbor at midnight. The man responds by claiming that he cannot rise up because "my children are with me in bed" (Luke 11:7). It would have been too unseemly for the man to say that he was in bed with his wife. The tendency to avoid such direct speech is universal. "To sleep with" in the sense of intercourse in ancient Egyptian upper-class circles (the meaning is also found in Akkadian, Hittite, Greek, Latin, German, and English but not in Ugaritic, Hebrew, Aramaic, Arabic and French) is even more toned down in the expression "to see" someone.[15] The taboo in our culture on such four-letter words as "cunt," "fuck," and "jism" is particularly observable among the middle class, because upward mobility and desexing often go together. Notions of what constitutes civilized life, what balance to strike between substance and show, between open acknowledgments of matters perceived to be unattractive and refinement of our sensibilities, come into play.

Desexing of biblical passages is particularly pronounced in the Septuagint (the third to first century BCE Greek translation of the Hebrew Bible). For example, it translates Judges 19:2: "And his [the Levite's] concubine played the harlot against him" as "his concubine was angry with him." Another example may be the omission in some of the Greek translations of 1 Samuel 2:22 about the sexual depravity of the priestly house of Eli. Matthew Goff points out that the immoral woman frequently depicted in Proverbs has her role in the Septuagint translation of Proverbs extended to function as a metaphor for abstract ideas.[16] I already cited at the beginning of this chapter the refined, pious Greek of Sir 51:13–30 in contrast to the robust sexual allusions of the Hebrew text. There is also the example of how the LXX translated Exodus 2:25 (to be discussed shortly). The negative attitude of Greek philosophers to the body and sexuality is doubtless a contributing factor to the tendency to desexualize. Socrates says to Simmias: "Do you think it is the part of a philosopher to be concerned with such so-called pleasures as those of food and drink?" Simmias answers, "By no means." Socrates then asks, "What about the pleasures of sex?" and Simmias says, "Not at all." We have the desexualizing of erotic dreams by the second-century CE dream analyst Artemidoros.[17]

In Chapter 6 I discussed the rule in Deuteronomy 24:5 granting a newly married man military exemption and no business duties for a year. Its rationale is that a newly married man should not be faced with danger from war or business (probably foreign) travel until such time as he has produced a (male) child. A common translation is: "When a man hath taken a new wife, he shall not go out to war, neither shall he be charged with any business: he shall be free at home one year; and [in the language of the translations] shall cheer up his wife which he has taken." What prompted the law's formulation, I suggested, was the lawgiver's interest in the first time the issue arises in the nation's history, when a married man without a child, but with the prospect of having one, encounters the threat of death. The biblical context that raises the issue is that of the aged Abraham and Sarah, long married, who are childless but learn that she will conceive, even though postmenopausal. Sarah says on the occasion, "After I am waxed old shall I have pleasure, my lord being old also?" (Gen 18:12). She means sexual pleasure (as well as conception). Before they come together they undertake what they perceive to be a dangerous journey to the kingdom of Gerar, and Abraham, fearing for his life, passes Sarah off as his sister (Gen 20:2). As it happens, despite the ruse being uncovered, the natives of the foreign country treat Abraham and Sarah well and spare his life; eventually the aged couple has intercourse that leads to the birth of Isaac (Gen 21:2).

The lawgiver drafts his rule on the basis of this highly idiosyncratic, saving moment in the nation's history. He does so by turning to the likeliest parallel in his time and thinks of a newly married man who might be faced with military duty or business that probably involves risky travel abroad. Rather than go through with such undertakings, the lawgiver permits the man to stay at home with his wife in order "to provide delight" (śimaḥ) to her. Referring back to Abraham and Sarah, the meaning is sexual pleasure with the expectation of conception. Sarah's "will I have ʾednah" comes through in the man's śimaḥ, "giving delight to his wife." Apart from being unaware of what prompted the writing down of the rule, translators (AV, RSV, JSB) gloss over, consciously or unconsciously, the sexual element in it when they give the sense that the man has "to cheer up" his new wife. The erotic aspect has thus been removed from the rule in standard translations.[18]

Sixty years ago in England divorce by agreement was not attainable. Because adultery was the only basis for obtaining one, a husband would spend a night at a hotel with a prostitute to "prove" that he was committing the offense. He might not have intercourse with her, but the law presumed that a married man, sharing a bedroom with an adult woman not his wife, engaged in sexual intercourse. Such a presumption for a married couple would be less pressing, because, in some ways, marriage is meant to draw attention away from sexuality. Among the Shi'ites of Iran, marriage contracts for periods as little as one hour are drawn up in order to avoid the appearance of irregular sex.[19] From one angle it is prostitution, from another it is marriage. In England, "Fleet marriages," in which clergymen carried out counterfeit ceremonies, were solely examples of irregular sex. The sham marriage ritual was supposed to conceal the practice. The notorious character of these fake marriages prompted a major change in the law of marriage (Lord Hardwicke's Act, 1753).[20] In a way, language about prostitutes restores sex to marriage. In the *Freudenhaus* ("house of pleasure") they refer to their clients as *Freieren* ("suitors"). As we saw in Chapter 7, Tamar seduces Judah by an act of prostitution in order to have him uphold the custom of levirate marriage, to make him, however irregularly, her husband. He condemns her action but then has to acknowledge that she has been "more righteous than I because I gave her not to Shelah my son" (Gen 38:26). Her act of prostitution is, in some legitimate sense, a marital one.

A most interesting text for the purpose of this analysis is God's role in the conception of Jesus, in particular, a text that comes from the story of the Exodus: "And God saw the children of Israel, and God knew" (Exod 2:25). In overturning a long-held view that attributed the Virgin Birth in the New Testament to a Hellenistic background, David Daube suggests that a divine conception for Moses is hinted at in the use of this Exodus text in the liturgy of the Jewish Passover seder.[21] In that section of the Haggadah where one biblical text is thought to illuminate another, the rabbis cite Exodus 2:25 by way of "proving" that another text, "And he [God] saw our affliction" (Deut 26:7), means abstention from sexual intercourse. If one is familiar with the rabbinic world of (to us) fanciful exegesis of scripture, it is understandable why the rabbis so interpret the latter text. They reasoned that the Israelites abstained from intercourse because—and this is biblical—the Pharaoh sought to kill the male children. Biblical rules about fasting from food and drink (Lev 16:29, 31, 23:27, 32) employ the verb "to abstain," and the rabbis had extended their scope to include abstaining from sexual relations. The puzzle is why they chose to cite Exodus 2:25 as proving the correctness of their interpretation.

Daube suggests that underlying the discussion is the question, why, if the Israelites are avoiding conjugal relations, Moses nonetheless comes to be born. The answer, he argues, is that we should read the verb "knew" in a sexual sense and infer a divine conception for Moses. Daube has worked out many links between the Passover Haggadah and the New Testament and thinks that the supernatural birth of Moses is the key to the story of the Virgin Birth in Matthew's and Luke's Gospels. For the Gospel writers, Jesus is a new Moses, and a story would have circulated at the time they wrote their Gospels about Moses' divine conception.

Dale Allison takes the suggestion a good deal further and argues that, extraordinary as it may be, Moses is regarded by the rabbis as having come from a virgin, even though his mother already had two children (Aaron and Miriam). Just as the topics of divorce and virginity are central aspects of the Virgin Birth story, so the two topics turn up in the tradition about the parents of Moses in Josephus and rabbinic sources. Early Jewish exegesis has it that the father of Moses, Amram, divorces his wife, Jochebed, before Moses is born and, like Joseph who almost divorces Mary but in the event refrains, takes up with her again even though she is pregnant. Equally interesting is the Talmudic view that before the birth of Moses, Jochebed has miraculously become a virgin again: "the symptoms of maidenhood were restored" (*b. B. B.* 120a).[22]

Indirect evidence to support the origin of the Virgin Birth in first-century Jewish interpretation of the Exodus story comes from the strained efforts of early Jewish authorities to desex the reference to "God knew" in translations and interpretations of the passage in Exodus 2:25. The Jewish translators that produced the Septuagint change the Hebrew to read, "And he [God] became known to them." The Targum Onkelos (written in Aramaic for reading in the synagogues because Hebrew was no longer the language of the congregants) has a radical change of meaning: "And the servitude of the children of Israel was revealed before the Lord, and the Lord said he would deliver them." The Jerusalemite Targum (also in Aramaic) has: "And the Lord saw the trouble of the servitude of the children of Israel, and the repentance which they practised in secret was revealed before the Lord, for they did not know of one another [that each secretly repented]." In both the Targums the verb "to know" is not used of God and certainly not of sexual relations. *Midrash Rabba* (a collective name for ten commentaries on different books of the Bible) on Exodus 2:25 reads: "And God saw—this means he saw their [sexual] abstention; and God knew—this means, he knew that the time had come which he had fixed to Abraham." This translation is all the more interesting because the idea of sexual abstention is present in the interpretation. The author of *Midrash Rabba,* however, seems to leave no trace of the idea that God becomes sexually involved unless in the more remote sense that he will cause the birth of a person to redeem the descendants of Abraham.

Many customs furnish examples of desexing. Each of the ones I look at in some detail has to do with the institution of marriage. Consider first the custom of circumcision in ancient Israel. At some point in the biblical past the rite occurred at the age of puberty, around twelve or thirteen. That is Ishmael's age when he is circumcised (Gen 17:25). That age is the time for sexual initiation and the Hebrew word for a bridegroom, *ḥatan* (one who undergoes circumcision), preserves the link between the boy's coming of age and the rite. The requirement, albeit involving deception, that the Shechemite males become circumcised before they can marry Hebrew women points to the link (Gen 34:14–24). So too does the action of the wife of Moses, Zipporah, in a strange incident in Exodus 4:24–26. She cuts off their son's foreskin and touches Moses' feet with it, that is, his genital "feet," and exclaims to Moses, "Surely you are a bridegroom of blood to me." Presumably, Moses himself had not been circumcised.[23]

In Israelite tradition the link between the custom of circumcision and a male's attainment of sexual maturity disappears. Circumcision occurs not at puberty but eight days after a male child is born. Isaac, according to the Bible, is circumcised then (Gen 21:4; cf. Lev 12:3). The odd episode of Zipporah's circumcising her son and then touching Moses' "feet" appears in some way to carry echoes of the transition. In any event, the significance of the rite changes from sexual initiation to spiritual inspiration. It becomes a sign that the Israelite male is a member of a community claiming a covenant with its god.

Genital mutilation is a literal form of desexing and denies a man entry into the "assembly of Yahweh," the ideal community of Israel whose chief aim is to increase in numbers because of the blessing of fruitfulness that began with Abraham (Gen 18:18, 19). A rule in Deuteronomy 23:2 prohibits a person who is reproductively impaired from entering the assembly: "He that is wounded in the stones, or hath his privy member cut off, shall not enter into the assembly of Yahweh." The rule is a product of the lawgiver's reflection on the incident involving Dinah in Genesis 34. The two sons of Jacob deceive the foreign Canaanite group, the Hivites, into thinking that by undergoing circumcision they could enter into conjugal and commercial relations with the incipient nation Israel. In light of the incident, the lawgiver has posed the question whether among Israelites there is any form of genital mutilation other than circumcision of the male member that would in fact exclude an Israelite man from entering Yahweh's assembly. Circumcision permits procreation and entry of the Israelite into the ideal national community, but the more drastic mutilation means infertility and the exclusion of the desexed Israelite from it.[24]

A ceremony involving a shoe in the history of levirate marriage in biblical tradition furnishes an example of a marital custom that becomes desexed in Talmudic times. In the Bible we have the dramatic instance of levirate marriage in the story of Judah and Tamar in Genesis 38. As I have argued in previous chapters, many issues posed by this remarkable story exercised the minds of biblical lawgivers. One such issue is the appropriate and more reasonable punishment for a brother, the levir, who refuses to give conception to the widow. The Deuteronomic lawgiver addresses it in the one law in the Bible where the sanction consists of public disgrace. The law reads:

> If brothers dwell together, and one of them die, and have no child, the wife of the dead shall not marry without unto a stranger: her husband's brother shall go in unto her, and take her to him as wife, and perform the duty of an husband's brother unto her. And it shall be that the firstborn which she beareth shall succeed in the name of his brother which is dead, that his name be not put out of Israel. And if the man like not to take his brother's wife, then let his brother's wife go up to the gate unto the elders, and say, My husband's brother refuseth to raise up unto his brother a name in Israel, he will not perform the duty of my husband's

brother. Then the elders of his city shall call him, and speak unto him: and if he stand to it, and say, I like not to take her; Then shall his brother's wife come unto him in the presence of the elders, and loose his shoe from his foot, and spit in his face, and shall answer and say, So shall it be done unto that man that will not build up his brother's house. And his name shall be called in Israel, The house of him that hath his shoe loosed. (Deut 25:5–10)

Most interpreters think that the significance of this penalty has to be worked out by relating it to a ritual found in the book of Ruth.[25] On closer inspection of both passages, however, the differences are more significant than the similarities, and we are left with the task of explaining precisely the point of the punishment in the Deuteronomic law. In Ruth the issue is also one that involves the denial of a child to a widow by a kinsman. However, what comes up first is not, as in the law, any complaint by the woman Ruth before the public authorities that an (unnamed) kinsman is denying her conception, but the issue as to whether he is willing to redeem the parcel of land that belongs to the family of Naomi's dead husband. A less close kinsman, Boaz, in a scene the night before on his threshing floor, has already responded positively to Ruth's request to act as redeemer. It is he who informs the nearer kinsman of his prior obligation and tells him that if he is unwilling to take it on, he, Boaz, will do so. The man says he will redeem the land. Boaz then informs him that in doing so he is also obliged to take Ruth as a wife and raise up a child to his dead relative. The man responds negatively and calls off the entire transaction. It is at this point that the author of Ruth explains to the reader the procedure by which in former times in Israel one person transferred to another the right to redeem land. The person holding the right took off his shoe and gave it to the new redeemer (Ruth 4:7). The kinsman so proceeds and Boaz then assumes the duty of buying the land and taking Ruth as his wife. In the absence of written documents, the kind of ceremony described for the transfer of a right to acquire an immovable object such as a piece of land makes sense. The new holder plainly cannot pick it up in front of witnesses. Nor is it seen to be necessary that he walk round the land before witnesses to indicate possession of a right to redeem. Instead he takes from the transferor the latter's shoe by way of symbolizing the acquisition.[26]

The symbolism of the shoe's removal in the book of Ruth is quite different in significance from its removal in the Deuteronomic law, where it expresses a levir's unwillingness to give the widow conception. For one thing, it is the man who takes off his shoe in Ruth, whereas it is the woman who removes the man's shoe in the law. For another, the verbs used to describe the removal of the shoe are different (*šalap* in Ruth, *ḥalats* in the law). Again, the purpose of the woman's removal of the man's shoe in the law is to disgrace him before his compatriots, whereas no obvious disgrace attaches to the handing over of the shoe from one redeemer to another in the Book of Ruth. Another line of inquiry is necessary to explain in the law the woman's dishonoring action with the man's shoe.

It is important to note that the woman is shaming the man, and because he refuses to raise up a child to his dead brother, his refusal of sexual intercourse is the central issue. Indeed, it is the implicit language about sexual activity that explains everything about the woman's gesture. My claim is that she disgraces her brother-in-law by likening him to Onan, because both deny an ongoing line of descent to their relative. The removal of the brother-in-law's shoe from his foot indicates withdrawal from intercourse à la Onan, and the spitting signifies what Onan did with his seed. What the woman does brings out matters of universal significance.

Consider first one of the many symbolic meanings attributed to shoes. In contemporary African American circles an expression for sexual intercourse is "to knock boots." Whatever the origins of this expression, the notion of a shoe symbolizing a woman's genitals is found at all times and places.[27] There are many examples. In a Bedouin divorce ceremony the man says, "She was my slipper; I have cast her off." When polyandry existed among the Manchus, a bride gave gifts of shoes to her husband's brothers, because as the younger siblings they had the right of sexual access to her. The shoes are decorated with the *lien hua,* in common speech the vulgar term for the female genitalia. In nursery rhymes, there are the following two examples:

> Cock-a-doodle-doo!
> My dame has lost her shoe
> My master's lost his fiddlestick
> And knows not what to do.

That is, the couple is no longer having sexual relations.

> There was an old woman who lived in a shoe
> She had so many children she didn't know what to do.

The old woman's reproductive function is her life. The slipper in the tale of Cinderella has similar symbolic meaning. Advice to a bridegroom in Germany is "Man muss nicht die Füsse in fremde Schuhe stecken" (he is not to go around sticking his feet into other shoes). A commonly observed custom is the attachment of shoes or boots to a bridal car.[28]

Feet (or foot) also have the transferred sense of male (or female) genitals, for example, in the French expression for fellatio, "prendre son pied." In biblical literature, urine is "water of the feet" (2 Kgs 18:27=Isa 36:12; cf. Jgs 3:24; Isa 6:2). As already noted, Moses' wife touches his "feet" with their son's newly circumcised foreskin (Exod 4:25). Deuteronomy 28:57 refers to a mother's afterbirth that "comes out from between her feet." When David tells Uriah, whom he has recalled from the battlefield, to go home and wash his feet he means that he should have sexual intercourse with his wife, Bathsheba. The sight of her washing herself initially triggered David's desire for her (2 Sam 11:2, 8, 11). The prophet Ezekiel indicts Jerusalem for acting the harlot and making herself available in the street by spreading wide her "feet" to any passerby (Ezek 16:25). The prophet Jeremiah describes Israel as a lusty female animal that gives herself to any partner and appeals to her to change her ways: "Keep thy feet from going unshod and thy throat from thirst" (Jer 2:25).

The term "skirt" also comes to stand for a woman in most cultures, a "skirt chaser" in English, for example. In his poem "Bagpipe Music," Louis MacNiece has the following lines:

> It's no go the Yogi-Man, it's no go Blatavsky
> All we want is a bank balance and a bit of skirt in a taxi.

In the Koran wives are "raiment for you and ye are raiment for them" (Q.2:187). In the Bible Ruth pays Boaz a nocturnal visit, waits until he is drunk, uncovers his feet, and lies down beside him on his threshing floor. When Boaz wakes up and finds the woman at his feet, she asks him to spread his garment over her (Ruth 3:9). She is suggesting that, taking off his garment, he put a new one on, namely, herself as a wife. The symbolic meaning when a male spreads his skirt over a woman to denote a forthcoming marital union is well illustrated in Ezekial 16:8: "Now when I [God] passed by thee [Jerusalem], and looked upon thee, behold, thy time was the time of love; and I spread my skirt over thee"; and in Deuteronomy 23:1: "A man shall not take his father's wife, nor uncover his father's skirt." Ruth's action of uncovering Boaz's feet is similarly with a view to offering herself—sexually—as his new shoes. In other words, "skirt" and "shoes" have similar symbolic sexual significance in this section of Ruth.

In order to shame the man for an action he refuses to engage in, the woman in the law likens him to the proverbial example of such a refusal, Onan's action, or rather nonaction, in Genesis 38. Onan takes his brother's widow, Tamar, but to avoid giving her a child he withdraws from intercourse and ejaculates outside her. As already indicated, the removal of the shoe from the man's foot indicates withdrawal from intercourse, and the spitting the ejaculation of seed. In the Egyptian creation myth Atum generates the cosmic pair Shu and Tefnut by masturbation, but in a variant tradition it is by spitting. The expression "spitting image" (better "spitten image," where spitten is the old past participle) may refer to the father's "spitting" that results in a son so resembling him ("c'est son père tout craché" [he is the spitting image of his father]). There is also the French sexual expression "tousser sans cracher" (to cough without spitting). The Talmud uses the term "spittle" for semen (e. g., *b. Nidd.* 16b). In fact, one rabbinic interpretation of the Deuteronomic ceremony is precisely the one for which I am arguing. In *Siphre* on Deuteronomy 25:9, the manuscript reads: "The removal [of the shoe] is in lying down and the spitting is in implantation of the seed."[29]

There are many parallels to shaming a person by likening him or her to a proverbial example in legend or history: a Peeping Tom (from the story of Lady Godiva), a sadist (from the marquis de Sade), a masochist (from Leopold von Sacher-Masoch), a Jezebel (a loose woman among African Americans), and a Lolita (from Nabokov's novel). In Hebrew the name Onan mockingly means "The Virile One."

In later times the ceremony of *ḥalitsah* (withdrawal of the shoe) no longer carries any of the sexual overtones of the original law. In the postbiblical period it does not serve to disgrace a man for failure to perform his duty to his dead brother. It becomes instead a means of freeing the widow from the bond of levirate marriage, now the proper thing for the levir to do. L. M. Epstein spells out the transformation that took place: "The rabbis retained all the features of the biblical 'taking off of the shoe,' but changed the spirit of it radically. In rabbinic times it was no longer a token of disgrace to the levir for not marrying the widow, such as is the spirit in Deuteronomy; it was the proper thing for the levir to do, in order to free the widow from the zikah bond [the legal situation of a woman after her husband's death and before her marriage to the levir] and thus afford her opportunity to marry the man of her choice." A reversal has taken place, and we have a classic instance of the desexing of a custom.[30]

As we saw in Chapter 1, the institution of marriage itself has been subject to desexing because of the doctrine of the androgynous being in New Testament and patristic sources. Jesus uses the doctrine to support his position that a marriage is indissoluble. There is, however, an added twist to his position. The appeal of the androgynous myth to him and early Christian interpreters is that it enables them to reject marriage as such. With their eschatological beliefs, a major one of which is that the end of time is a return to the ideal order intended at the beginning of time, there is a stage after the unity of the male and the female, namely, union with God. As we saw for Matthew 19:10–12, Jesus gives out the esoteric teaching that being a eunuch is the preferable state to marriage. He is hinting at a mystical union with the Christ figure, just as Paul spells out the preference more explicitly in 1 Corinthians 7 (e.g., v. 32: "He that is unmarried careth for the things that belong unto the Lord, how he may please the Lord. But he that is married careth for the things of the world, how he may please his wife"). Ideally one should have no attachments whatever that detract from mystical union in Christ. In the Gospel according to the Egyptians, Salome, the daughter of Herod, asks Jesus when his kingdom would finally arrive. He replies, "When ye have trampled on the garment of shame [the wedding night cloth such as plays a role in the law of Deut 22:14, 15; see Chap. 4], and when the two become one and the male with the female is neither male nor female."[31] Not only is there a clear reference to the ideal, androgynous being and the disappearance of the distinction between the sexes, but the primary concern is the need to be rid of sexual passion. The view that the passions are the source of so many problems has a long history. Maimonides is a later representative of the position when, in his *Guide to the Perplexed*, he states that "the philosophers have proved that in youth the bodily forces prevent the attainment of most ethical virtues" (bk. 3, chap. 51).

It is not surprising that the examples I cite for the desexing of customs all have to do with the institution of marriage. To be sure, there are examples unconnected with that institution. Among the Roma (Gypsies) it has been traditional for a woman to lift her skirt or toss her shoe by way of cursing an offender. The gesture's genital, shaming element, however, has been downplayed in more recent times, and the woman is likely to end up by having impurity visited upon her instead.[32] The idea that marriage should be thought of as an institution is in some ways odd. Why should the state or religious authorities legislate for marital unions? The unions themselves are fundamentally linked to human physiology, to Eros, which is not easily controlled. Doubtless, it is the control of sexuality by state and church, with a view to controlling other areas of life, that is a major factor.[33] The point might also be made that the imposition of a duty to procreate leads to the control of marriage, one result being that no same-sex marriages would be recognized. To be sure, Paul's condemnation of lesbian and homosexual behavior in Romans 1:26, 27 comes from his notion of what constitutes the "natural." Paul views God as the power behind the "unnatural" sexuality, an attribution indicating that au fond the activity in question is viewed as beyond human (Paul's) comprehension.

In all the above examples the earlier customs focus on sexual activity, and the later developments neutralize the sexual dimension (marital union as understood by Jesus and Paul) or remove all focus from it (circumcision, withdrawal of a shoe [ḥalitsah], and the Manchu custom). The change points to the clash between physiological demand and institutional control. Perhaps in earlier times there was less repression of sexuality, but in later times the interests of state and religion reverse the position, with the phenomenon of desexing coming more into play. Karel Van Der Toorn is of the opinion that "the ancients, including most of the Israelites, were less inimical to the practice of 'free love' than we generally are."[34] In the Talmudic era we find increasing opposition to marriages—fully valid, informal marriages—by intercourse alone.[35]

David Daube has argued that there is a rational reason why sexual intercourse typically takes place in private and why the emotion of shame—shame in the sense of avoidance of notice—originates in such an elemental human activity.[36] Fear is an integral component of shame, and two people, engaged in what gives them the greatest pleasure, are most vulnerable to attack if they expose themselves in public. An onlooker, who is aroused by envy or anger, might seek to appropriate the woman. Daube expanded his observation by pointing out that shame is a universal phenomenon, and civilizations largely differ from one another insofar as shame spreads out from its locus in sexual activity to other, nonsexual areas of life. An illustration was how, in the Freiburg of Daube's youth, it was not proper to be seen eating when walking along a street. Yet the enjoyment of food in public, in a restaurant or a café, is a desirable aim when people wish to socialize. The point was that one would desist from eating in the street for fear of arousing envy among those not having the means to eat much food. Gerald Brenan reports that some eighty years ago in Andalusia shame could attach to eating: "I once knew a family of well-to-do people, of partly gipsy descent, each of whom cooked his own food and ate it a separate table, with his back to the others." Brenan comments: "One must expect such feelings to arise in a country where for many people food is scarce and any sort of eating an act of daring and extravagance. Old women in particular developed the sort of prudery about it that in other countries they develop about sex."[37]

If shame is indeed integrally linked to sexuality—a sixteenth-century quotation in the *Oxford English Dictionary* reads: "the dark-some nyght, sharpe enemye to shame, by candles light, betrayethe many a dame"—and if shame's effect can spread to other areas of life not involving sexuality, then desexing parallels this profound phenomenon.[38] Not surprisingly, desexing shows up in almost every facet of life. The above observations constitute but a small part of a very large topic. The following example well illustrates.

A most interesting way in which desexing plays out and appears in unexpected places is the world of childhood. I noted that, as well as the desexing of the custom of circumcision, the rite entailed a switch from a focus on the beginning of manhood to a focus on the male infant. This instance of a transformation taking us to childhood provides one of many where a matter of great moment is but dimly preserved in the life of children, in customs, games, rhymes, and the like. An example is the maze or labyrinth, which originally carries meaning about the mystery of the passage of life, but ends up in the playground. Nursery rhymes about adult sexuality include the two I cited about the old woman and her shoe and the master and his fiddlestick. A German version of the children's game of tag, in which one child touches another by way of putting the devil into the playmate, preserves the link in many languages between the verb "to sin" and the verb "to be." When one child tags the other, he or she says, "You are" (Du bist), not "You are it" (Du bist es).[39] In ancient versions of the Passover service, the *aphikoman*, the piece of unleavened bread broken off from the larger piece to represent the Messiah and which, when eaten, enables the participant to unite mystically with his redeemer, becomes in later Jewish celebration of the Passover the focus of a children's game of hide-and-seek.[40]

Abbreviations

AB	Anchor Bible
AJCL	*American Journal of Comparative Law*
AJT	*American Journal of Theology*
ANET	*Ancient Near Eastern Texts Relating to the Old Testament*, ed. J. B. Pritchard, 3rd ed. (Princeton, 1969)
AOAT	*Alter Orient und Altes Testament* (Neukirchen-Vluyn, Germany, 1973)
ATD	Das Alte Testament Deutsch
AV	Authorized Version
BCOT	Biblical Commentary on the Old Testament
BDB	F. Brown, S. R. Driver, and C. A. Briggs, *A Hebrew and English Lexicon of the Old Testament* (Oxford, 1906)
BEATAJ	Beiträge zur Erforschung des Alten Testaments und des Antiken Judentums
BLL	*Studies in Comparative Legal History: Collected Works of David Daube,* vol. 3, *Biblical Law and Literature,* ed. Calum Carmichael (Berkeley, 2003)
BO	*Bibliotheca Orientalis*
CB	Century Bible
CBQ	*Catholic Biblical Quarterly*
CBQMS	Catholic Biblical Quarterly Monograph Series
CBSC	Cambridge Bible for Schools and Colleges

CH	Code of Hammurabi
Colum.L.Rev.	*Columbia Law Review*
Cornell L.Rev.	*Cornell Law Review*
ELR	*Edinburgh Law Review*
EOW	*Studies in Comparative Legal History: Collected Works of David Daube*, vol. 4, *Ethics and Other Writings*, ed. Calum Carmichael (Berkeley, 2009)
HJ	*Heythrop Journal*
HL	Hittite Laws
HLR	*Harvard Law Review*
HTR	*Harvard Theological Review*
HUCA	*Hebrew Union College Annual*
IB	Interpreter's Bible
ICC	International Critical Commentary
IDB	*Interpreter's Dictionary of the Bible*, ed. G. A. Buttrick (Nashville, 1962)
JBL	*Journal of Biblical Literature*
JJS	*Journal of Jewish Studies*
JLAS	*Jewish Law Association Studies*
JLR	*Journal of Law and Religion*
JPS	Jewish Publication Society
JPSTC	Jewish Publication Society Torah Commentary
JR	*Juridical Review*
JSB	Jewish Study Bible
JSJ	*Journal for the Study of Judaism*
JSNT	*Journal for the Study of the New Testament*
JSOT	*Journal for the Study of the Old Testament*
JSOTSS	Journal for the Study of the Old Testament Supplement Series
KAT	Kommentar zum Alten Testament
LCL	Loeb Classical Library
LE	Laws of Eshnunna
LQR	*Law Quarterly Review*
LXX	The Septuagint
MT	The Massoretic Text
NCBC	New Century Bible Commentary
NEB	New English Bible
NIV	New International Version
NovTSup	Supplements to Novum Testamentum
NRSV	New Revised Standard Version
NTJ	*Studies in Comparative Legal History: Collected Works of David Daube*, vol. 2, *New Testament Judaism*, ed. Calum Carmichael (Berkeley, 2000)
NTS	*New Testament Studies*
NTSuppl.	New Testament Supplement Series

OTL	Old Testament Library
RIDA	*Revue Internationale des Droits de l'Antiquité*
RJ	*Rechtshistorisches Journal*
RSV	Revised Standard Version
RV	Revised Version
SVT	Supplement *Vetus Testamentum*
TDOT	*Theological Dictionary of the Old Testament*, ed. G. J. Botterweck and H. Ringgren (Grand Rapids, 1980)
U.Chi.L.Rev.	*University of Chicago Law Review*
VT	*Vetus Testamentum*
WBC	Word Bible Commentary
WC	Westminster Commentary
ZAW	*Zeitschrift für die alttestamentliche Wissenschaft*
ZSS	*Zeitschrift der Savigny-Stiftung*

Notes

Introduction

1. Most recently, Richard Davidson, *Flame of Yahweh: Sexuality in the Old Testament* (Peabody, MA, 2007).

2. J. G. A. Pocock, *The Ancient Constitution and the Feudal Law: A Study of English Historical Thought in the Seventeenth Century* (Cambridge, Eng., 1957), 1–29.

3. On language, David Daube, "Word-Formation in Indo-European and Semitic," in *Lex et Romanitas: Essays for Alan Watson,* ed. Michael H. Hoeflich (Berkeley, 2000), 15–18 [*BLL,* 429–431]; on the art of storytelling, Walter Benjamin, *Illuminations: Essays and Reflections* (New York, 1968), 89.

4. Contrast the bewilderingly naive comments of Albert Einstein about the Bible: "A collection of honourable, but still primitive legends which are nevertheless pretty childish. No interpretation no matter how subtle can (for me) change this"; *Guardian,* May 13, 2008, reporting a letter written by Einstein to the philosopher Eric Gutkind on January 3, 1954.

5. John Locke, *Some Thoughts Concerning Education,* par. 189, l. 325.

6. See Douglas Templeton, *The New Testament as True Fiction: Literature, Literary Criticism, Aesthetics* (Sheffield, 1999), 76.

7. *Studies in Comparative Legal History: Collected Works of David Daube,* ed. Calum Carmichael: vol. 1, *Talmudic Law* (Berkeley, 1992) [*TL*]; vol. 2, *New Testament Judaism* (Berkeley, 2000) [*NTJ*]; vol. 3, *Biblical Law and Literature* (Berkeley, 2003) [*BLL*]; vol. 4, *Ethics and Other Writings* (Berkeley, 2009) [*EOW*]. In *Ideas and the Man:*

Remembering David Daube (Frankfurt am Main, 2004), I give an account of Daube's intellectual achievements.

8. Cited by Jacob Haberman in "A Jewish View of the Idea of Progress," *JJS* 35 (1984), 70.

Chapter 1: Procreation

1. Daniel Boyarin brings out well the problems of commenting on historical and social life from biblical and rabbinic texts, *Carnal Israel: Reading Sex in Talmudic Culture* (Berkeley, 1993), 3.

2. See Thomas Brodie, *Genesis as Dialogue: A Literary, Historical and Theological Commentary* (Oxford, 2001), 48.

3. "Both are given the command to be fruitful and multiply," in Davidson's recent study, *Flame of Yahweh,* 39; Meir Malul consistently refers to Gen 1:28 as a commandment, in *Knowledge, Control, and Sex: Studies in Biblical Thought, Culture and Worldview* (Tel Aviv, 2002), 250 n. 65, 467, 479 n. 190; and P. J. Budd, NCBC, *Leviticus* (Grand Rapids, 1996), 218, states: "To be fruitful and multiply is a basic requirement of the priestly creation ordinance." On Gen 1:28 as a blessing, not a duty, see David Daube, *The Duty of Procreation* (Edinburgh, 1977), 1–42; also *Proceedings of the Classical Association* 74 (London, 1977) [*BLL,* 951–969]. Daube further notes that in Gen 1:22, concerning the fish and the fowl ("And God blessed them, saying, Be fruitful, and multiply, and fill the waters in the seas, and let fowl multiply in the earth"), it makes no sense to think of these creatures as under a moral or legal duty to reproduce.

4. See *b. B. Q.* 91b; Augustine, *City of God,* bk. 1, chaps. 16–27.

5. Plato, *Laws* 4.721B, 6.773E f., 776B.

6. Stobaeus, *Anthology* 67.16; Plutarch, *Lysander* 30.5, *Lycurgus* 15.1–2, *Sayings of Spartans, Lycurgus* 14 (Mor. 227F); Plato, *Laws* 4.11.721, 6.17.774.

7. Plato, *Republic* 5.9.460E.; cf. also *Laws* 11.930C.

8. Dio Cassius, *Roman History* 53.13.2, 54.16.1, 55.2.6, 56.10; Ulpian, *Regulae* 13ff.

9. Justin, *Apology for Christians* 1.29; Athenagoras, *Legation on Behalf of Christians* 33; Clement of Alexandria, *Stromata* 2.23.140.1. See the magisterial discussion of John T. Noonan, *Contraception: A History of Its Treatment by the Catholic Theologians and Canonists* (Cambridge, MA, 1965), 30–106.

10. On the difficulties of the task, e.g., the lack of any evidence of problems in the Jewish community in Roman times of a need to increase numbers, see Jeremy Cohen, "*Be Fertile and Increase, Fill the Earth and Master It*": *The Ancient and Medieval Career of a Biblical Text* (Ithaca, 1989).

11. The right to procreate can be taken away by a court. The *San Francisco Chronicle,* July 13, 2001, A10, reports the decision of the Wisconsin Supreme Court to uphold an order to David Oakley, a thirty-four-year-old father of nine who owed $25,000 in child support, to father no more children during a five-year probation period imposed in 1999. He faced eight years in prison should he fail to comply with the order. See Calum Carmichael, *Remembering David Daube,* 35.

12. See *Aristotle: The Nicomachean Ethics,* ed. H. Rackham (Cambridge, MA, 1945), x.

13. See David Daube, *Ancient Jewish Law: Three Inaugural Lectures* (Leiden, 1981), 10 [*NTJ*, 471].

14. Michael Novak, *The Spirit of Democratic Capitalism* (Lanham, MD, 1991), 112.

15. Robert Graves and Raphael Patai, *Hebrew Myths: The Book of Genesis* (London, 1964), 67.

16. In Chap. 3 I draw attention to the discussion of God's gender by a Palestinian *Amora* of the earlier part of the third century, Rabbi Samuel.

17. The prophet Isaiah had spoken of the lifting of the primeval curse laid on Eve: "Before she travailed, she brought forth; before her pain came, she was delivered of a man child. Who hath heard such a thing, who hath seen such things? Shall the earth be made to bring forth in one day or shall a nation be born at once? For as soon as Zion travailed, she brought forth her children" (Isa 66:7, 8).

18. *Against Jovinian* 1.16

19. Gen 9:7, with its repetition of "Be fruitful and multiply," follows the injunction about homicide. One result of the juxtaposition of these two texts was a rhetorical rabbinic view that someone who did not procreate was committing homicide and diminishing the divine image; Boyarin, *Carnal Israel,* 134–135.

Chapter 2: The Marriage at Cana

1. See Peter Kalkavage's discussion in *Plato's Timaeus* (Newburyport, MA, 2001), 33.

2. Quoted by Lord Westbury in Knox v. Gye, LR, E. and I. App. 656, 676, 5 HL (1871).

3. For details of the *imitatio creatio* for all seven days of creation in John's Gospel, see Calum Carmichael, *The Story of Creation: Its Origin and Interpretation in Philo and the Fourth Gospel* (Ithaca, 1996).

4. Speaking about the relationship between Gen 1 and John 1, Ellen J. van Wolde aims "to understand their different modes of cognition." She fails to recognize, however, the Philonic-like allegorical mode of interpreting an ancient text in John's time; "Crossing Border, Speaking about the Beginning in Genesis 1 and John 1," in *Recognising the Margins: Developments in Biblical and Theological Studies,* ed. Werner Jeanrond and Andrew Mayes (Dublin, 2006), 91–111.

5. C. H. Dodd, *The Interpretation of the Fourth Gospel* (Cambridge, Eng., 1965), 297.

6. Ibid., 299.

7. Ibid., 297–300.

8. Daniel Boyarin well demonstrates how fundamental the creation stories in Gen 1–4 were to views on sex, gender, and marriage in Philo, Paul, and Hellenistic and Palestinian Judaism; *Carnal Israel* (Berkeley, 1993).

9. H. Strack and P. Billerbeck, *Kommentar zum Neuen Testament aus Talmud und Midrasch* (Munich, 1924), 2:371; also 1:858.

10. Dodd, *Interpretation,* 83.

11. See Hugo Odeberg, *The Fourth Gospel Interpreted in Its Relation to Contemporaneous Religious Currents in Palestine and the Hellenistic-Oriental World* (Uppsala, 1929), 48–71. He attributes the rabbinic speculation to a time before John.

12. David Winston, *The Wisdom of Solomon,* AB (New York, 1979), 325.

13. In producing the miracle, Jesus gives instructions to the servants at the wedding. For Philo, parts of the universe were made to serve God's purpose in the way in which a slave ministers to a master (*Mos.* 1.202).

14. See C. A. Briggs, *The Book of Psalms,* ICC (Edinburgh, 1907), 2:334.

15. "Creation in 4 Ezra: The Biblical Theme in Support of Theodicy," in *Creation in the Biblical Traditions,* ed. R. J. Clifford and J. J. Collins, CBQMS 24 (Washington, DC, 1992), 133.

16. The author of this section of 2 Esdras was a Palestinian Jew who, as already indicated, wrote around the time of the composition of John's Gospel. For another comparison between a cistern and the sea, note Sir 50:3. Dr Milton Horne, William Jewell College, Missouri, drew my attention to the possible link between the six water pots and the passage in 2 Esdras.

17. R. E. Brown, *The Gospel According to John I–XII,* AB (New York, 1966), 100; B. F. Westcott, *The Gospel According to St. John* (Grand Rapids, 1954), 84.

18. On Cana, see Birger Olsson, *Structure and Meaning in the Fourth Gospel* (Lund, Sweden, 1974), 26; on Heracleon, see E. H. Pagels, *The Johannine Gospel in Gnostic Exegesis: Heracleon's Commentary on John* (Nashville, 1973), 52; on John's place names, see Thomas Brodie, *The Quest for the Origin of John's Gospel* (Oxford, 1993), 161.

19. It would be the spiritual androgynous union that Boyarin attributes to Philo and Gnosticism; *Carnal Israel,* 42 n. 23.

20. See Calum Carmichael, *Women, Law, and the Genesis Traditions* (Edinburgh, 1979), 63.

21. R. Alan Culpepper, *Anatomy of the Fourth Gospel* (Philadelphia, 1983), 110.

22. Strack and Billerbeck, *Kommentar,* 2:401.

23. Culpepper, *Anatomy,* 133, 134.

24. On this aspect of Paul's conversion, see David Daube, *Appeasement or Resistance and Other Essays on New Testament Judaism* (Berkeley, 1987), 67, 68 [*NTJ,* 533].

25. See J. Duncan M. Derrett on the Jewish custom of the time about the provision of wine by guests at a wedding; *Law in the New Testament* (London, 1970), 229–235.

26. See Dodd's comments, *Interpretation,* 135.

27. See C. K. Barrett, *The Gospel According to St. John* (London, 1955), 24, 25. On the difficulty of deciding whether John uses a Hebrew text or the Septuagint, see E. D. Freed, *Old Testament Quotations in the Gospel of John,* NovTSup 11 (Leiden, 1965).

28. See the discussion in R. E. Brown, *The Death of the Messiah* (New York, 1993), 2:1356–1373.

29. Albert Schweitzer, *The Quest of the Historical Jesus,* trans. W. Montgomery (London, 1911), 369.

Chapter 3: A Sexual Encounter

1. See Carmichael, *Story of Creation,* 90–98, for the detailed correspondences between the Baptism of John and the fifth day of the creation.

2. For illuminating comments on female wombs and wellsprings and the reproductive cycle and the creation, see R. W. Whitekettle, "Levitical Thought and the Female Reproductive Cycle: Wombs, Wellsprings, and the Primeval World," *VT* 46 (1996), 383–390.

3. J. Bligh, "Jesus in Samaria," *HJ* 3 (1962), 336, drew attention to this parallel with Jacob's marriage. See also Brodie, *Origin of John's Gospel*, 83.

4. On the role of these women and their sexual intentions, see Karel Van Der Toorn, "Female Prostitution in Payment of Vows in Ancient Israel," *JBL* 108 (1989), 199.

5. See Odeberg, *Fourth Gospel*, 51–68. As I pointed out in "Marriage and the Samaritan Woman," *NTS* 26 (1980), 336, the term *water* in Jesus' request to the Samaritan woman, "Give me to drink," is understood and is consequently one clue that a figurative sense is intended.

6. Joachim Jeremias, *Jerusalem in the Time of Jesus* (Philadelphia, 1967), 356 n. 19.

7. Odeberg, *Fourth Gospel*, 159.

8. Dale Allison, *The New Moses: A Matthean Typology* (Minneapolis, 1993), 146–150.

9. And not "the prophet like Moses" of Deut 18:18, as some commentators think, e. g., W. A. Meeks, *The Prophet-King*, NovTSup 14 (Leiden, 1967), 34, and Brown, *John I-XII*, 171. The woman refers to *a* prophet, not to *the* prophet. In rabbinic sources, it might be noted, Jeremiah was identified with "the prophet like Moses" in Deut 18:18, e. g., *Midrash Tehillim* 1:1.

10. See Barrett, *St. John*, 24, 25.

11. As commentators point out, the success among the Samaritans is the high point in John's account of the life of Jesus; J. Edgar Bruns, "The Use of Time in the Fourth Gospel," *NTS* 13 (1996), 288.

12. Odeberg, *Fourth Gospel*, 169.

13. See Olsson, *Structure and Meaning*, 221. For the personification of a piece of food as the Messiah, the *aphikoman*, "The Coming One," the piece of food eaten on Passover Eve and at the Last Supper, see Robert Eisler, "Das Letzte Abendmahl," *ZAW* 24 (1926), 161–192.

14. Cf.. Rudolf Schnackenburg, *The Gospel According to St John* (New York, 1980), 1:447 and 452: "So long as Jesus is dwelling in this cosmos, he is the only one who works with his Father."

15. For a rabbinic parallel to the notion that one day in the future the earth will be sown and bear fruit in one and the same day, see *Torath Kohanim Behukothai*, M. M. Kasher, *Encyclopedia of Biblical Interpretation* (New York, 1953), 1:42, no. 163.

16. G. F. Moore, *Judaism in the First Centuries of the Christian Era: The Age of the Tannaim* (Cambridge, MA, 1966), 1:366 n. 4.

17. Barrett, *St. John*, 203.

18. See Moore, *Judaism*, 1:369, 453; 2:204, 352, 370–371.

19. See Carmichael, *Story of Creation*, 115–126.

20. See David Daube, "Two Cases of Hypostatizing," *Annales de la Faculté de Droit d'Istanbul*, 4,5 (1955), 24–26 [*TL*, 377–80].

21. See Daube, *Appeasement*, 23–26 [*NTJ*, 54–56].

Chapter 4: Seduction

1. *West-östlicher Diwan, Noten und Abhandlungen: Hebräer*, Goethe's Werke 21 (Stuttgart, 1820).

2. See David Daube, *The New Testament and Rabbinic Judaism* (London, 1956), 32–36; *Appeasement*, 33–38 [*NTJ*, 60, 137–139].

3. E. F. Campbell, *Ruth*, AB (New York, 1975), 64, 65, acknowledges that it is overly coincidental and very tentatively suggests some lost custom, possibly hinted at in Cant. 3:4 and Gen 24:28, whereby a girl who contemplates marriage discussed and planned it first with her mother. Jack M. Sasson, *Ruth: A New Translation with a Philological Commentary and a Formalist-Folklorist Interpretation* (Baltimore, 1979), 23, has no reservations in accepting some such view on the basis that the above two texts indicate it. Neither text, in fact, has to do with a daughter consulting her mother about a marriage.

4. Wilhelm Rudolph, *Das Buch Ruth, Das Hohe Lied, Die Klagelieder*, KAT 17/3 (Gütersloh, 1962), 171–172. Marvin Pope renders Hebrew *šorek* not as "navel" but as cognate with Arabic *sirr*, "secret part, pudenda"; *Song of Songs*, AB (New York, 1977), 617; also BDB, 1057.

5. Noted by D. F. Rauber, "Literary Values in Ruth," *JBL* 89 (1970), 35.

6. On the extensive wordplay in Ruth, see Campbell, *Ruth*, 13, 14.

7. See Rudolph, *Das Buch Ruth*, 48. The synonymous term ʿoz in Ezek 19:11, 12, 14, occurs in a description of Israel's failed potential to become a strong royal line. For the name Onan as meaning "voll Lebenskraft," see Martin Noth, *Die israelitischen Personennamen im Rahmen der gemeinsemitischen Namengebung* (New York, 1980), 225.

8. F. Buhl already made this point; "Some Observations on the Social Institutions of the Israelites," *AJT* 1 (1897), 736.

9. In CH 160 a bride's father who wrongs the bridegroom by failing to deliver his daughter for the consummation of the marriage has to repay double the value of the gifts he received from the girl's suitor. Cf. also LE 25 in Reuven Yaron's discussion, *The Laws of Eshnunna* (Jerusalem, 1969), 33, 127–129.

10. Aside from complicated links that he draws to non-Israelite, Near Eastern legal sources, Bruce Wells' attempt to address the issues in the law founders on his assumption that the law about false accusation in Deut 19:16–21 is a general statement that applies to all cases, including the one about the slandered bride. The law in Deut 19:16–21, in fact, concerns but a single example, that of a man who accuses another of apostasy (*sarah*) and not wrongdoing in general as Wells thinks (44). Hebrew *sarah* never has this general sense but always the sense of defection from God. There is then no clash between the false accusation by the husband in one rule and the false accusation of apostasy in the other, a distinction central to Wells' argument. See "Sex, Lies, and Virginal Rape: The Slandered Bride and False Accusation in Deuteronomy," *JBL* 124 (2005), 41–72.

11. On aspects of the history of the rule in later Jewish law, see Ruth Langer, "*Birkath Betulim:* A Study of the Jewish Celebration of Bridal Virginity," *Proceedings of the American Academy for Jewish Research* 61 (Jerusalem, 1995), 53–94, and Joseph Fleishman, "The Husband's Sin and Punishment in Deuteronomy 22:18–19 in Early Jewish Law," *JLAS* 18 (2008), 70–87.

12. The RSV translation, for example, reads as follows: Hamor "saw her, he seized [*laqah*] her and lay with her ['*innah*] by force." So similarly does the JSB, only it tones down the seizing and has him "taking" her. JSB is correct in toning down the verb *laqah*, "to take." In any sexual encounter, there is a physical taking hold of and it may well be mutual. Potiphar's wife takes hold of (*tapaś*) Joseph's garment with a view to seducing him. It is not a description of the beginnings of a rape. Not alert to the legal significance of the term '*innah*, Yael Shemesh, "Rape Is Rape Is Rape: The Story of Dinah and Shechem (Genesis 34)," *ZAW* 119 (2007), 2–21, insists that psychological considerations have priority in judging the offense. Lyn Bechtel rightly rejects that Dinah is raped: "What If Dinah Is Not Raped? (Genesis 34)," *JSOT* 62 (1994), 23–31.

13. S. R. Driver, *Genesis*, WC (London, 1913), 307–308.

14. On the characteristics of the sayings in Gen 49, see A. H. J. Gunneweg, "Uber den Sitz im Leben der sogenannte Stammessprüche," *ZAW* 76 (1964), 248–255. Herodotus (5.68) records how the anti-Dorian Cleisthenes mocked the Sicyonians, who had been invaded by the Dorians in the ninth to eighth centuries BCE, by replacing heroic names for their tribes with words for pig and ass. His intent was to "destroy the sense of dignity of people who called themselves after their Dorian ancestors"; *Herodotus: The History,* trans. David Greene (Chicago, 1987), 384 n. 34.

15. See I. M. Casanowicz, "Paronomasia in the Old Testament," *JBL* 12 (1893), 107, 114, 139, 155.

16. In claiming that there is no idea present of Gentile ritual impurity when an Israelite marries a Canaanite but only moral-religious objections, Christine Hayes does not pay sufficient attention to the view of Simeon and Levi, the sons of Jacob, which is also the position of Deut (22:10, 7:1–5). These sons do not want an uncircumcised Canaanite, the son of the ass (house of Hamor) to marry an Israelite woman, the daughter of the Ox (house of Jacob). The disappearance of Dinah from the record after her deflowering by Shechem also suggests that she is beyond the pale in terms of ritual, not just moral defilement, which is how Jub 30 views her. Hayes' distinction between ritual and moral defilement is difficult to sustain; "Intermarriage and Impurity in Ancient Jewish Sources," *HTR* 92 (1999), 6, 7, 18.

17. "A unique moralizing judgment, and a late addition, absent in the Ethiopic version and the LXX"; J. A. Montgomery and H. S. Gehman, *The Books of Kings,* ICC (Edinburgh, 1951), 274.

Chapter 5: Contamination

1. J. P. Fokkelman, *Narrative Art and Poetry in the Books of Samuel* (Assen, 1986), 2:245.

2. Major claims about the meaning of a rule are made based upon the subject matter of the surrounding rules. For example, Howard Eilberg-Schwartz claims that sexual intercourse with a menstruant must constitute a heinous offense because the rule is found with rules about incest, adultery, bestiality, and homosexuality; *The Savage in Judaism: An Anthropology of Israelite Religion and Ancient Judaism* (Bloomington, 1990), 183.

3. Jacob Milgrom speaks of the "virulent holinesss" of the Ark in *Leviticus 1–16*, AB (New York, 1991), 638.

4. For details, see Calum Carmichael, *Illuminating Leviticus: A Study of Its Laws and Institutions in the Light of Biblical Narratives* (Baltimore, 2006), 11–26.

5. The term *baśar*, "flesh," can, as here, refer to the male member. Cf. that in English we find an expression "body and person exposed," where the term *person* refers to the private parts. Robert Megarry, *A Second Miscellany at Law: A Further Diversion for Lawyers and Others* (London, 1973), 165. It is a synecdoche where, in this instance, the whole stands for the part.

6. Milgrom, *Leviticus 1–16*, 927, is unaware of the difficulty. Another reason to discount a nocturnal emission is that *škb*, with its basic meaning of "to lie down," which comes through in the expression "an emission of semen" (literally, a lying of seed), is commonly used of sexual congress. That is, sexual relations are perhaps assumed in the reference to the male's emission of seed in Lev 15:16. For the common view that Lev 15:16 concerns a nocturnal emission, see Barry Bandstra and Allen Verhey, "Sex; Sexuality," *International Standard Bible Encyclopedia* (Grand Rapids, 1988), 4:434–435.

7. P. Kyle McCarter, *1 Samuel*, AB (New York, 1980), 343.

8. Robert Alter, *The David Story* (New York, 1999), 134.

9. Moshe Garsiel, *The First Book of Samuel: A Literary Study of Comparative Structures, Analogies and Parallels* (Ramat-Gan, 1989), 130–131. Other telling examples of such links are: S. McDonough, "'And David was old, advanced in years': 2 Samuel xxiv 18–25, 1 Kings i, and Genesis xxiii–xxiv," *VT* 49 (1999), 128–131; Craig Y. S. Ho, "The Stories of the Family Troubles of Judah and David: A Study of Their Literary Links," *VT* 49 (1999), 514–531; Dominic Rudman, "The Patriarchal Narratives in the Books of Samuel," *VT* 54 (2004), 239–249; John Harvey, "*Tendenz* and Textual Criticism in 1 Samuel 2–10," *JSOT* 96 (2001), 71–81.

10. J. D'ror Chankin-Gould (with six others) carelessly refers to the husband's seed of copulation in Lev 15:18; "The Sanctified Adulteress and Her Circumstantial Clause: Bathsheba's Bath and Self-Consecration in 2 Samuel 11," *JSOT* 32 (2008), 345.

11. So Christophe Nihan (and other authors cited by him), *From Priestly Torah to Pentateuch*, Forschungen zum Alten Testament, 2 Reihe, 25 (Tübingen, 2007), 282.

12. Milgrom, *Leviticus 1–16*, 926; Nihan, *Priestly Torah*, 282–283; Daube, *Suddenness and Awe in Scripture* (London, 1964), 18 [*BLL*, 451].

13. Bruce L. Gerig provides one of the better discussions in www.epistle.org, "Saul's Sexual Insult and David's Losing It."

14. Many critics so read it: the "son of Jesse"; e.g., R. W. Klein, *1 Samuel*, WBC 10 (Waco, 1983), 209.

15. At the time of David's problems with Saul, he has his family take refuge with his Moabite relatives (1 Sam 22:1–4). Robert Alter notes that Saul's words to David ("You are more in the right than I") in 1 Sam 24:17 "echo the ones pronounced by Judah, referring to his vindicated daughter-in-law Tamar, who will become the progenitrix of David's line"; *David Story,* 151.

16. Budd, *Leviticus,* 218; Eilberg-Schwartz, *Savage in Judaism,* 186–189; Malul, *Knowledge, Control, and Sex,* 384–394, esp. 390.

17. Milgrom, *Leviticus 1–16,* 947.

18. Nihan, *Priestly Torah,* 310.

19. McCarter, *The HarperCollins Study Bible,* ed. Wayne A. Meeks (London, 1993), 450; Shimon Bar-Efrat, *Jewish Study Bible,* ed. Adele Berlin and Marc Zvi Brettler (Oxford, 1999), 601.

20. See William McKane, *I & II Samuel: Introduction and Commentary* (London, 1963), 129; McCarter, *1 Samuel,* 345.

21. Alan Rodger, "Roman Gifts and Rainwater," *LQR,* 100 (1984), 77–85; see also Dieter Nörr's extended discussion, "Spruchregel und Generalisierung," *ZSS* 89 (1972), 18–93.

22. D'ror Chankin-Gould (with six others) is correct to concentrate on Bathsheba's act of sanctifying herself ("David lay with her while simultaneously she is in a state of self-sanctifying"), but the reason is hardly that the biblical author is intent on legitimizing the future mother of Solomon, especially when the context is her adultery with David; "The Sanctified Adulteress," 339–352.

23. See Chap. 9 for Dale Allison's major contribution to our understanding of the virgin birth story.

24. See Peter Conradi, *Iris: The Life of Iris Murdoch* (New York, 2001), 127.

Chapter 6: Adultery

1. Stefan Heym, *The King David Report* (Evanston, 1973), 158; Malul, *Knowledge, Control, and Sex,* 306–309; E. A. Speiser, "The Wife-Sister Motif in the Patriarchal Narratives," in *Biblical and Other Studies,* ed. Alexander Altmann (Cambridge, MA, 1963), 15–28.

2. See David Daube, "Historical Aspects of Informal Marriage," *RIDA* 25 (1978), 95–107 [*TL,* 153–163].

3. Yet, curiously, that is just the position in the nonstory of Isaac and Rebekah at Abimelech's court in Gen 26. The king looks out a window of the palace and sees Isaac with Rebekah "and, behold, Isaac was sporting with Rebekah his wife" (Gen 26:8).

4. E. P. Thompson, *Customs in Common: Studies in Traditional Popular Culture* (New York, 1993), 408. On Cato, see Plutarch, *Lives: Cato the Younger,* LCL (London, 1919), 25.2ff.; Susan Treggiari, *Roman Marriage* (Oxford, 1991), 145, 470.

5. See Jonathan Magonet, "The Themes of Genesis 2–3," *A Walk in the Garden,* JSOT Suppl. 136, ed. Paul Morris and Deborah Sawyer (Sheffield, 1992), 42–44. In general, prior to the introduction of a written document, divorce was effected by the husband's expelling his wife. See Z. W. Falk, *Hebrew Law in Biblical Times* (Jerusalem, 1964), 154.

6. Herodotus (1.8–10) recounts how Candaules, the ruler of Sardis, had his bodyguard Gyges slipped into his bedroom to view his unsuspecting wife naked. Her nakedness is not shameful in her own bedroom but, as the story makes clear, certainly becomes so with Gyges present. I do not think that the expression in the law automatically includes the notion that the woman contributes by going out of her way to look attractive to a man not her husband.

7. See Ronald Paulson, *Popular and Polite Art in the Age of Hogarth and Fielding* (Notre Dame, IND, 1979), 15; and Thompson's major study, *Customs in Common*, 404–466.

8. For other examples of conduct that appears to be in order but is in fact the product of crooked motive, see David Daube's discussion of purists and pragmatists in later Talmudic law and New Testament literature; "Neglected Nuances of Exposition in Luke-Acts," *Principat* 25 (Berlin, 1985), 2329–2356 [*NTJ*, 857–873].

9. See Treggiari, *Roman Marriage*, 288–290.

10. See John Calvin, *Commentaries on the Last Four Books of Moses Arranged in the Form of a Harmony*, trans. C. W. Bingham (Grand Rapids, 1950), 3:94; also G. P. Hugenberger, *Marriage as Covenant*, SVT 52 (1994), 76–78.

11. What the Roman legal scholar Georg Beseler calls "completomania" and Reuven Yaron *Herzverfettung* ("fatty degeneration"), that later stage in legal development when every contingency is covered; "On Defension Clauses in Some Oriental Deeds of Sale, from Mesopotamia and Egypt," *BO* 15 (1958), 18.

12. I am indebted to Professor Tony Honoré, when Regius Professor of Civil Law, University of Oxford, for raising the issue with me.

13. See David Daube, *Law and Wisdom in the Bible: David Daube's Gifford Lectures*, comp. and ed. Calum Carmichael (West Conshohocken, PA, 2010), 2: chap. 2.

14. It should be clear, however, that I cannot go along with the reading of this law as depicting the historical realities of ancient Hebrew society. Here is a typical treatment of how such a law is understood: "In pre-prophetic times all that a man had to do if his wife 'found no favor in his eyes' was to write her a bill of divorcement and send her out of his house. He might not, however, remarry her." See the entry "Marriages, Law of," *Encyclopedia Americana*, vol. 18 (New York, 1965), 315.

15. *Guardian*, Fri., Jan. 25, 2008, p. 29 of the *International* section.

16. See J. K. Campbell, *Honour, Family, and Patronage: A Study of Institutions and Moral Values in a Greek Mountain Community* (Oxford, 1964), 12.

17. See Calum Carmichael, "The Giving of the Decalogue and the Garden of Eden," BEATAJ, 55 (2008), 21–24; "The Decalogue as Myth," *Jewish Law Association Newsletter* (2008), 7–15.

18. For an analysis of all the rules in the second tablet, see Calum Carmichael, *The Spirit of Biblical Law* (Athens, GA, 1996), 83–104.

19. A. P. Herbert, *Holy Deadlock* (Garden City, 1934).

20. For the following account, I lean heavily on the arguments of David Daube, "Biblical Landmarks in the Struggle for Women's Rights," *JR*, 90 (1978), 177–197 [*NTJ*, 231–247]. He discusses the preceding topics in *The Exodus Pattern in the Bible* (London, 1963) [*BLL*, 101–156] (social laws pertaining to slavery); *Studies in Biblical*

Law (Cambridge, Eng., 1947), 186, 158–160 [*BLL*, 494–495, 474–475] (family curse in Greek saga and keeping the law in order to break it); *New Testament and Rabbinic Judaism,* 71–89 [*NTJ*, 252–66] (prohibition of divorce); *Appeasement,* 19–23 [*NTJ*, 52–56]; "Pauline Contributions to a Pluralistic Culture: Re-Creation and Beyond," in *Jesus and Man's Hope,* ed. D. G. Miller and D. Y. Hadidian (Pittsburgh, 1971), 2:223–245 [*NTJ*, 537–552] (incest; see also Chap. 8).

Chapter 7: The Suspected Adulteress

1. See G. R. Driver and J. C. Miles, *The Babylonian Laws* (Oxford, 1952), 1:283–284.

2. See Baruch Levine, *Numbers 1–20,* AB (New York, 1993), 198, 201. As G. B. Gray points out, the phrase *wenizreʿah zaraʿ* is similar to the one in Lev 12:2, where the meaning is "to bring forth seed" (*hizriʿah*); *Numbers,* ICC (Edinburgh, 1903), 55. Some translations avoid the concrete sense and give the meaning as retaining the capacity to bear children.

3. See Roland de Vaux, *Ancient Israel* (New York, 1961), 1:158. Tikva Frymer-Kensky is correct to point out that what happens to the woman in the biblical law is not an ordeal along the lines that the woman in CH 131, 132, experiences; "The Strange Case of the Suspected Adulteress (Numbers V 11–31)," *VT* 34 (1984), 24. Frymer-Kensky, 25, points to some elements in the law that may reflect Near Eastern background, as does Levine, *Numbers 1–20,* 210–211.

4. See Chap. 8, on incest, for further examples.

5. Milgrom rightly translates Num 5:5 as "feels guilty"; *Leviticus 1–16,* 339, 368. As for the added payment by way of a penalty, we might recall how Abimelech has not only to return Sarah to her husband, Abraham, but also to pay the latter, as her brother, an additional payment (Gen 20:16). Repentance of a wrong requires in many systems of law giving over the ill-gotten gain or its equivalent. In *Hamlet* (act 3, sc. 3, ll. 53–55), the king who murders his predecessor says that he cannot pray because "I am still possessed/Of those effects for which I did the murder/My crown, mine own ambition, and my queen."

6. Gray, *Numbers,* 41. Levine, *Numbers 1–20,* 187, is less clear when he answers his own question: "As long as the original victim was alive, or if deceased had left no heirs, how would the system work?" He explains that the payments would go to a priest. The law, in fact, concentrates on the situation where it is assumed that both the wronged person and any kinspeople of his are dead. When Levine later comments (with an exclamation mark) about there being "no relatives, no heirs at all!" he presumably expresses his surprise about the law's narrow focus (190).

7. See *TDOT,* entry maʿal, 8:460.

8. In Num 5:6, the unique language of the offense, *mikkol-ḥaṭṭot haʾadam,* is probably best understood as "any wrong toward a man, a fellow human" (as in JSB). The reference to *haʾadam* (man and woman) may be influenced by the nature of the promise Judah made to Tamar and hence to Er, namely, that in line with God's original blessing of procreation on the man and the woman in Gen 1:27, 28, increase of seed would be forthcoming. The use of *haʾadam* suggests some universal matter.

9. Levine, *Numbers 1–20,* 190.

10. Ibid., 191.

11. Milgrom thinks that the only link between the preceding law in Num 5:6–10 (betrayal) and Num 5:12–31 (adultery) is the use of the term *ma'al; Numbers,* JPSTC (Philadelphia, 1990), 37.

12. For the rabbis, "the ziqah bond is similar to the marriage bond in that the widow cannot marry outside the family"; L. M. Epstein, *Marriage Laws in the Bible and the Talmud* (Cambridge, MA, 1942), 109. The term *ziqah* means "being chained." As Epstein states, "The widow, on the one hand, is freed from her husband by his death, yet she is chained to him; on the other hand, she is given by Heaven to the levir, yet he has not come into possession of her" (104).

13. Judah can exert full authority over Tamar because his rights or, perhaps from his standpoint at the time, those of his dead son have apparently been violated. See the comments of A. van Selms on the situation; also on the importance of the father-in-law–daughter-in-law relationship in Ugarit, Israel, and Babylonia, in *Marriage and Family Life in Ugaritic Literature* (London, 1954), 36.

14. *Oxford English Dictionary,* 2nd ed. (1989), s.v. "regular." See Jacob Levy, *Neuhebräisches und Chaldäisches Wörterbuch über die Talmudim und Midraschim* (1889), 4:250; Jonathan Katz, *The Invention of Heterosexuality* (New York, 1995), 21, 22.

15. See Levine, *Numbers 1–20,* 203–204.

16. E.g., ibid., 196; Gordon Wenham, *Numbers: An Introduction and Commentary* (Leicester, 1981), 83.

17. Contrary to the view of Jaejoung Joon, who argues that somehow, by some far from obvious cultural transference, the two rules in CH 131 (oath) and CH 132 (water ordeal) have become intertwined to produce one biblical rule and also, most puzzling, caused the single biblical rule to be the antithetical equivalent of the two Babylonian rules; see his "Two Laws in the Sotah Passage (Num. v 11–31)," *VT* 57 (2007), 181–207. In CH 132, the woman is subjected to the ordeal of the river-god if some other member of the community reports suspicious behavior on her part. In Gen 38:24, associates of Judah inform him that Tamar has played the harlot. Presumably, their report is based on the fact that she is carrying a child, that they know she is legally bound to Judah's family, and that they do not think Shelah or Judah has caused her pregnant condition because she has been staying at her father's home (Gen 38:11).

18. Frymer-Kensky, "Strange Case," 25; Milgrom, *Numbers,* 348.

19. Hayes, "The Midrashic Career of the Confession of Judah (Genesis xxxviii 26)," pt. 1, *VT* 45 (1995), 77, 78; pt. 2, *VT* 45 (1995), 184, 186. On Tamar and the treatment of the suspected adulteress, see pt. 1, 71.

20. Gen 38 describes Tamar as both an ordinary harlot and a sacred one. Ordinary and sacred prostitution is also the subject of Hos 4:12–14, a text that the rabbis were later to claim voided the bitter water test. As I indicated in the previous chapter, they understood Num 5:31 to mean that the man could proceed against his wife only if he himself were free from licentiousness in deed and intent (*Siphre* on Num 5:31; *y. Sot.* 24a; *b. Sot.* 47b). In support they quoted Hos 4:14, in which the prophet claims that

there will be no divine punishment for unfaithful wives because their husbands forsake Yahweh for heathen sacred prostitutes. In Hosea, a "spirit of harlotry" (*ruaḥ zenunim*) has caused the nation, Yahweh's wife, to err. It would be appropriate to say that, in response, a "spirit of jealousy" (*ruaḥ qinʾah*) comes upon the husband Yahweh. The latter is jealous if the Israelites worship other gods (Exod 20:5, 34:14), an activity thought of as adultery. In the law in Num 5:14, a "spirit of jealousy" drives the husband to bring his wife before the priest.

21. Levine, *Numbers 1–20*, 215; Gray, *Numbers*, 60; A. R. Radcliffe-Brown, *Structure and Function in Primitive Society* (New York, 1965), 50.

22. On gender, Levine, *Numbers 1–20*, 187, 218, and Van Der Toorn, "Female Prostitution," 196; on grape products, Timothy Ashley, *The Book of Numbers*, NICOT (Grand Rapids, 1993), 142; on uncleanness, Milgrom, *Numbers*, 46, 304 n. 18.

23. I am skeptical about Van Der Toorn's suggestion that we should not think of a particular office of cultic prostitution in either Canaan or Israel, which was associated with religious sanctuaries, but of women who resorted to prostitution in order to pay sacred vows that they had made to a sanctuary without their husbands' knowledge; "Female Prostitution," 201–205.

24. "*Post vinum Venus*," attributed to Christopher Guise; Douglas Bush, *English Literature in the Earlier Seventeenth Century, 1600–1660*, 2nd ed. (Oxford, 1962), 17.

25. For the role of wordplays in Gen 49, see Gunneweg, "Stammessprüche"; see also Chap. 4, on seduction.

26. See *Apocrypha and Pseudepigrapha of the Old Testament*, ed. R. H. Charles (Oxford, 1913), 2:319. For an analysis of this interpretation in the Testament of Judah, see Hayes, "Midrashic Career," 68.

27. On Hos 3:1, C. F. Keil and F. Delitzsch, *Numbers*, BCOT (Grand Rapids, 1951), 4:35. Pope has an extensive discussion of the erotic associations of the "raisin cakes" (*ʾašišot*) of Hos 3:1 and Cant 2:5 and views them as aphrodisiacs for both sexes. He notes that the "custom of baking cakes in the shape of the genitalia was widespread in antiquity"; *Song of Songs*, 379.

28. Milgrom, *Numbers*, 356; Levine, *Numbers 1–20*, 221. Other commentators also suggest that the term for the priestly crown or diadem, *nezer*, "consecration," is used of the Nazirite's uncut hair (Lev 8:9; 21:12); see Wenham, *Numbers*, 86, and Ashley, *Book of Numbers*, 143. Like *nezer* as a synecdoche for the Nazirite, so *šaʿatnez* (a garment made solely of linen, not from a mixture of two materials, as is commonly assumed) is a synecdoche for a prostitute in the rule about forbidden mixtures in Deut 22:11, and Tamar is again the focus. See Calum Carmichael, "Forbidden Mixtures," *VT* 32 (1982), 406–411.

29. Keil and Delitzsch, *Numbers*, 4:36.

30. Milgrom thinks that the only link between the two laws is the role of the priest in each and possibly the shared use of the term *paraʿ*, "let loose" (the hair); *Numbers*, 43.

31. Levine, *Numbers 1–20*, 221.

32. Gray, *Numbers*, 69; Levine, *Numbers 1–20*, 229.

33. So Levine, *Numbers 1–20*, 222.

34. Gray, *Numbers*, 67.

35. A. H. McNeile, *Book of Numbers,* CBSC (Cambridge, Eng., 1911), 36. Cf. Gray, *Numbers,* 71.

Chapter 8: Incest

1. See Keith Hopkins's major study, "Brother-Sister Marriage in Roman Egypt," *Society for Comparative Study of Society and History* 22 (1980), 303–354.
2. Discussed by David Daube in *Ancient Jewish Law: Three Inaugural Lectures* (Leiden, 1981), 14–18 [*NTJ,* 474–477].
3. Even more so than the headline in the London *Times,* July 1984: "Man's wish to marry his ex-mother-in-law to be considered by Parliament." See Sybil Wolfram, *In-Laws and Outlaws: Kinship and Marriage in England* (New York: 1987), 42, and her discussion of the increasing tendency to permit marriage between affines.
4. For illuminating remarks about scholars' avoidance of the topic of new birth in regard to the Jewish law of conversion, see Daube, *Appeasement,* 64 [*NTJ,* 531].
5. Montesquieu, *My Thoughts,* trans. Henry C. Clark (Indianapolis, 2007), no. 205; Fariborz Nozari, *The 1987 Swedish Marriage Code* (Washington, DC, 1989), 11–13.
6. L. B. Jorde, "Inbreeding in Human Populations," *Encyclopedia of Human Biology* (San Diego, 1992), 4:431–441.
7. See R. D. Jamieson, *Three Lectures on Chinese Folklore* (Peiping, 1932), 75.
8. In regard to the incest laws, the titles of studies reveal this bias: e.g., S. F. Bigger, "The Family Laws of Leviticus 18 in Their Setting," *JBL* 98 (1979), 196; in his commentary *Leviticus,* WBC (Dallas, 1992), 280, J. E. Hartley has the heading "Laws Governing the Extended Family"; Baruch Levine has an excursus, "Family Structures in Biblical Israel," in his commentary *Leviticus,* JPSTC (Philadelphia, 1989), 253–255.
9. Wolfram, *In-Laws and Outlaws,* 161, 162, 168–169.
10. See David Daube, "The Self-Understood in Legal History," *JR* 85 (1973), 126–134; *Ancient Jewish Law,* 123–129 [*NTJ,* 225–229]; "The Contrariness of Speech and Polytheism," *JLR,* 11 (1995), 1601–1605 [*EOW,* 3–25].
11. James Twitchell, *Forbidden Partners: The Incest Taboo in Modern Culture* (New York, 1987), 26–32.
12. In the Hittite Laws (HL 189) both a son (with a mother, cf. CH 157) and a father (with a daughter, cf. HL 189, a father with a son) are targeted.
13. See "Marriage," IDB Suppl. (Nashville, 1976), 574; also Levine, *Leviticus,* 253.
14. See Clark's contribution "Law," in *Old Testament Form Criticism,* ed. J. H. Hayes (San Antonio, 1974), 128. All lists of rules about incest have something of this character. The philosopher John Locke expresses the matter as follows: "To know whether his idea of adultery or incest be right will a man seek it anywhere among things existing? Or is it true because anyone has been witness to such an action? No; but it suffices here that men have put together such a collection into one complex idea that makes the archetype and specific idea, whether ever any such action were committed in *rerum natura* or no"; in "Names of Mixed Modes and Relations," *An Essay Concerning Human Understanding,* ed. A. C. Fraser (Oxford, 1894), 2:44.

15. For those who think the incident between Ham and Noah involved a homosexual act, see the opposing views of Anthony Phillips, "Uncovering the Father's Skirt," *VT* 30 (1980), 39, 40, and of Davidson, *Sexuality in the Old Testament,* 142–145. Those who see physical sex involved speculate, wrongly, I think, that because the act was so abhorrent the biblical author did not spell it out. My view is that a lawgiver found the narrative suggestive of the topic of sexual encroachment on a father. See the comments of S. D. Kunin, *The Logic of Incest: A Structuralist Analysis of Hebrew Mythology* (Sheffield, 1995), 173–175.

16. See Stanley Brandes, *Metaphors of Masculinity: Sex and Status in Andalusian Folklore* (Philadelphia, 1980), 99.

17. E.g., S. F. Bigger, "Family Laws," 196.

18. Phillips, "Uncovering the Father's Skirt," 39, 40.

19. On the role of hypothetical constructions in legal culture ancient and modern, see, for ancient Near Eastern codes, F. R. Kraus, "Ein zentrales Problem des altmesopotamischen Rechts: Was ist der Codex Hammurabi," *Geneva* 8 (1960), 283–296; for Roman Law, H. F. Jolowitz, *Historical Introduction to Roman Law* (Cambridge, Eng., 1952), 93, 95. For contemporary America, there is the role of the Restatements of the Law by the American Law Institute. Judges typically treat its formulations with respect, and some even regard them as the "law." See R. S. Summers, "The General Duty of Good Faith—Its Recognition and Conceptualization," *Cornell L.Rev,* 67 (1982), 810–840.

20. August Dillmann, *Die Genesis* (Leipzig, 1892), 227.

21. Deborah Ellens supports Susan Rattray's translation of *moledet* in Lev 18:9 and 11 to mean "family" or "kindred," not "begotten." The result is to forbid three kinds of women to the man in Lev 18:9: a half-sister born of the man's father and a stepmother and two other half sisters, one born of his mother and a male relative of his father and one born not of a male relative of his father. Lev 18:11, in turn, forbids to the man a woman born of the father's wife and his relative, that is, a stepsister and not a half-sister. The interpretation is prompted by unwillingness to accept duplicate rules; yet such duplication is a common enough feature in biblical material and in Lev 18 and 20 specifically. The interpretation of *moledet* appeals to a less usual meaning of a Hebrew word. Context, however, is crucial to determine a word's meaning, not its semantic range. See Deborah Ellens, *Women in the Sex Texts of Leviticus and Deuteronomy* (New York, 2008), 88–91.

22. If S. A. Naber's emendation of "sister" into "niece" is correct, Plutarch cites a prohibition in Roman Law for marriage with a niece (but not, I repeat, between a man and his grandniece). See F. C. Babbitt, *Plutarch's Moralia,* LCL, 4 (Cambridge, MA, 1936), 16 n. 2.

23. S. D. Kunin states that the rule is about incest, because a man who marries one sister automatically creates a kin relationship with the other; *Logic of Incest,* 265 n. 2. If this were the case, however, there would have been no need for the lawgiver to bring up the issue of rivalry as the ground of the prohibition. Kunin's view seems to come from the history of the interpretation of the Levitical incest rules in English Law (see next note). The term ʿalehah, "upon her," in the sense of beside the other sister as a wife,

occurs also in Gen 28:9 (Esau's acquiring other wives) and Gen 31:50 (Jacob's acquiring wives in addition to Leah and Rachel).

24. I do not accept the view of Angelo Tosato that the two-sisters rule has been properly interpreted by the Dead Sea community; "The Law of Leviticus 18:18: A Reexamination," *CBQ* 46 (1984), 199–214. CD 4:20–21 paraphrases the rule as a prohibition of bigamy, not as prohibiting marriages to two sisters while both are alive. English Law also reads the rule as prohibiting polygamy, but this understanding derives from the Parity of Reason interpretation of Lev 18 on which English Law came to be based. I agree with Tosato that we should not introduce the notion of incest into this rule—a major part of his argument—but his interpretation that the rule is a general prohibition of bigamy still does not follow. He finds himself in considerable difficulty when he argues against the usual view that the rule is about two sisters. Thus he comments (212): "One cannot forget that Jacob-Israel had at the same time two sisters as wives. . . . It is hard to believe that such personages were made into breakers of the Law on account of incest, with the counterproductive consequence for these 'sons of Israel' of portraying themselves as a people irremediably unclean (just the opposite of the holiness sought!)." Not incest, to be sure, but on other grounds the lawgiver condemns marriages comparable to Jacob's marriages. One wonders what Tosato would have to say about Abraham's marriage to Sarah in light of the Leviticus prohibition against that incestuous union, and also about Moses' rule in Lev 18:12, 13, legislating against the union his parents contracted.

25. For a detailed analysis of the above rules and narratives, see Calum Carmichael, *Law, Legend, and Incest in the Bible: Leviticus 18–20* (Ithaca, 1997), 45–61. J. E. Millar sees the key to the Lev 18:19–23 non-incest laws in terms of wrongful placement of semen (in menstrual fluid, in a woman married to another man, offspring as seed to Molech, in another producer of semen, homosexuality, in an animal, or in a woman from an animal). Aside from the problem with the Molech rule, his solution does not work for Lev 18:18 (marriage to two sisters); "Notes on Leviticus 18," *ZAW* 112 (2000), 401–403.

26. Harry Hoffner points out how sparse, for example, is the evidence for bestiality and homosexuality (prohibited in Lev 18:22, 23; 20:13, 15, 16) in Syro-Palestine and Mesopotamia: "Incest, Sodomy, and Bestiality in the Ancient Near East," in *Orient and Occident, AOAT* 22 (Neukirchen-Vluyn, Germany, 1973), 82.

27. Cited by R. N. Frye, "Zoroastrian Incest," *Orientalia Josephi Tucci memoriae dicata,* ed. G. Gnoli and L. Lanciotti (Rome, 1985), 448. I am indebted to my friend Ian Smith, Professor of Infectious Diseases, University of Iowa Medical School, for information on the history of syphilis.

28. In his *Logic of Incest,* 92, 266, S. D. Kunin argues that a mythological, but stresses only a mythological, analysis of the Genesis narratives suggests that in some of the instances of incest there is positive assessment in order to resolve some of the fundamental issues that the redactors of the material confronted.

29. See David Daube, "Neglected Nuances of Exposition in Luke-Acts," 2329–2356 [*NTJ*, 857–873].

30. A. Tosatu forgets this fact; hence his difficulty when he states, "It is hard to believe that such personages [the patriarchs] were made into breakers of the Law"; "Law of Leviticus 18:18," 212.

31. Without realizing just how important is the connection, commentators have long drawn attention to the notices about the iniquity of these cultures in Genesis (13:13; 18:20ff.; 19:1ff.; 20:11) and the similar ones in Lev 18:24–28; 20:22–24. See Dillmann, *Die Genesis*, 251; also M. A. Fishbane, *Biblical Interpretation in Ancient Israel* (Oxford, 1985), 420, who states that while Abraham on divine authority would inherit the land defiled by the Amorites (Gen 15:7, 16), Abraham's descendants would forfeit it if they defiled it with those sins decried by Ezekiel. Fishbane then cites Ezek 33:25, 26, and Lev 18:20, 26–30.

32. See Moore, *Judaism in the First Centuries*, 2:115, 116.

Chapter 9: Desexing

1. J. A. Sanders, *The Dead Sea Psalms Scroll* (Ithaca, 1967), 113–117.
2. See *Aprocrypha and Pseudepigrapha*, ed. Charles, 29.
3. Eric Blackall, "Don Juan and Faust," *Seminar* 14 (1978), 71–83. Daniel Boyarin speaks of how the celibate Rabbi ben Azzai's erotic desire went into the study of the Torah. Boyarin entitles the chapter in which he discusses the topic "Lusting after Learning: The Torah as 'the Other Woman,'" *Carnal Israel*, 135.
4. I use the participial "desexing" because the topic is not sufficiently recognized to warrant conceptualization as an action noun, "desexualization." In recent times desexing for good or ill has been an important issue in feminist circles, and not just in regard to the use of language. On language, see Robert Baker, "'Pricks' and 'Chicks': A Plea for 'Persons,'" in *Racism and Sexism: An Integrated Study*, ed. Paula S. Rothenberg (New York, 1988), 280–295. Singling out the publications of the philosopher John Rawls, Carole Pateman argues that liberal social-contract theorists work with abstract, desexed players to the detriment of the position of women in society; *The Sexual Contract* (Stanford, 1988), 41–43. See also Linda Hirshman, "Is the Original Position Inherently Male-Superior?" *Colum.L.Rev.* 94 (1994), 1860–1881. Although these feminist critics use the term "desexed," their focus is really on gender, not on sexuality as such.
5. See Calum Carmichael, *The Spirit of Biblical Law* (Athens, GA, 1996), 99.
6. *The Complete Poetry of Robert Herrick*, ed. J. Max Patrick (New York, 1963), 41; Montesquieu, *Thoughts*, no. 499.
7. In the comparable but much more dramatic Egyptian Tale of Two Brothers, the Egyptian hero Bata cuts off his phallus to declare his virtue in the face of the false accusation of his brother's wife that he had tried to seduce her. See *ANET*, 15, 16.
8. See my analysis in *Law and Narrative in the Bible* (Ithaca, 1985), 206–210.
9. See the entry "Song of Songs," in *Encyclopaedia Judaica* (Jerusalem, 1972), 15:146–147.
10. See Pope, *Song of Songs*, 17.
11. On the more common phenomenon whereby bawdy folktales for adults are transformed into sanitized versions suitable for children, see Maria Tatar's major study, *Off with Their Heads: Fairytales and the Culture of Childhood* (Princeton, 1992).
12. The late Professor Walter Weyrauch, College of Law, University of Florida, Gainesville, who kindly read this chapter, drew my attention to these examples.

13. See Van Selms, *Marriage and Family Life*, 45–48.

14. See BDB, 993. On euphemisms in biblical and later Jewish writings, see the entry "Euphemism and Dysphemism," in *Encyclopaedia Judaica*, 6:961.

15. See David Daube, "Perchance to Dream," *ELR* 3 (1999), 191–201 [*BLL,* 459–468], with my added note about the use or nonuse of "to sleep with" in other languages. Increasingly, and misleadingly, the verb "to sleep with" in the sense of intercourse is being introduced into modern translations of the Bible, e.g., *The New Oxford Annotated Bible,* 3rd ed. (Oxford, 2001), in Num 31:17, 18, for instance. On delicacy of presentation in regard to female sexuality (Leah, Bathsheba, and Mary), see Daube, *Appeasement,* 33–38 [*NTJ,* 84–86].

16. See Carmichael, *Illuminating Leviticus,* 82–85; E. L. Greenstein, "Removing the Women Who Served at the Entrance," *Studies in Historical Geography and Biblical Historiography,* ed. G. Galil and M. Weinfeld (Leiden, 2000), 170; Harvey, "Tendenz and Textual Criticism," 72–73; Matthew Goff, "Hellish Females: The Strange Woman of Septuagint Proverbs and 4QWiles of the Wicked Woman (4Q184)," *JSJ* 39 (2008), 20–45.

17. See J. J. Winkler, *The Constraints of Desire: The Anthropology of Sex and Gender in Ancient Greece* (London: 1990), 33–41. On Socrates, see *Phaedo* 64d in *Plato: Five Dialogues,* trans. G. M. A. Grube and rev. John M. Cooper (Indianapolis, 2002), 101.

18. François Rabelais correctly understands the rule; *Gargantua and Pantagruel,* bk. 3, chap. 6. See *Works of Rabelais,* trans. Sir Thomas Urquhart and Peter Motteux (London, 1927), 1:462.

19. See Shahla Haeri, *The Law of Desire: Temporary Marriage in Shi'i Iran* (Syracuse, NY, 1989). While noting (19) that there is a structural parallelism between prostitution and *muta* (marriage of pleasure), Haeri also observes (x) that it is a complex and dynamic institution: "The ambiguities inherent in this form of marriage have sustained it through its long history and allowed it to be intimately interconnected with other aspects of social life."

20. See Albert Jacobs and Julius Goebel, *Cases and Other Materials on Domestic Relations,* 4th ed. (Brooklyn, 1961), 80–81.

21. See Daube, *New Testament and Rabbinic Judaism,* 5–9 [*NTJ,* 583–588].

22. Dale Allison, *The New Moses: A Matthean Typology* (Minneapolis, 1993), 146–151.

23. See J. I. Durham, *Exodus,* WBC (Waco, 1987), 56–59.

24. See Carmichael, *Law and Narrative,* 226–228. On the association of circumcision with fertility and descent, see Eilberg-Schwartz, *Savage in Judaism,* 141ff.; Malul, *Knowledge, Control, and Sex,* 394–395.

25. A. D. H. Mayes, *Deuteronomy,* NCBC (Grand Rapids, 1979), 329.

26. Compare in the promise to Amenophis III: "You will be king of Egypt and ruler of the desert. All lands are under your surveillance, the boundaries lie united under your sandals"; W. Helck, *Urkunden der 18. Dynastie* (Berlin, 1961), cited by Claus Westermann, trans. J. J. Scullion, *Genesis 1–11* (Minneapolis, 1986), 159.

27. See Geneva Smitherman, *Black Talk: Words and Phrases from the Hood to the Amen Corner* (New York, 1994), 151. Her explanation that the meaning is possibly from taking (*knockin*) off one's lover's boots before engaging in sex is, I think, wrong.

28. On the Bedouin, see W. Robertson Smith, *Kinship and Marriage in Early Arabia* (Cambridge, Eng., 1903), 105; G. W. Freytag, *Lexicon arabico-latinum* (Halle, 1837), lists "coniunx viri" (wife of the husband) as one of the meanings of *naʿal*, "shoe." The Ethiopic word for the wife of the levirate seems to be derived from the word for a shoe; *Lexicon Linguae Aethiopicae* (repr., New York, 1955), col. 676. See my comments in "A Ceremonial Crux: Removing a Man's Sandal as a Female Gesture of Contempt," *JBL* 96 (1977), 330 n. 29. On the Manchus, see Jamieson, *Three Lectures*, 75, and S. M. Shirokogoroff, *Social Organization of the Manchus* (Shanghai, 1924), 111 n. 3. On Cinderella, see Bruno Bettelheim, *The Uses of Enchantment: The Meaning and Importance of Fairy Tales* (New York, 1976), 264–277. A Yorkshire version of the Cock-a-doodle-doo rhyme (see the *Oxford Dictionary of Nursery Rhymes,* I. and P. Opie [Oxford, 1952], 128–129) reveals similar sexual meaning (not brought out by the Opies): "Cock-a-doodle-doo, My dad's gone to ploo, Mummy's lost her pudding-poke, And knows not what to do." "To plough" has the sense of penetrating a woman, "pudding" is a penis, and "to poke" also signifies sexual intercourse.

29. See H. S. Horovitz and Louis Finkelstein, *Sifre on Deuteronomy* (New York, 1969), par. 291, 310 (in Hebrew).

30. See Epstein, *Marriage Laws,* 122. A comparable reversal seems also to be found in the history of Chinese marriage. Nowadays (in Cantonese custom) it is the groom who gives shoes to his future wife's younger brothers. I am not competent to probe the complex issues in the development of the Manchu custom. In a letter on file with me, Dr Liz Ngan, of Baylor University, suggests that the Manchurians who ruled China and who imposed their own customs and fashions may have imported the particular custom in question. If so, one question is why a version of it has persisted in a southern province such as Canton. In any event, the sexual symbolism has again, as in the Hebrew example, been rendered unintelligible. A comparable development of a custom losing its original import comes from the Finnish Roma (Gypsies). In other Roma societies women cannot be physically above men because a woman's genital area, which is unclean, should not come near a man's upper body, which is clean. Among the Finnish Roma the prohibition has extended to younger men in relation to older men (as well as younger women in relation to older women). The more comprehensive prohibition owes much to the extreme denial of sexuality among the Finnish Roma. See Martti Grönfors, "Institutional Non-Marriage in the Finnish Roma Community and Its Relationship to Rom Traditional Law," *AJCL* 45 (1997), 313 n. 18.

31. See M. R. James, *Apocryphal New Testament* (Oxford: 1966), 11.

32. See Calum Carmichael, "Gypsy Law and Jewish Law," *AJCL* 45 (1997), 288.

33. For an analysis of the problems of social control and the regulation of sexuality in ancient Greek society, see David Cohen, *Law, Sexuality, and Society: The Enforcement of Morals in Classical Athens* (Cambridge, Eng., 1991).

34. Van Der Toorn, "Female Prostitution," 205.

35. See David Daube, "Historical Aspects of Informal Marriage," 95–107 [*TL,* 154–56]; also Walter Weyrauch, "Informal Marriage and Formal Marriage: An Appraisal of Trends in Family Organization," *U.Chi.L.Rev.* 28 (1960), 88–110. See also Chap. 7 on the increasing trend to emphasize marriages as sacramental. Last century, the transition

from tzardom to the Soviet Republic provides an example, albeit short-lived, of the opposite phenomenon, namely, a move away from the institutionalization of marriage. The Bolsheviks annulled church regulations and introduced civic offices for voluntary registration. See Nicholas Timasheff, *The Great Retreat: The Growth and Decline of Communism in Russia* (New York, 1946), for the classic statement of the Bolsheviks' original revolutionary enthusiasm in social legislation and their gradual retreat from it in the 1930s.

36. See his "The Culture of Deuteronomy," *Orita* 3 (1969), 40 n. 5 [*BLL*, 1005 n. 64]; also *The Jottings of David Daube: Reflections from the Twentieth Century by One of Its Foremost Legal Minds,* ed. Calum Carmichael (New York, 2008), 1–2.

37. Gerald Brenan, *South from Granada* (London, 1957), 158.

38. *Oxford English Dictionary,* 2nd ed. (1989), s.v. "shame."

39. How interesting that children playfully and generously incorporate Satan into their world. In a pantomime some years ago in Liverpool, England, the Devil, having done his business, disappeared. When the obligatory puff of smoke cleared, he was seen stuck halfway down the shoot at the side of the stage and a child shouted out, "Hooray! Hell's full oop."

40. For the maze, see W. H. Matthews, *Mazes and Labyrinths: Their History and Development* (New York, 1970); for the aphikoman, see D. B. Carmichael, "David Daube on the Eucharist and the Passover Seder," *JSNT* 42 (1991), 45–67; on Latin *sons* ("guilty") and *insons* ("innocent") as originally the present participle of the verb "to be," see Calvert Watkins, "Latin *sons,*" in *Studies in Historical Linguistics in Honor of George Sherman Lane,* ed. Walter Arndt (Chapel Hill, 1967), 186–194; for the preservation of the original significance of the verb "to be" in the children's game of tag, see David Daube, "*Pecco Ergo Sum,*" *RJ* 4 (1985), 137–139.

Index of References

Biblical Sources

Genesis
1, *12, 14, 16, 19, 28, 42, 183*
1–4, *183*
1–11, *x*
1:1–5, *14*
1:3, *14*
1:6–8, *18*
1:9–13, *15, 18*
1:11–13, *19*
1:12, *20*
1:14, 15, *14*
1:22, *182*
1:24–31, *29*
1:26, *40*
1:26–28, *30*
1:26–31, *29*
1:27, *7, 8, 29, 32, 191*
1:28, *1, 2, 7–9, 35, 100, 182, 191*
1:29, *38, 39*
1:30, *38*
2–4, *110*
2:23, 24, *102*
3:3, *100*
3:7, *158, 159*
3:10, 11 *159*
4:1, *100, 102*
4:6, 7 *101*
4:17, *102*
5:1–2, *10*
6:9, *156*
9:5, *3*
9:6, *10*
9:7, *183*
9:20–27, *143*
9:22, *90*
11:27, *149*
11:29, *137, 148, 149*
11:31, *148*
12, *85, 87, 94, 98, 99*
12:10, *97*
12:10–20, *147*
12:11, *85*
12:13, *147, 148*
12:19, *86*
13:13, *197*
15:7, 16, *197*
17:25, *166*
18, *154*
18:10, *97*
18:10–15, *149*
18:12, *98, 163*
18:18, 19, *167*
18:20ff., *197*
19, *155*
19:1ff., *197*
19:29, *149*
19:30–38, *47, 49, 137, 144*
19:31, *149*
20, *85–88, 94, 98, 99, 154*
20:1, *97*

201

Genesis (continued)
20:2, 163
20:3, 87, 93, 99
20:9, 10, 94
20:11, 197
20:12, 137, 147, 148
20:16, 191
21, 154
21:2, 163
21:4, 166
22, 154
22:17, 154
24:3, 156
24:28, 186
26, 94, 189
26:6-11, 147
26:8, 189
28:9, 196
29, 53, 59, 72, 99, 137
29:7, 30
29:21-23, 112
29:25, 26, 53
30:14-16, 91
30:14-18, 152
30:25-43, 138
31, 67
31:30, 34, 132
31:32-35, 78
31:34, 79
31:50, 196
33:19, 60
34, 57, 59, 60, 61, 62, 155, 156, 167
34:2, 57
34:3, 58
34:5, 61
34:12, 58, 59
34:14-24, 166
34:30, 59, 60, 61, 155
34:31, 57, 58, 60
35, 67
35:16-20, 78
35:22, 145
38, 51, 64, 67, 72, 74, 82, 109-12, 115, 117, 119, 120, 122, 124, 127, 130, 150, 167, 171, 192
38:2, 115
38:6, 151
38:7, 10, 115
38:11, 47, 114, 192
38:15, 125, 128
38:16, 122
38:18, 137
38:21, 125, 127
38:22, 125
38:24, 192
38:25, 122
38:26, 108, 113, 115, 119, 122, 164
38:29, 67, 134
39, 160
42:9, 90
45:11, 52
49, 61, 187, 193
49:4, 145, 146
49:5-7, 60
49:6, 61, 155
49:12, 126, 127
Genesis–2 Kings, x–xi, 1, 56, 57, 70, 72, 91, 99, 100, 102, 110, 134, 137, 142

Exodus
2:25, 162, 164-66
4:24-26, 166
4:25, 170
6:20, 33, 137
19:12, 13, 15, 100
20:5, 193
20:13, 3
20:14, 99
22:7-13, 114
22:16, 17, 56
23:9, 110
34:14, 193
34:16, 45

Leviticus
6:1-7 [5:20-26], 113, 114
8:9, 193
11, 68
11-15, 68
12, 65, 68
12-14, 82
12-15, 68
12:2, 191
12:3, 166
13, 65, 68
14, 65, 68
15, 65-69, 74, 82
15:2-13, 71
15:2-15, 69, 70, 82
15:4, 6, 12, 72
15:16, 69, 72, 73, 188
15:16-18, 72-74, 76
15:16ff., 73
15:17, 72, 73, 74
15:18, 73, 76, 188
15:19, 20, 77, 79
15:19-24, 72
15:19-30, 78
15:22, 23, 72
15:24, 65
15:25-30, 80
15:26, 72
15:31, 67, 83
15:32, 33, 76
16:29, 31, 165
18, 137, 140, 142, 153, 155, 195, 196
18-20, 143
18:1-3, 135, 155
18:3, 126
18:6, 143
18:6-18, 138, 152
18:7, 143, 145, 150
18:7-17, 153
18:8, 145
18:9, 195
18:9-11, 147
18:10, 150
18:11, 195

18:12, 13, 33, *196*
18:14, *145*
18:15, *115*, *119*, *125*, *150*
18:16, *119*, *151*
18:18, *152*, *196*
18:19-23, *153*, *196*
18:20, *197*
18:22, 23, *196*
18:24-28, *197*
18:24-30, *155*
18:26-30, *197*
19:16, *10*
20, *137*, *140*, *142*, *195*
20:11, *145*
20:12, *119*, *125*
20:13, 15, 16, *196*
20:21, *119*
20:22-24, *197*
21:12, *193*
22:13, 47
23:27, 32, *165*

Numbers
2-4, *110*
3:12, 13, *110*
5, *109*, *121*, *122*
5:1-4, *111*
5:2, *111*
5:5, *191*
5:5-10, *111*, *113*
5:6, *191*
5:6-10, *113*, *115*, *192*
5:11-31, *111*
5:12, *119*, *122*
5:12-31, *117*, *192*
5:13, *122*
5:14, *193*
5:18, *129*
5:19, 20, *122*
5:28, *109*, *122*
5:30, *105*
5:31, *105*, *192*
6, *110*, *112*, *126*, *132*
6:2, *130*
6:2-21, *124*, *126*

6:3, *128*
6:5, *128*, *129*, *130*
6:9, *131*
6:11, *129*
6:13, *132*
6:19, *129*
6:22-27, *133*, *134*
12, *120*
15:30-31, *115*
15:37-41, *160*
16, *10*
23:22, *61*
24:7, *120*
24:8, *61*
25, 45
25:1, *60*
26:59, 33, *137*, *157*
30:16, 47
31:17, 18, *198*

Deuteronomy
1:1, *96*
5:17, *3*
5:18, *99*
6:20, 21, *78*
7:1-5, *61*, *187*
7:3, *62*
7:4, 45
18:18, *185*
19:16-21, *186*
20:7, *96*
20:19, 20, *51*
21:1-9, *144*
21:20, *43*
22:1-4, *2*
22:10, *61*, *187*
22:11, *193*
22:12, *160*, *161*
22:13-21, 53, 54, 99
22:14, 15, *172*
22:21, 47
22:22, *91*, *98*, *99*
22:24, 57
22:28, 29, 56
22:30, *50*, *146*
23:1, *171*

23:2, *167*
23:10-15, *144*
23:15, *90*
23:18, *125*
24:1-4, *5*, *88*, *92*, 95
24:4, 95
24:5, 96, *163*
24:19-22, *2*
25:5, *118*
25:5-10, *2*, *168*
26:7, *164*
28:30, *161*
28:57, *170*
32:11, *17*
33:1-34:12, 96
33:7, *61*

Joshua
2, *82*
11:6, 9, *61*

Judges
3:24, *170*
6:4, *51*
8:33, *126*
9, 9:28, *60*
13:1-7, *124*
13:2-5, *133*
16:1, 17:6, 18:1, *133*
19:2, *162*
21:25, *133*

Ruth
1:2, *46*
1:6, 8, 47
1:20, 47
1:22, *47*, 48
2:1, 47
3, 49, *82*
3:7, 48
3:9, *44*, *46*, 48, *170*
3:14, 15, *50*
4, *82*
4:1, *50*
4:7, *128*, *168*
4:11, 52, 53
4:12, *51*, *52*, *128*
4:15, *52*

Ruth (continued)
  4:18, 51, 64, 74
  4:18–22, 134
1 Samuel
  1:1–11, 124
  1:11, 13, 15, 16, 133
  2–6, 68
  2:17, 68
  2:22, 162
  9:1, 21, 10:2, 74, 78
  18, 72
  20, 67, 68, 72
  20:26, 64, 65
  20:27, 74
  20:30, 66, 74
  20:31, 74
  20:33, 84
  20:36, 77
  21, 66, 68
  21:2, 4, 66
  21:5, 66, 71
  21:13, 71
  22:1–4, 189
  22:7, 8, 13, 74
  24:6, 7, 67
  24:17, 189
  25, 127
  25:10, 74
2 Samuel
  3:8, 66
  4:12, 66
  6:3, 66
  8:4, 61
  11, 82, 84, 88
  11:2, 170
  11:4, 82
  11:8, 170
  11:9, 66
  11:11, 84, 170
  12, 82, 84
  13, 139
  13:11, 12, 57
  13:13, 137
  13:23–28, 127
  16:21–23, 66
  19:32, 33, 52
  20:1, 74
  21:20, 138
1 Kings
  3:12, 88
  3:14, 62
  4:7, 53
  5:27, 53
  11:1, 62
  11:33, 38, 62
  13:4, 120
  14:8, 62
  15:5, 62, 63
  16:31, 45, 62
  18:4, 13, 53
  21:10, 92
2 Kings
  5, 120
  8:17, 45, 62
  16:3, 17:17, 154
  18:27, 170
  21:6, 23:10, 154
1 Chronicles
  20:6, 138
2 Chronicles
  1:12, 88
  21:6, 45
Job
  3, 78
  38:5–8, 20
Psalms
  80:9–20 [8–19], 127
  104:6–8, 14, 15, 19
  128:3, 22, 127
  132:5, 61
Proverbs
  1:9, 160
  2:16, 31
  3:3, 160
  4:15, 122
  5:3, 31
  5:15, 31, 32
  5:18, 20, 31
  6:6, 81
  7:5, 31
  7:19, 20, 97
  7:25, 122
  9, 158, 159
  9:17, 22:14, 31
  23:26–35, 23:29, 127
  23:33, 31
  31:3–7, 127
Song of Songs
    (Canticles)
  2:5, 128, 193
  3:4, 186
  4:12, 31
  7:1–3, 49
Isaiah
  6:2, 170
  13:16, 161
  16:7, 128
  36:12, 170
  40:12, 14
  49:15, 9
  57:8, 161
  66:7, 8, 183
  66:10, 98
  66:13, 9
Jeremiah
  2:2, 13, 20–25, 34
  2:25, 170
  3, 34
  3:1, 8, 95
  3:2, 161
  7:18, 128
  11:19, 51
  20:14–18, 78
  20:15, 98
  32:35, 154
  44:17, 74
  44:19, 128
Lamentations
  5:11, 57
Ezekiel
  16, 126
  16:8, 171
  16:8–14, 50
  16:25, 170
  19:10–14, 127

19:11, 12, *186*
33:25, 26, *197*
Hosea
  1:2, 3, 2:2–13, *158*
  2:14, *45*
  3:1, *128, 193*
  4:11, *127*
  4:12–14, *192*
  4:14, *106, 125, 192*
Amos
  2:7, 9, 11–12, *130*
Zechariah
  14:2, *161*
  14:8, *41*
Malachi
  3:11, *51*
Matthew
  1, *64, 82*
  1:3, 5, 6, 18, 19, 20, *82*
  5:31, *92*
  9:10–17, *43*
  11:19, *43*
  19:4, *9*
  19:9, *92*
  19:10–12, *172*
  19:10–13, 4, *6*
  19:12, 13, *6*
  19:14, *7*
Mark
  2:15–22, *43*
  12:25, 6, *9*
Luke
  1:35, *46*
  5:29–39, 7:34, 36–50, *43*
  11:5–7, *3*
  11:5–11, *81*
  11:7, *162*
  15:1–10, *43*
John
  1, *183*
  1:1–5, *13*
  1:1–42, *14*
  1:3, *19*
  1:6, *14*

1:14, 16, 6, *25*
1:32, 45, 51, *17*
2:1, *12, 14*
2:1–5, *23*
2:1–11, *12*
2:1–12, *15*
2:2, *22*
2:4, 22, 23, *24*
2:5, *24*
2:6, 20, *21*
2:7, *21*
2:11, 24, *25*
2:12, *23*
3:23, *29*
3:29, 22, 36, *98*
3:30, *98*
4:1–54, *29*
4:5, *42*
4:7, *21*
4:7–18, *30*
4:12, 32, *34*
4:15, *21*
4:18, 19, *31*
4:19–26, *34*
4:21, *30*
4:25, 42, *44*
4:26, *44*
4:27, 28, 29, *30*
4:27–30, *35*
4:31–42, *38*
4:32, 34, *39*
4:35, 40, *45*
4:37, *40*
4:39–42, *44*
4:46, *37*
4:46–54, *37*
4:49–53, *19*
4:50, 54, *37*
5, *14, 42*
5:16–18, *39*
5:17, *42*
5:37, *34*
5:39, *42*
5:46, 26, *42*
5:47, *14, 26*

8, *108*
8:1–11, *102*
8:48–58, 32, *34*
8:58, *32*
9:7, *22*
9:39–41, *13*
10:7, 9, 11, *25*
15:1–8, *24*
15:5, 24, *25*
15:11, *98*
16:21, 23, 41, *98*
17:1–4, *24*
17:13, *98*
19:14, *27*
19:25–27, *23*
19:26, *22*
Acts
  5, *120*
Romans
  1:26, 27, *173*
1 Corinthians
  3:2, 7, *9*
  5, *135*
  7, *4*
  7:32, *172*
2 Corinthians
  5:17, *7*
Galatians
  1:15, *23*
Colossians
  2:13, *136*
  3:10, *7*
Hebrews
  5:12, *7*
1 Peter
  1:3, 2:2, *7*
Revelation
  17:15, *120*

Targums

On Genesis (Pseudo-Jonathan and Neofiti)
  38:25, 26, *122*

On Genesis (Onkelos)
38:26, *122*
On Exodus (Jerusalemite)
2:25, *166*
On Exodus (Onkelos)
2:25, *165–66*

Apocrypha and Pseudepigrapha

2 Baruch
57:1, *120*
1 Esdras
3:1–4:41, *158*
4:15, *159*
2 Esdras
6:42, *20, 21*
6:43, 44, *19, 20, 21*
16:57, 58, *20*
1 Enoch
17:4, *17*
54:8, *31*
Jubilees
30, *187*
30:3, 4 *62*
33:1–17, *145*
Sirach
50:3, *184*
51:13–30, *158, 162*
Testament of Judah
12:2, 3, *127*
Wisdom of Solomon
19:7, *19*

Dead Sea Scrolls

Covenant of Damascus
4:20–21, *196*

Josephus

Antiquities
2:205–23, *33*

Philo

De Abrahamo
7.36ff., *156*
18, *26*
De agricultura
8–10, *39*
De confusione
190, *26*
Legum allegoriae
3.163, *18*
3.97–103, *42*
De opificio mundi
27, 38, 39, *18*
40, *19, 40*
41, *40*
82, *18*
De plantatione
15, *18*
De praemiis et poenis
46, *42*
Questions on Genesis
2.47, *19*
2.66, *20*
4.215, *18*
Questions on Exodus
2.46, *33*
De sacrificiis Abelis et Caini
13.52ff., *101*
De specialibus legibus
3.30, 31, *92*
De vita Mosis
1.202, *184*

Talmudic Sources

Mishnah
Eduyoth
5:2, *136*
Nazir
2:7, *128*
Shebiith
8:10, *32*
10:9, *136*
Yoma
3:10, *105*
Babylonian Talmud
Baba Bathra
120a, *33, 165*
Baba Kamma
91b, *182*
Berakoth
19b, *10*
Menahoth
37b, *10*
44a, *160*
Niddah
16b, *171*
Pesachim
25b, *10*
Sanhedrin
58a, *102*
74a, *10*
Sotah
47b, *192*
Yebamoth
22a, *7*
47b, *62*
48b, *7*
97a, *xii*
Palestinian (Jerusalem) Talmud
Sotah
24a, *192*
Taanith
64b, *18*

Midrashim and Other Jewish Sources

Mekilta on Exodus
12:14, *8*
21:37, *10*

Siphra on Leviticus
   89b, *11*
Siphre on Numbers
   5:31, *192*
Siphre on Deuteronomy
   25:9, *171, 199*
Genesis Rabba
   1:26, *8*
   4:3ff., *101*
   5:1, *20*
   5:1–2, *11*
   6:9, *156*
   8:9, *40*
   13:13, 14, *18, 31*
   38:9, *48*
   42:3, *41*
Exodus Rabba
   1:19, *33*
   2:25, *166*
Ruth Rabba
   1:16ff., *62*
Midrash on Psalms (Tehillim)
   1:1, *185*
Pesikta Rabbathi
   2.4, *xii*
Maimonides
   Guide to the Perplexed
      3.51, *173*

Early Christian Sources

Athenagoras
   Legation on Behalf of Christians 33, *182*
Augustine
   City of God, bk. 1, chaps. 16–27, *182*
Clement of Alexandria
   Stromata 2.23.140.1, *182*
Jerome
   Against Jovinian 1.16, *183*
Justin
   Apology for Christians 1.29, *182*

Ancient Legal Sources

Code of Hammurabi (CH)
   131, *109, 121, 191, 192*
   132, *109, 121, 191, 192*
   157, *194*
   160, *186*
Digest
   48.5.30[29], *81*
   50.17.167 pr., *81*
Hittite Laws
   189, *194*
Laws of Eshnunna (LE)
   25, *186*
Ulpian
   Regulae 13 ff., *182*

Classical Authors

Aristotle
   Poetics 1459.6–8, *x*
   Topics 139.34, *13*
Athenaeus
   Deipnosophists 13.555C, *182*
Dio Cassius
   Roman History 53.13.2, 54.16.1, 55.2.6, 56.10, *182*
Dio Chrysostom
   Discourses 33.16, *13*
Herodotus
   1.8–10, *190*
   1.10, *143*
   1.215–16, *86*
   5.68, *187*
Homer
   Odyssey 8.312, *78*
Plato
   Laws
      11.930C, *182*
      4.11.721, 4.721B, *182*
      6.17.774, 6.773E f., 776B, *182*
   Phaedo
      64d, *198*
   Republic
      5.9.460E, *182*
Plutarch
   Parallel Lives
      Lycurgus 15.1–2, *182*
      Lysander 30.5, *182*
   Moralia
      Sayings of Spartans 14 (227F), *182*
Seneca
   On Providence 3.10, *86*
Sophocles
   Oedipus the King 1310, *144*
Stobaeus
   Anthology 67.16, *182*

Later Sources

Koran
   2:187, *146, 170*
Rabelais
   Gargantua and Pantagruel 3.6, *198*
Shakespeare
   Hamlet 3.3.53–55, *191*

Subject Index

Androgyny, 8, 9, 24, 25, 32, 41, 102, 172, 184
Authorities, 103, 104, 105, 165, 173
Authority, 10, 106, 192

Benediction, 133–34
Bestiality, 141, 153, 155
Betrothal, 46, 56–57, 64, 82, 99, 111, 151
Biography, x, 26
Bitter water test, 104–6, 109, 116–17, 192
Bride-price, 55, 56, 58–59, 66, 72

Chastity, 46, 48
Childbirth, 23, 65, 68, 80, 83, 97, 183
Childhood, 161, 174–75
Children: disciples, 6–7; indelicacy, 161, 162, 197; play, 200; pregnancy, 119–21, 170; procreation, 2–4, 182; sacrifice, 141, 153–54; sick, 37, 138
Christian missionaries, 16
Circumcision, 16, 58, 59, 61, 62, 66, 136, 161, 166, 167, 170, 173, 174, 187, 198
Clothing: betrothal, 46, 48, 50, 170, 171; seduction, 143, 187, 193; shame, 146, 160, 172, 173; unclean, 72, 73, 76
Collocatio, 105
Collusion, 70, 93, 96
Conscience, 95, 104, 109, 120
Contraception, 97

Control of body, 43, 73, 75–76, 108–9, 173
Conversion, 7, 16, 23, 62, 105, 136, 160, 194
Cosmology, 13, 18, 23, 39, 42
Curse, 66, 67, 69, 75, 77–78, 103, 109, 116–17, 120, 143, 183, 191
Custom, 22, 70, 112, 117, 125, 153, 159, 166, 167, 170, 172, 174, 184, 186, 193, 199. *See also* Marriage, Levirate

Decalogue, 98–102, 110, 160
Decency, 87, 91, 161
Dignity, 7
Discrimination, 100–101

Dishonor, 4, 58, 75, 86, 101, 109, 129, 156, 167–72, 187
Divorce, 5–7, 9, 56, 82, 88–95, 102, 103, 164, 165, 169, 189
Double standard, 105, 108
Dreams, 86, 87, 89, 163
Drunkenness, 16, 43, 45, 46, 47, 48 49, 51, 52, 82, 90, 126, 127–28, 130, 133, 144, 149, 170

Eden, 100–101, 160
Ejaculation, 48, 51, 65, 74–77, 83, 131, 171
Elitism, 13
Emotion, 23, 90, 100, 173
Equality, 8, 10, 39
Eros, 173
Erotic language, 48, 49, 158, 161, 163, 164, 193, 197
Ethnic purity, 61
Eunuchs, 5, 167, 172, 197

Fables, 13
Family life, 10, 37, 58–59, 65, 75, 79–80, 100–101, 110, 139
Female sexual initiative, 49, 79, 118, 128, 143, 152, 155
Fertility, 18, 19, 22, 25, 48, 52, 53, 87, 93, 94, 127, 134, 139, 167, 198
Fetus, 120
Firstborn, 2, 110–11, 115, 132, 145, 152
Fornication, 127

Gender of God, 9, 42, 183
Genetics, 138–39
Gnosis, 17

God's moral code, 100, 101
Greek rationalism, xi
Guilt, 109, 113, 120–21
Gypsies, 173, 174, 199

Hereditary, 67, 73, 74, 78, 125, 134, 169, 186
Hire of a husband, 91
Homosexuality, 74, 141, 153–55, 156, 173, 188, 195, 196
Host culture, 157
Household gods, 72, 78, 79, 80, 83, 132
Human rights, 10

Identity, 55, 60, 93, 118, 122
Image of God, 7–10, 29, 40, 183
Impregnation, 79, 115, 117, 120–21, 128, 149
Insult, 77, 103
Intercourse, 65, 75, 76, 77, 159, 162, 164, 165, 169, 173, 188, 198, 199
Intermarriage, 58, 61, 62, 187
Interpretation of scripture, 2, 8, 14, 26, 28, 32, 40, 92, 105–6, 108, 127, 161, 165–66, 171, 172, 183, 195, 196

John the Baptist, 7, 14, 22, 29, 36, 40, 43

Law: drafting, 89, 92, 163; hypothetical, 59, 70, 122, 126, 142, 147, 195; implicit, 79, 100, 102, 109, 110, 151; machinery, 91, 92, 93; narrative, ix, x, 56–57, 67, 68, 70, 72, 78–79, 81, 91, 98–99, 100, 102, 109–13, 121, 140, 144, 145, 151, 152; parables, 81–82; proverbs, 81–82
Legal fiction, 2, 114, 117
Licentiousness, 104, 106, 127, 137, 192
Logos, 13, 14, 16, 18, 19, 20, 32, 34, 35
Love, 10–11, 31, 34, 56, 95, 154, 158, 161, 171, 173
Lovemaking, 91, 126–27, 152

Marriage: arrangements, 55, 57, 58, 59; brother-sister, 86, 135, 136, 138, 147–48; Cain's 101–02; centralized control, 3, 173; consummation, 53, 87, 89, 151, 186; contracts, 89, 103, 135, 164; created order, 12, 102; deity's, 45, 50; downgrading, 4, 6, 7, 9, 172; fraught, 153–54; group, 139; indissolubility, 172; informal, 173; institution, 173, 198, 199, 200; levirate, 2, 75, 111, 114, 117, 118, 119, 121, 128, 129, 130, 151, 164, 167, 171, 199; sacrament, 119–20, 199; same-sex, 173; sex, 167, 172–73, 198; unwanted bride, 54–56
Mary, 33, 46, 64, 82, 165, 198
Master-disciple relationship, 6, 7, 12, 24, 26, 184

Milieu, 136, 156–57
Miracles, 15–21, 24, 26, 30, 33, 37, 39, 40, 136, 154, 160, 165, 184
Miscarriage, 109
Mortality, 130–32
Mosaic writings, 26, 34, 35, 42
Mothers, 64, 132, 141, 144–45, 156, 186, 189
Myth, x–xi, 8, 26, 86, 101, 171, 172, 196

Nakedness, 50, 77, 88–91, 100, 143, 144–47, 150–53, 160, 161, 190
Natural law 138
Nazirite, 123–34

Oath, 109, 114, 116–17, 121, 192
Obscenity, 77, 126, 162
Oral tradition, xii

Paradise, 9
Passion, 172–73
Passivity, 51
Patrimony, 114–15
Personification, 26, 42–43, 60, 185
Philo, 14, 26, 42, 140
Philosophy, xi, 3, 4, 8, 13, 26, 162
Pimping, 85–95
Polygamy, 51, 139, 196
Prostitution, 34, 54–55, 57, 60, 64, 74, 82, 83, 92, 106, 115, 116, 118, 119, 121, 122, 125, 126, 127, 128, 129, 132, 133, 151, 156, 160, 162, 164, 170, 192, 193, 198
Psychological distress, 120

Puberty, 131, 150, 166
Public policy, 136

Rape, 57–58
Rebellious son, 43
Rebirth, 7, 18, 23–25, 29, 32, 41, 136, 194
Re-creation, 14, 19, 34, 36, 135–37
Repentance, 7, 166, 191

Sacred offenses, 79–80, 83–84, 111, 126, 129
Sanitizing tendency, 88, 161, 197
Sexuality: abstention, 4, 164–66; control, 173, 199; decadent, 126, 156, 160, 162; delicacy, 53, 198; denial, 6, 162, 172, 199; deviant, 46; disease, 125, 131, 156; foreigners, 156; heightened state, 49, 128, 154; hospitality, 86; idolatry, 44–45, 59, 60, 62, 63, 128; initiation, 166; Jesus, 12, 28–33, 43, 44; knowledge, 159, 162; menstruation, 153–54; pleasure, 96–98, 154, 163, 174; rivalry, 152, 195; sacred, 74, 79, 83, 84, 100, 109, 119, 126–28, 192, 193; Sinai, 100; suppression, 160, 164, 173; symbolism, 31, 48, 49, 100, 160–61, 169–71, 199; transaction, 119; unnatural, 173; violence, 139; vulnerability, 89–90, 174; wisdom, 45; world's origin, 32

Shame, 77, 81, 90, 95, 129, 143, 169, 171–74, 190
Shoes, 48, 49, 50 167–73, 198–99
Sinai, 100–101
Sinning, 5, 7, 13, 94, 103–4, 113, 122, 159, 175, 197
Slander, 53, 55, 99, 186
Spitting, 69, 71, 168, 169, 171
Status, 7, 10, 87, 98, 99, 119, 125, 137, 143, 149
Storytelling, x–xii, 26, 56, 111, 137
Suicide, 2, 3
Supernatural, 14, 26, 97, 120, 136, 161, 165
Surrogate husband, 118

Taboo, 66, 76, 84, 119, 125, 141, 151, 162
Tainted origin, 67, 78
Topographical references, 21–22
Trust, 109, 112, 112–14, 119

Unworthy company, 29, 43, 77

Virginity, 9, 33, 54–58, 82, 164–65

Weddings, 14, 15, 19, 22–25, 30, 32, 53–55, 99, 103, 135, 172, 184
Wife-selling, 91
Wordplay, 50, 61, 127
Wrongful looking, 90, 143, 144, 174, 189, 190

Zeal, 60